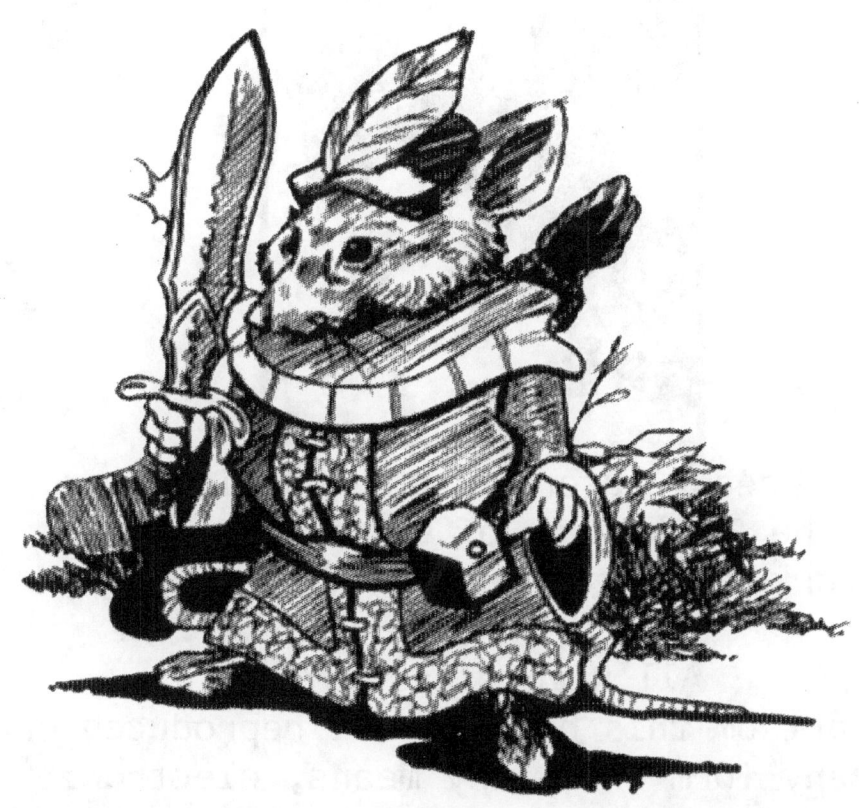

FOR WILLIAM ELWANGER, A WIZARD WHO TOOK HIS NEPHEW AS AN APPRENTICE AND TAUGHT HIM HOW TO CREATE REAL MAGIC FROM THE HUMAN IMAGINATION.

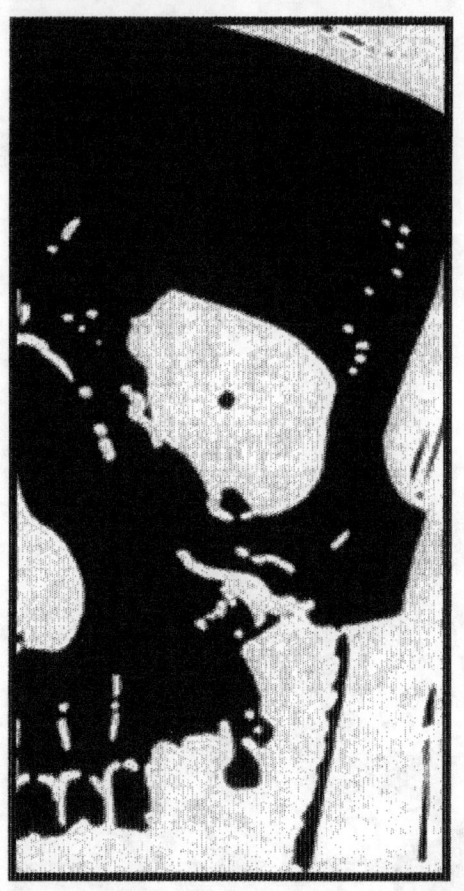

DREAM CHASER

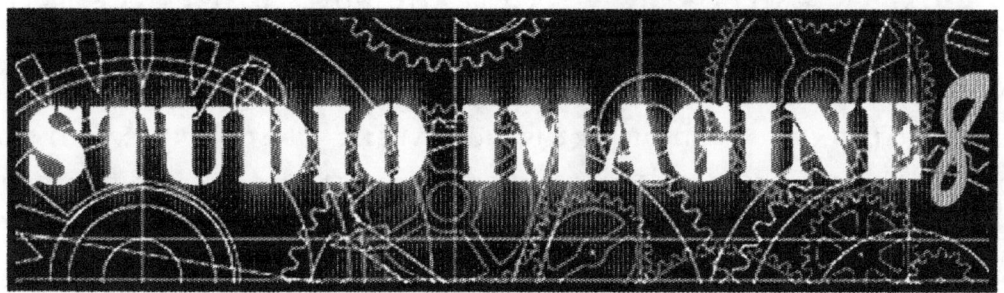

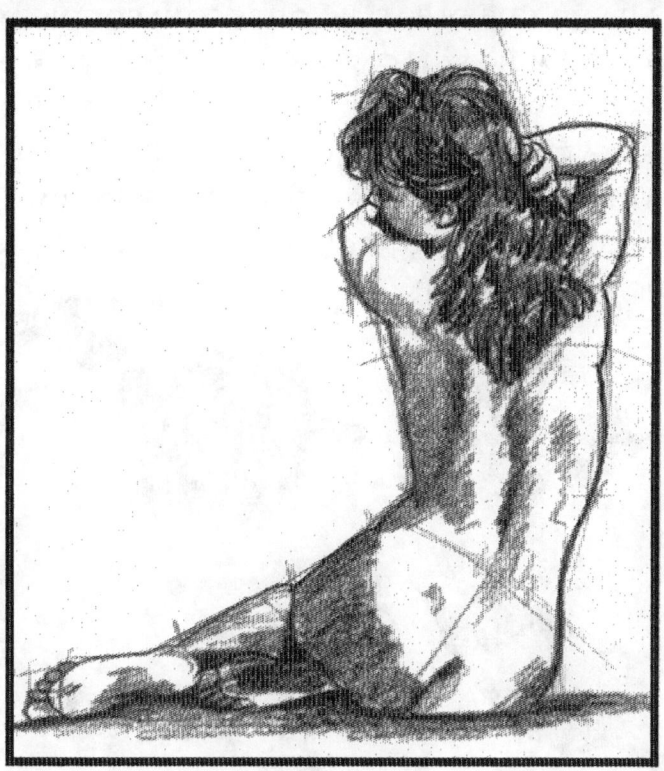

THE RENDERINGS OF JONATHAN MYERS

Introduction

Jonathan Myers is a showcase of artistic talent that spans a variety of styles. I remember the first time I met him back in 2003 at a small comic convention in upstate NY. He was selling his creator owned book, Swamp Fox. It was a beautifully illustrated all ages retelling of the Revolutionary War hero Francis Marion that would have made Walt Disney himself jealous. Needless to say I was quite impressed, not only with his artistic talents, but also with how generous and cool he was. My adolescent-self pestered him for a good two hours, trying to absorb all the information I could about commercial art and the business of illustrating. Flash forward ten years later, and I have the pleasure of reconnecting with Jonathan, and let me tell you, I am now blown away with the art I see. From Star Wars to Tarzan, classic literature to classic movies, Jon's Sci-Fi and Fantasy illustrations are gorgeously rendered depictions that cross between Hal Foster and that collectively awesome feeling of childhood adventure and wonder. His artwork is all quality and all class. Just like the man himself.

~V Ken Marion

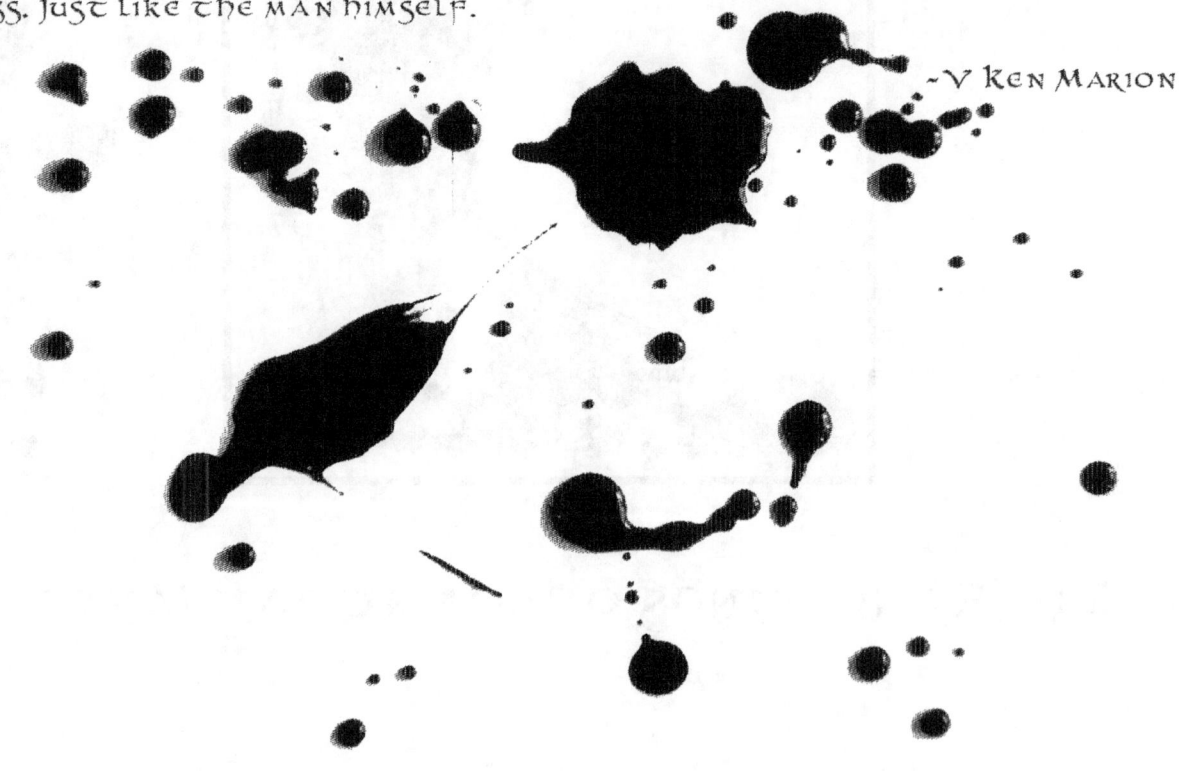

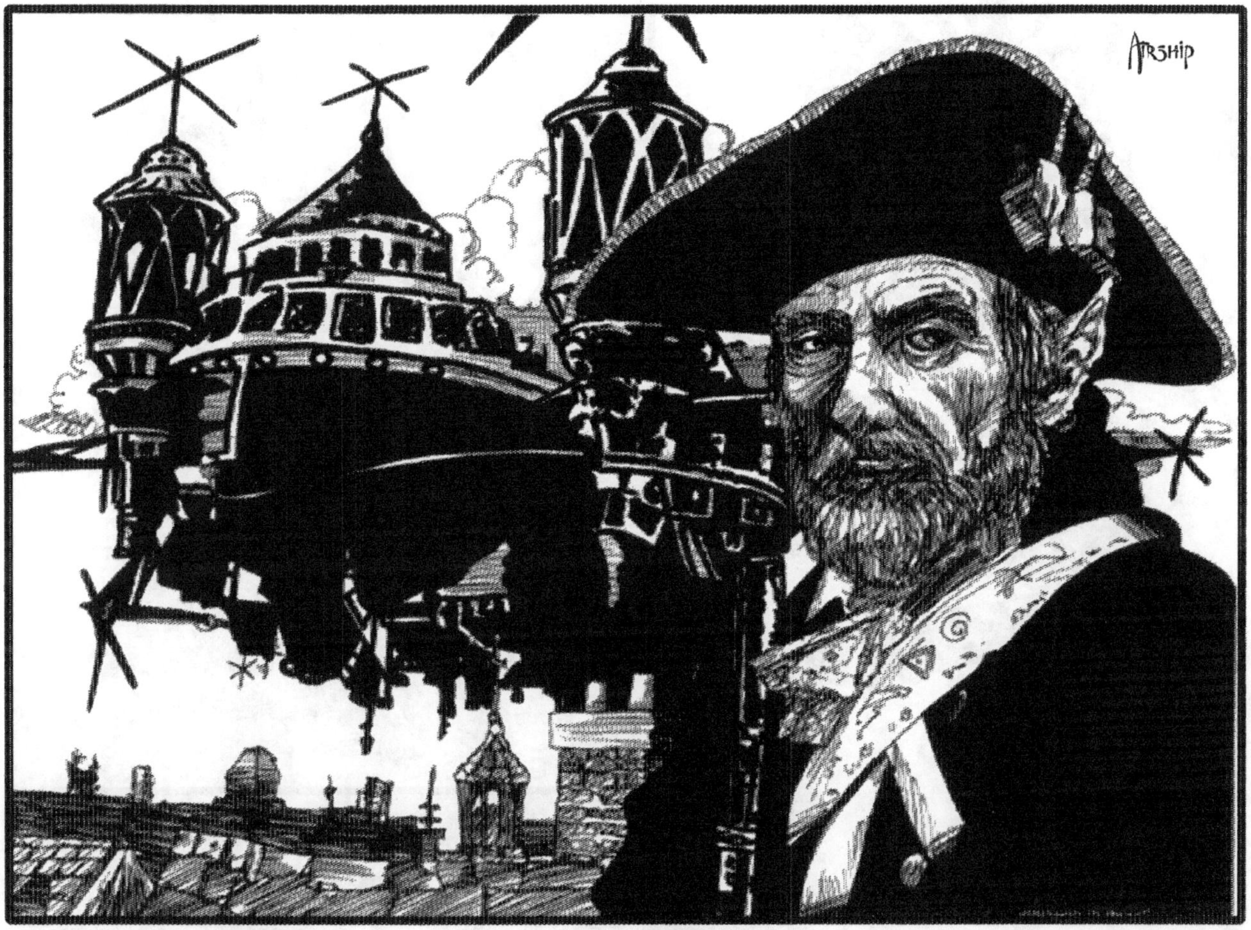

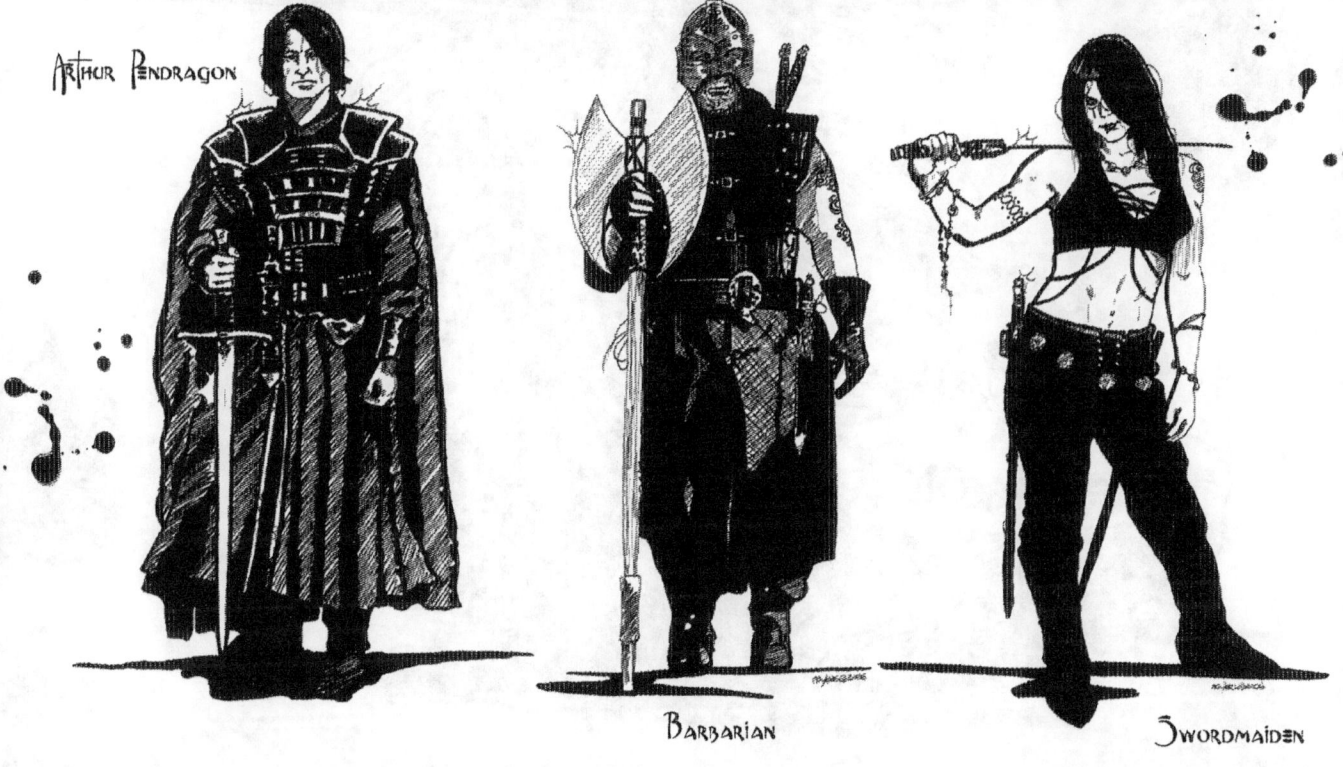

AIRSHIP

ARTHUR PENDRAGON

BARBARIAN

SWORDMAIDEN

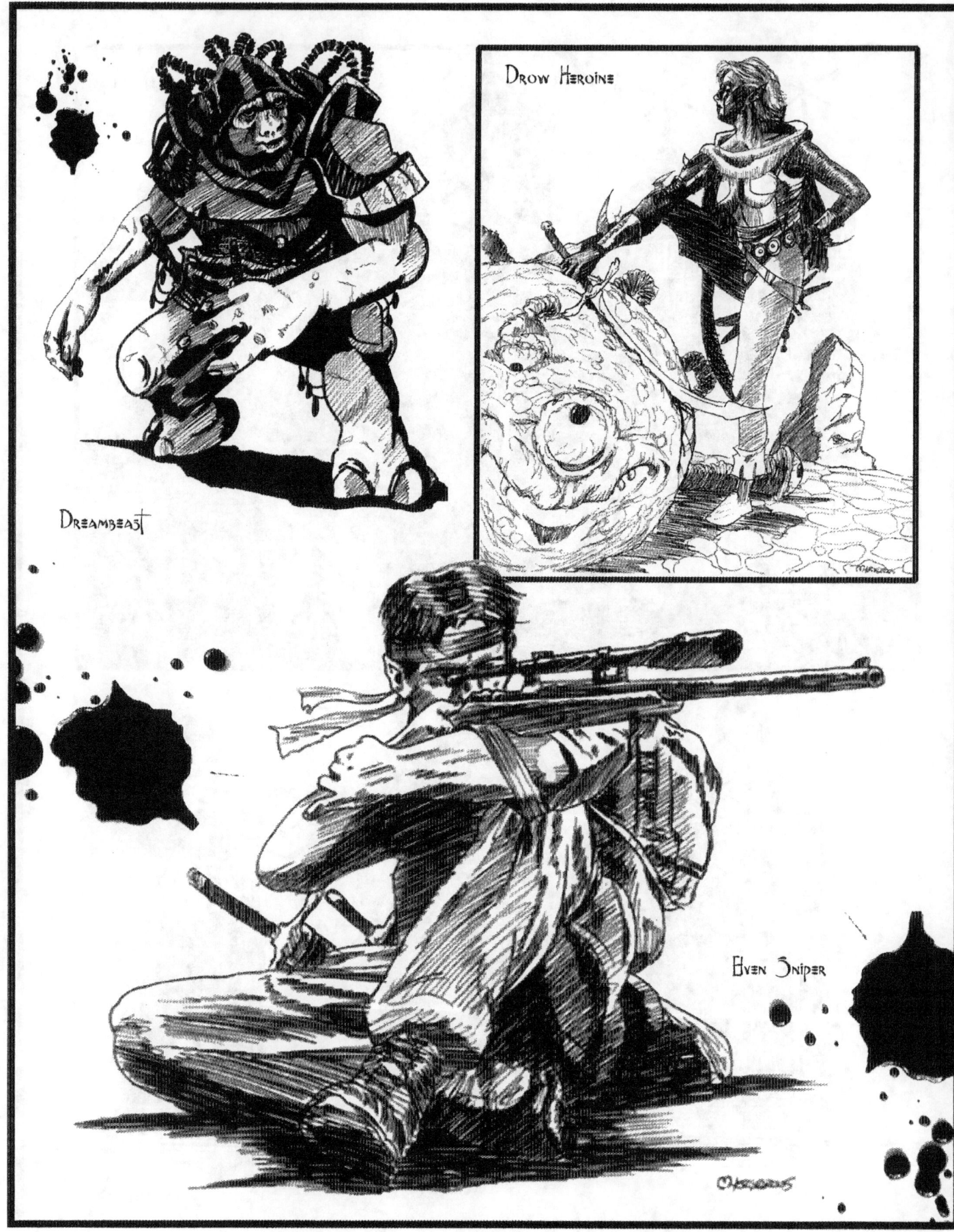

DREAMBEAST

DROW HEROINE

ELVEN SNIPER

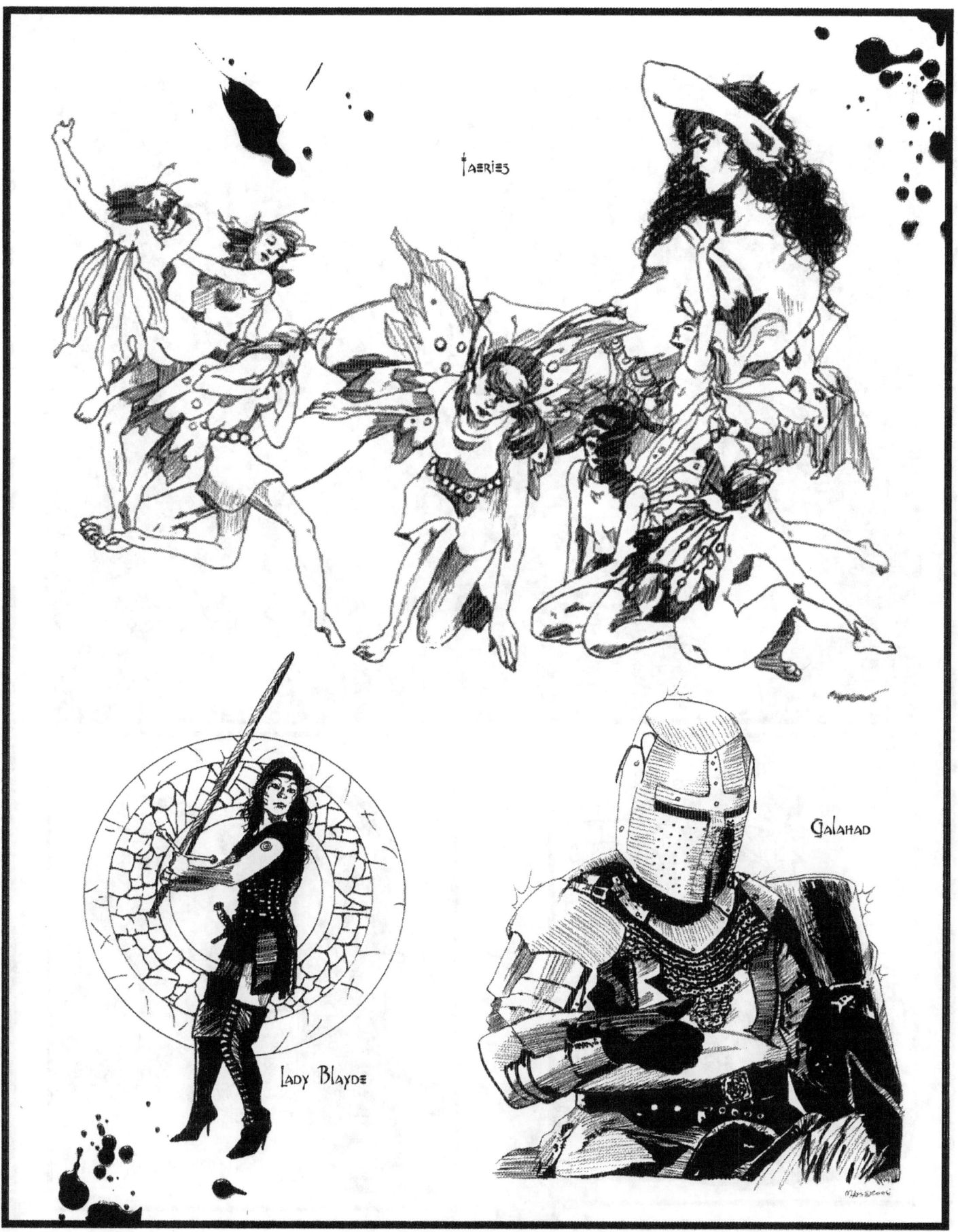

Faeries

Lady Blayde

Galahad

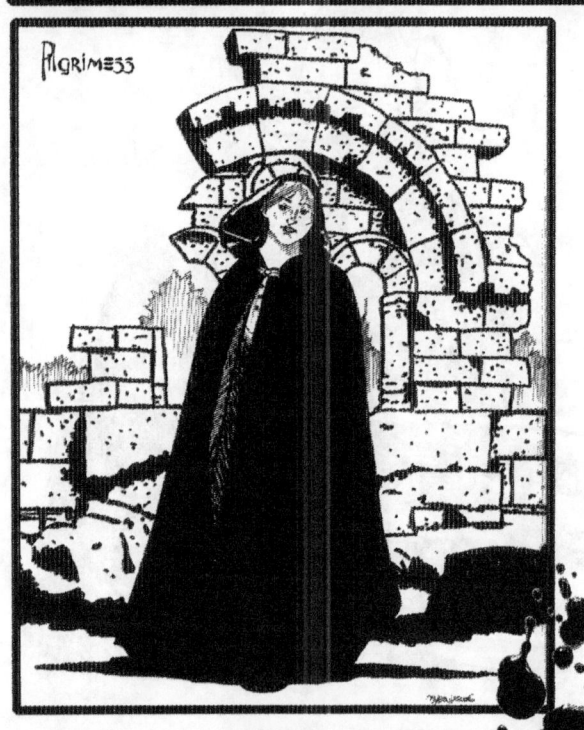

Pilgrimess

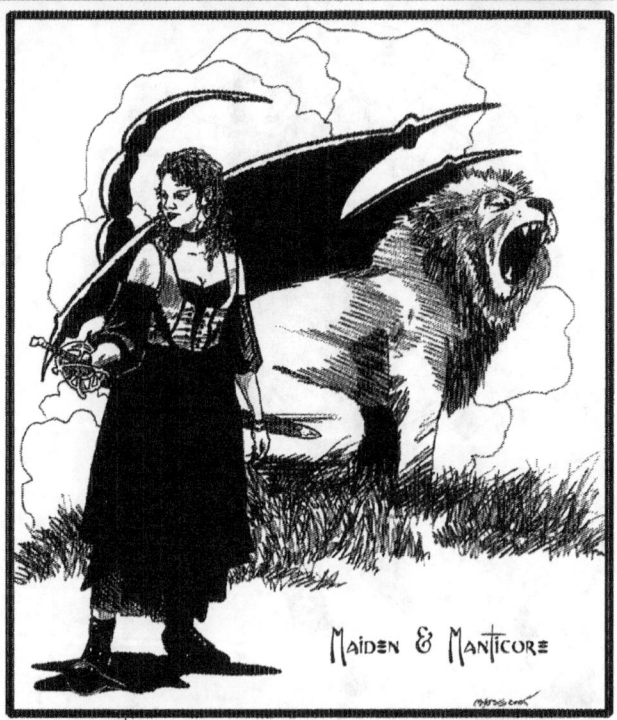

Maiden & Manticore

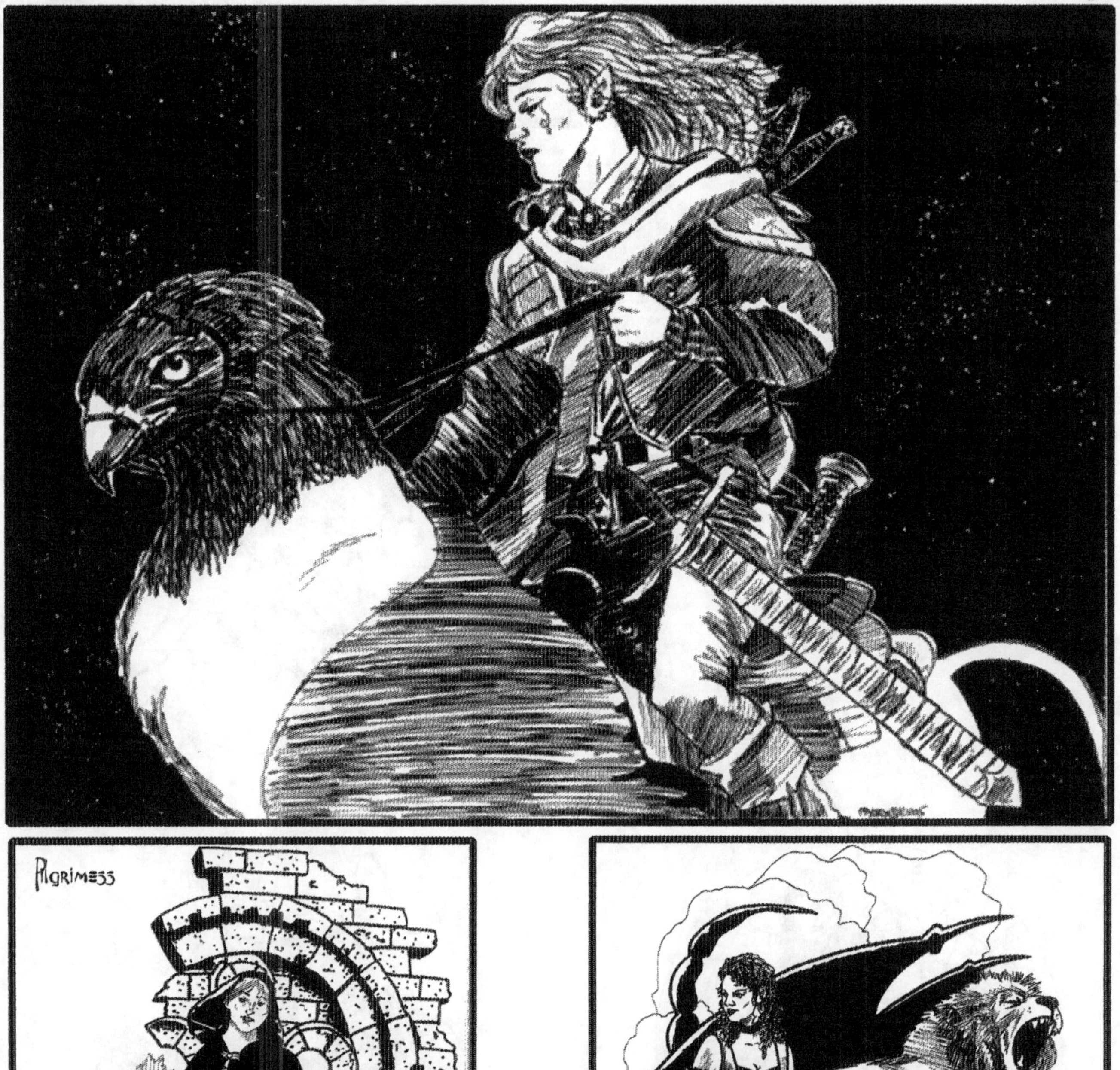

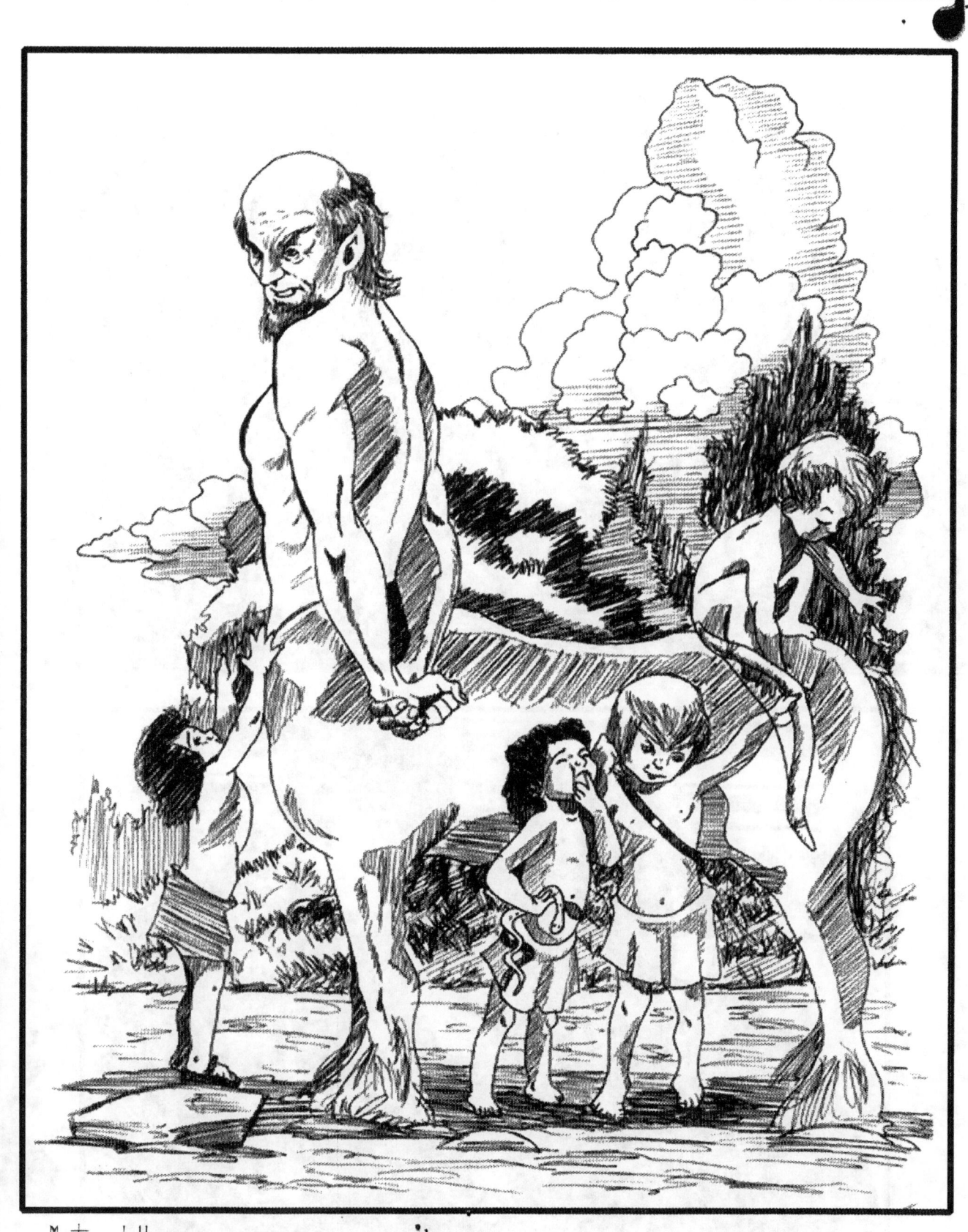

MENTOR of HEROES

Guilds

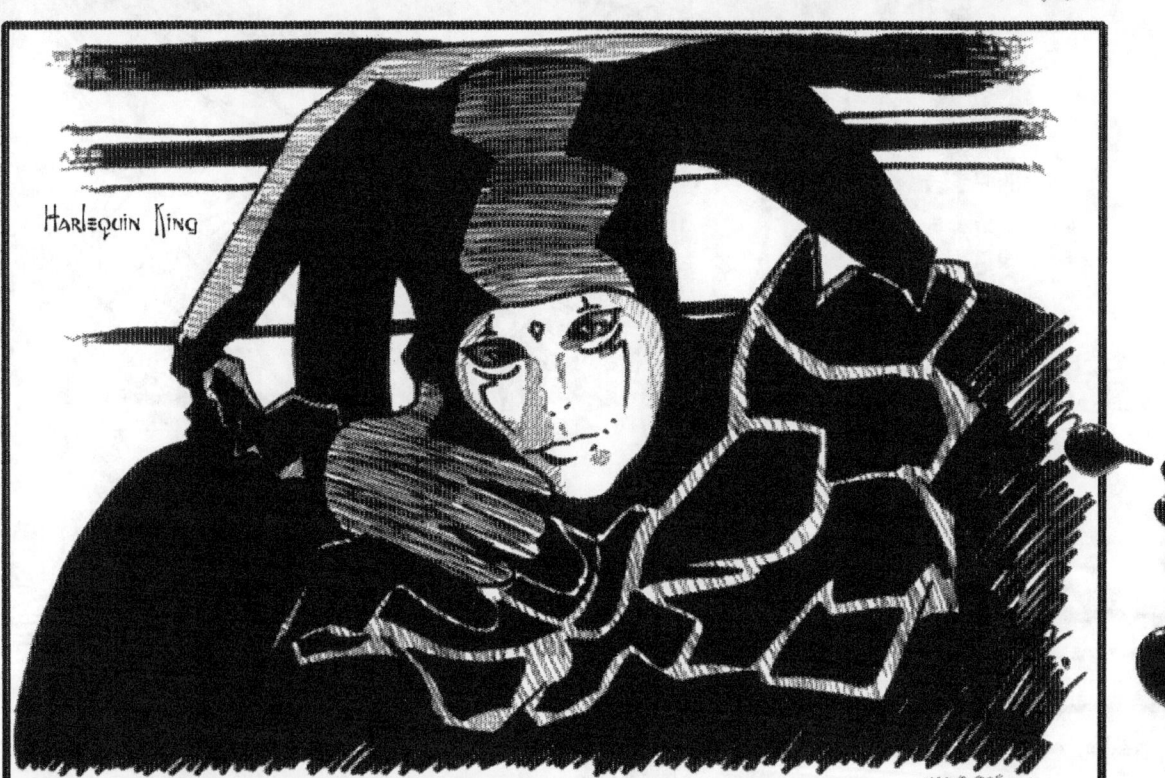

Harlequin King

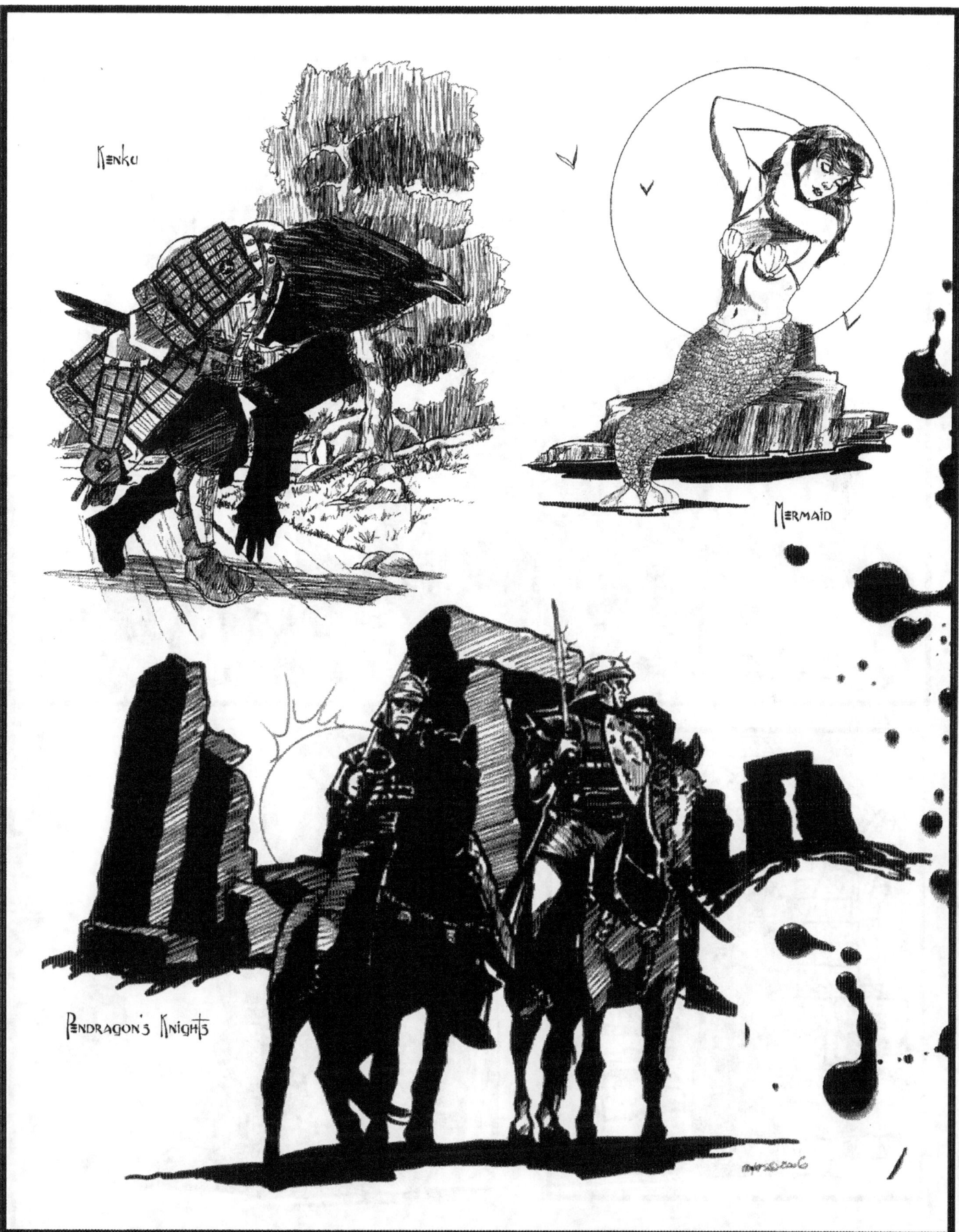

Kenku

Mermaid

Pendragon's Knights

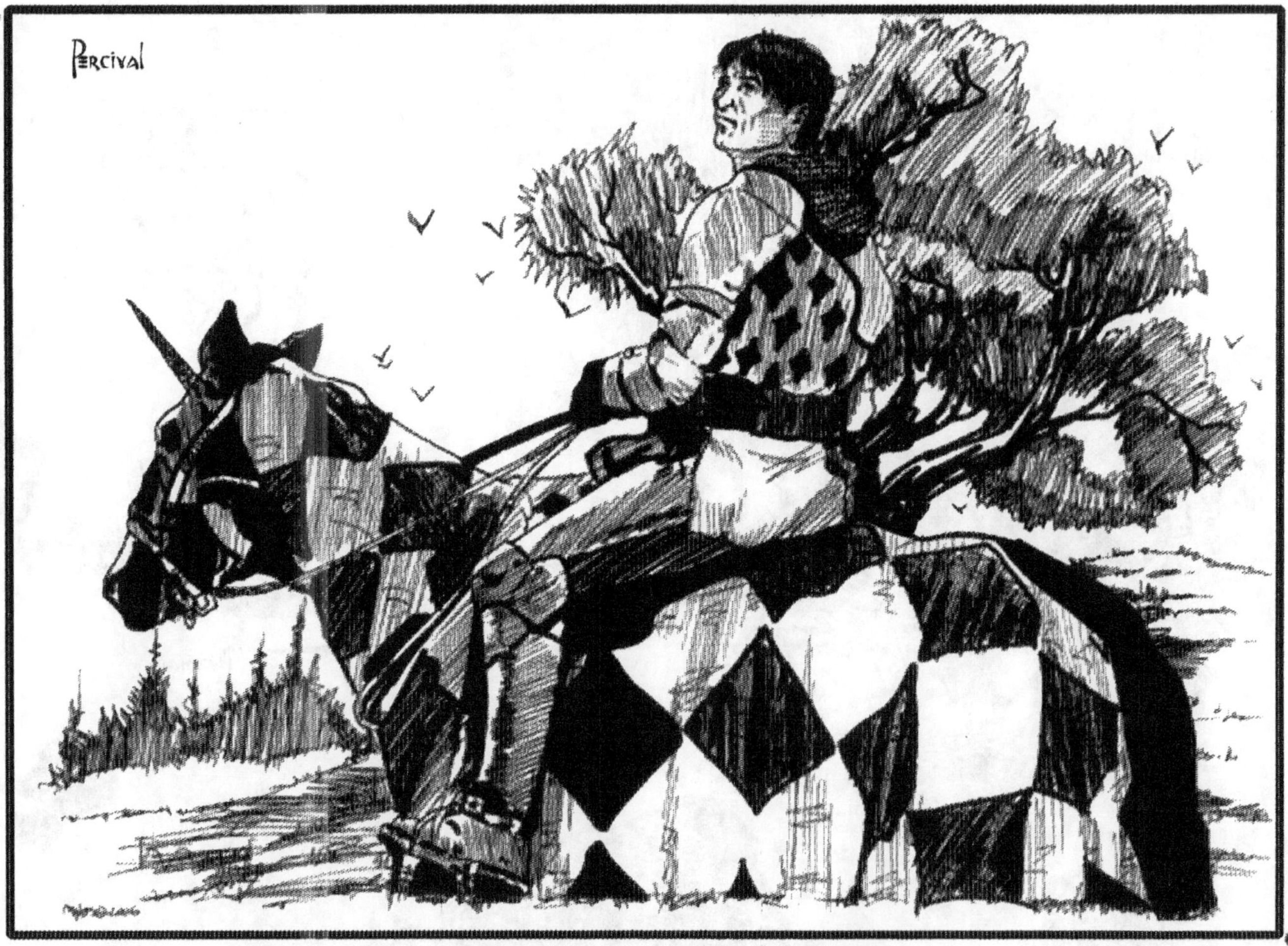

Percival

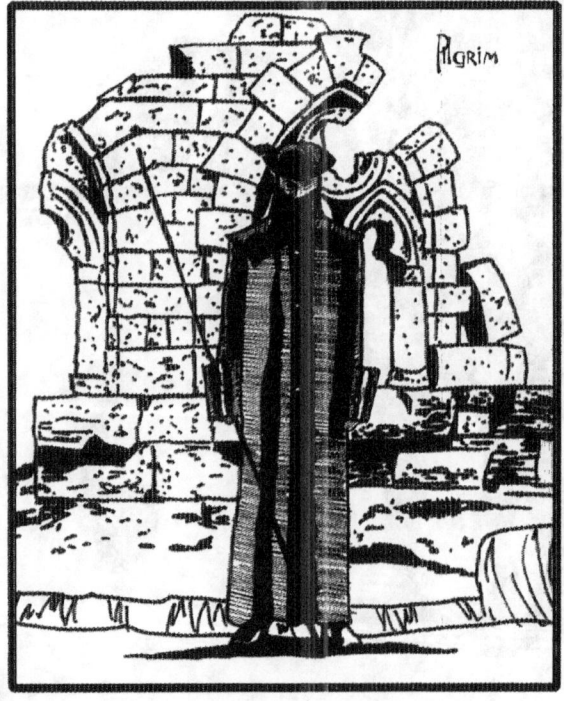

Pilgrim

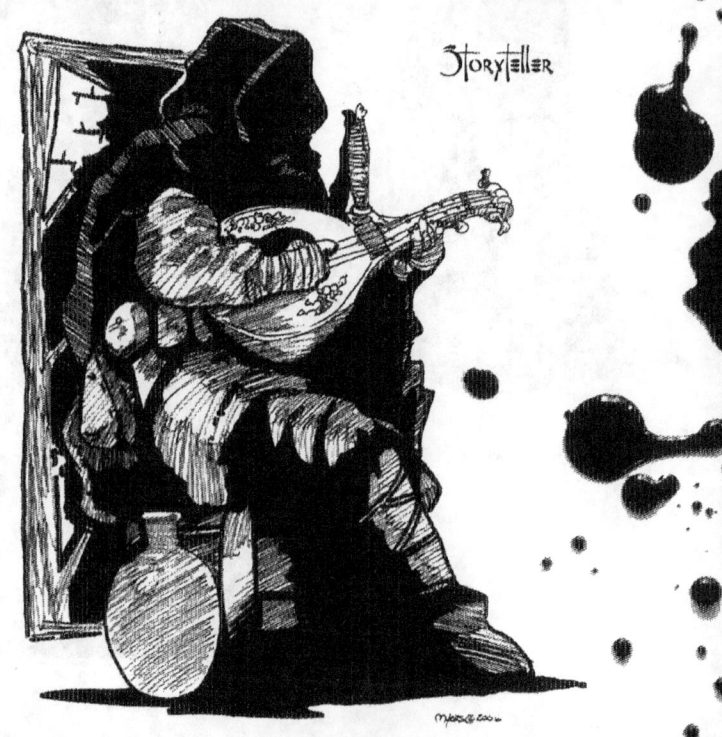

Storyteller

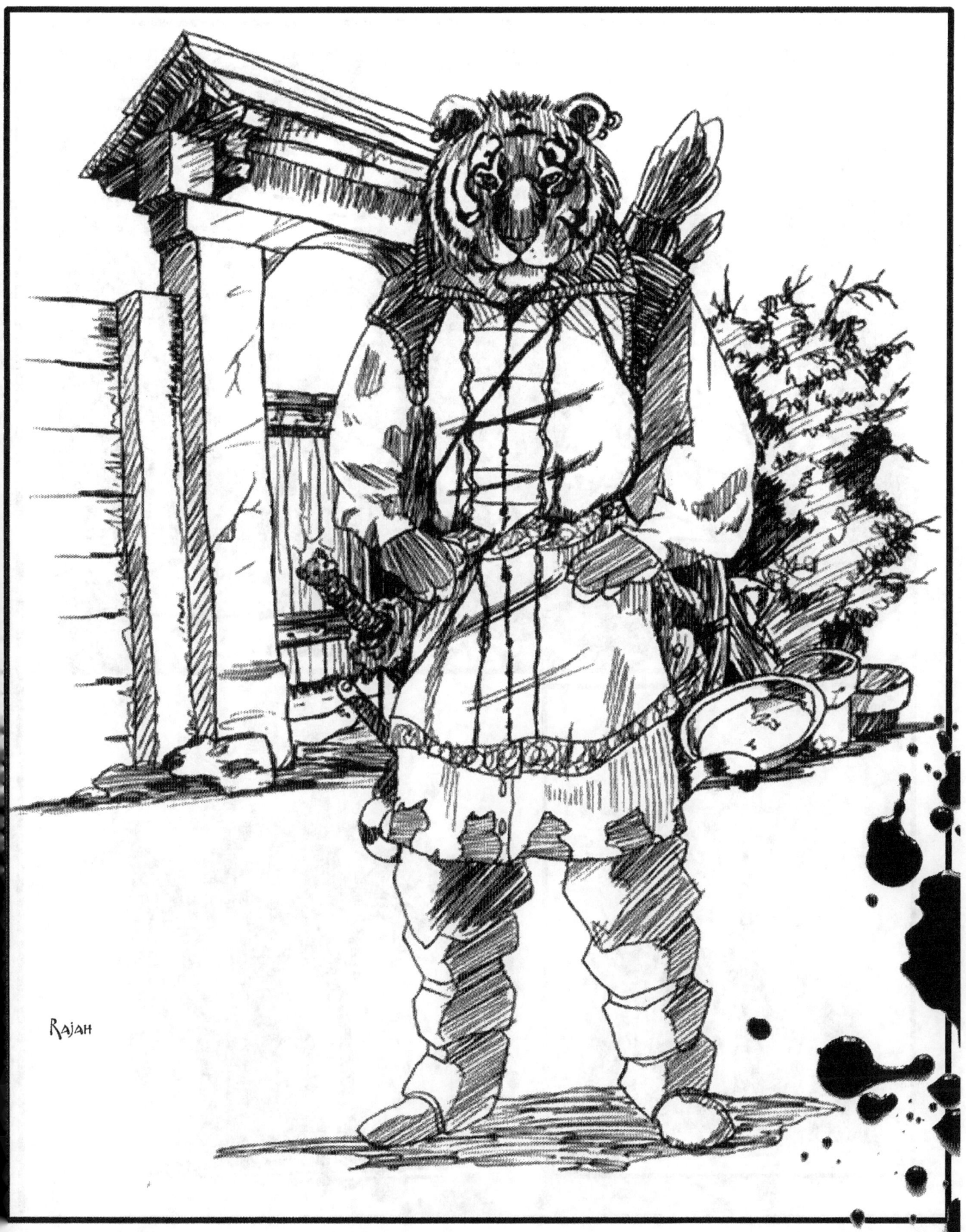

Rajah

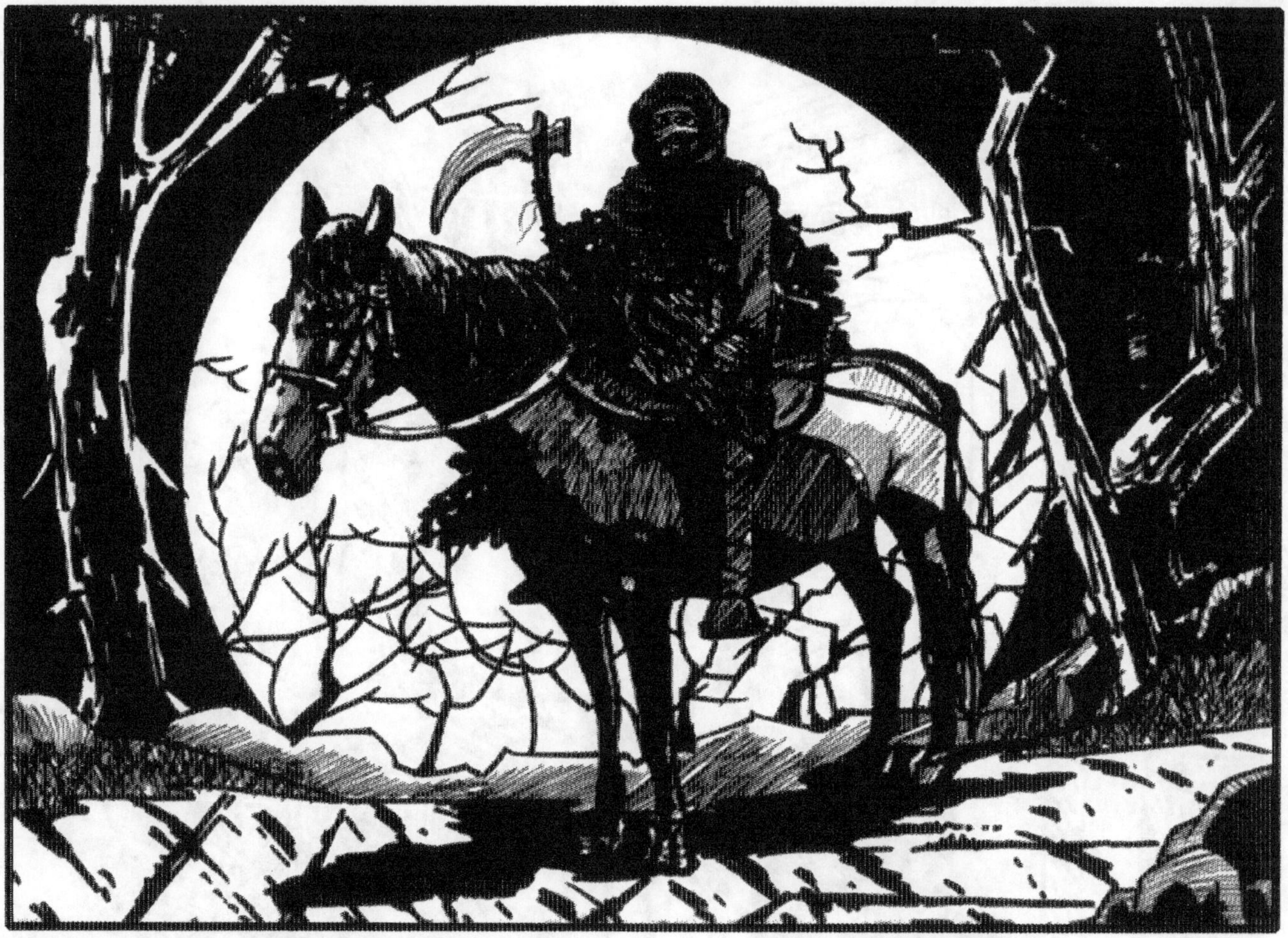

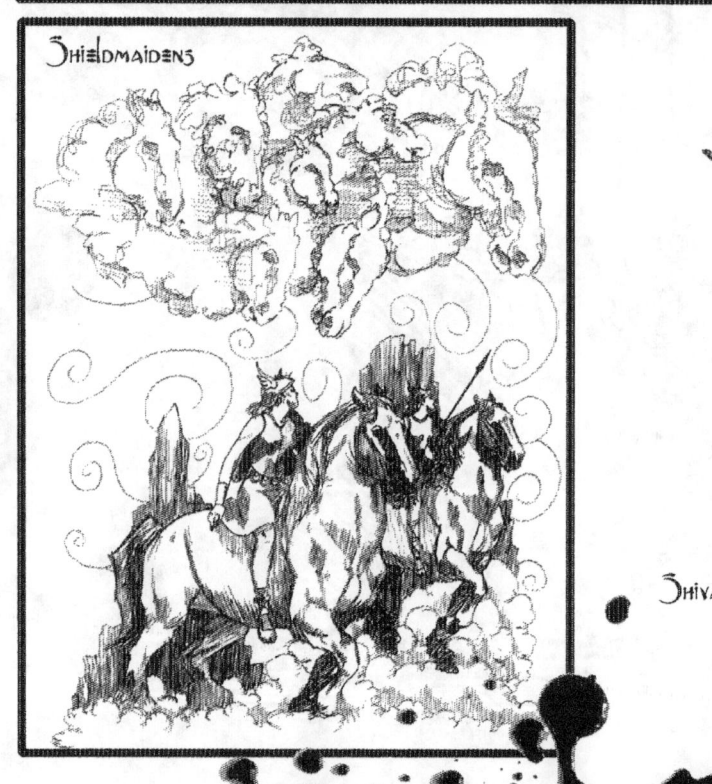

SHIELDMAIDENS

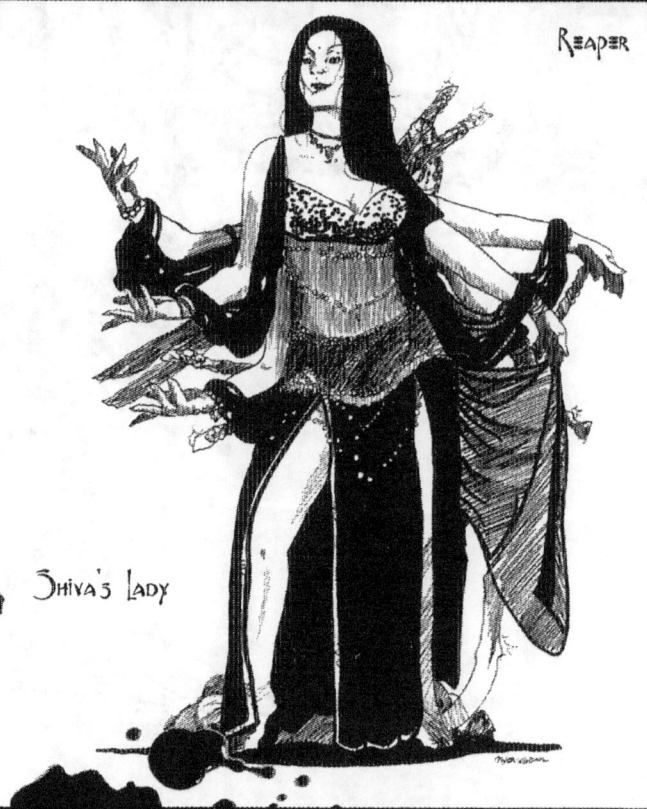

REAPER

SHIVA'S LADY

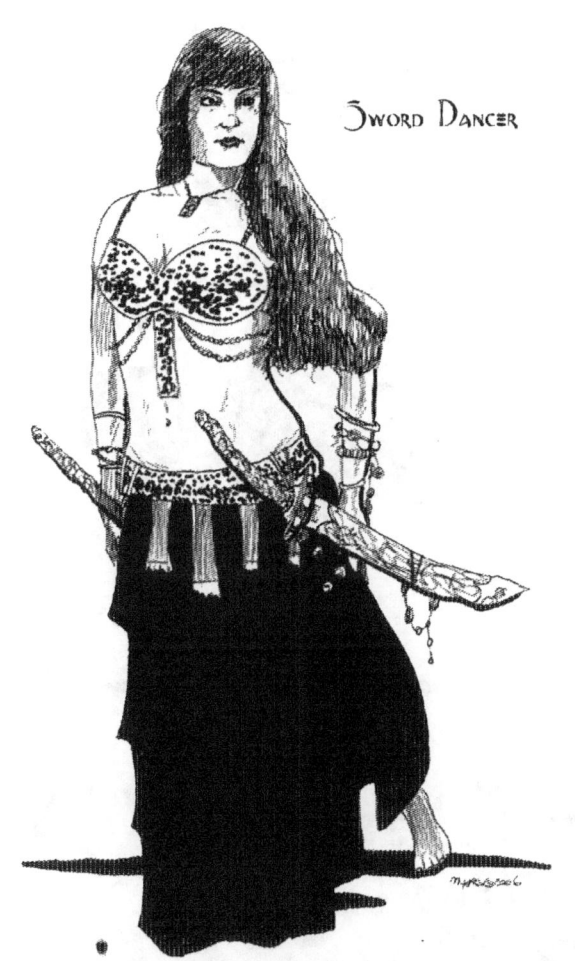

Sword Dancer

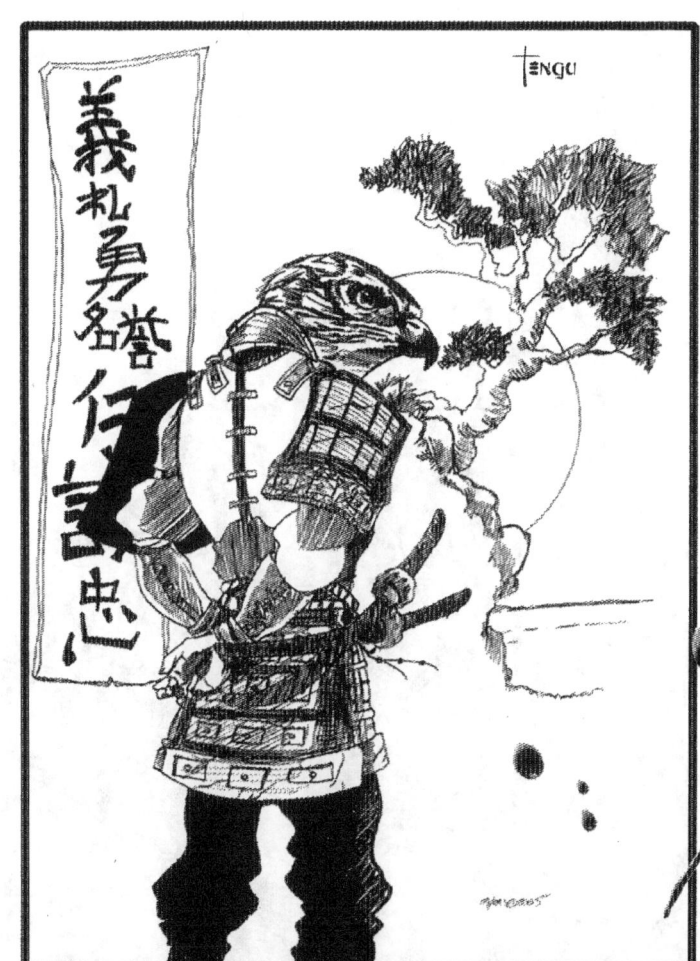

Tengu

義礼勇誉仁言忠

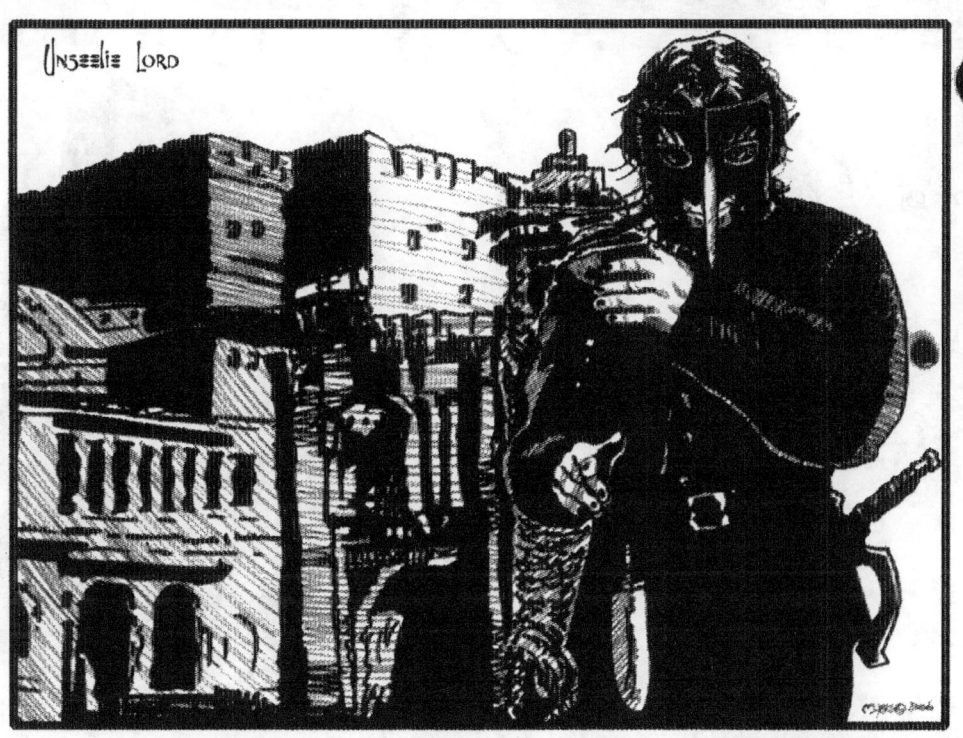

Unseelie Lord

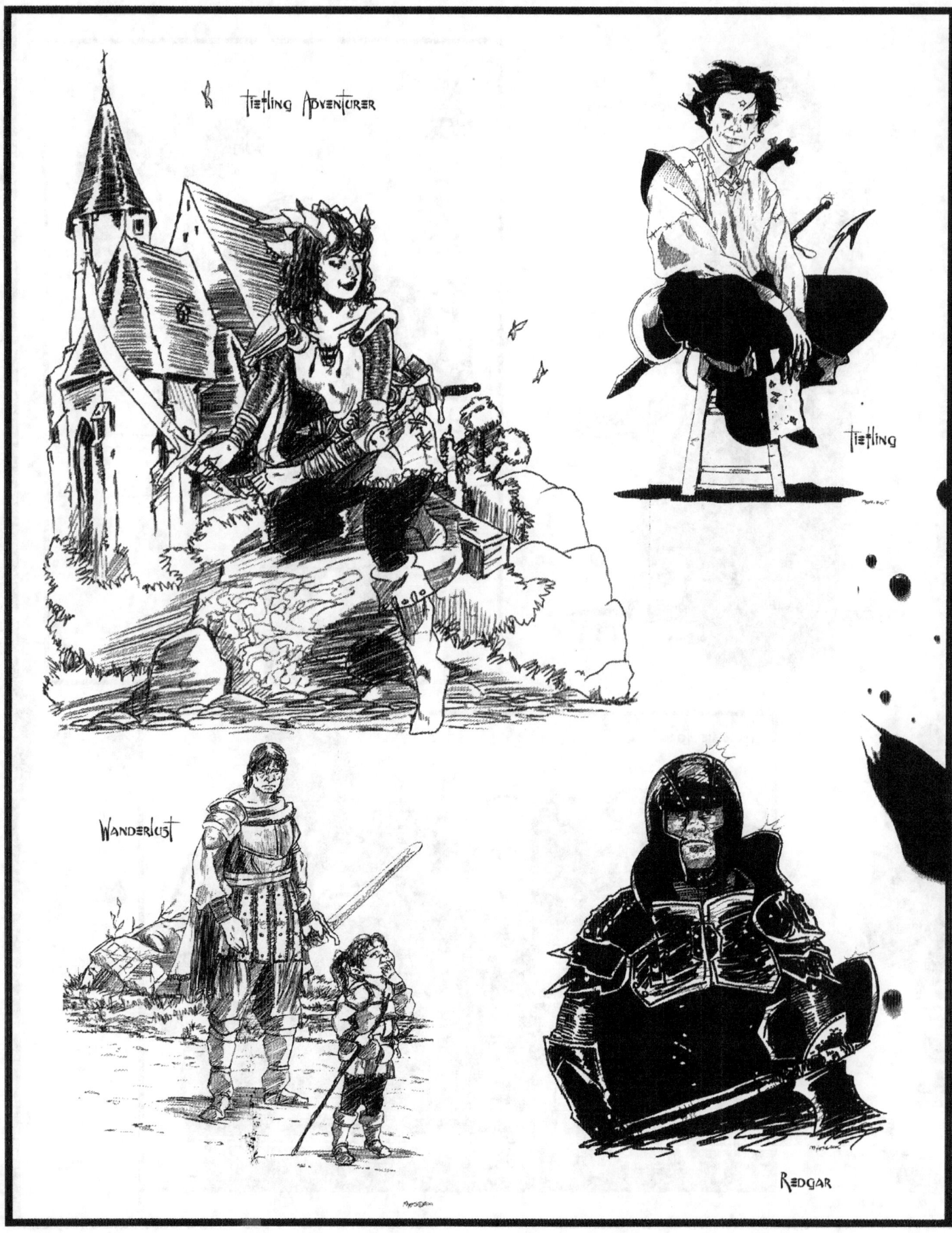

TIEFLING ADVENTURER

TIEFLING

WANDERLUST

REDGAR

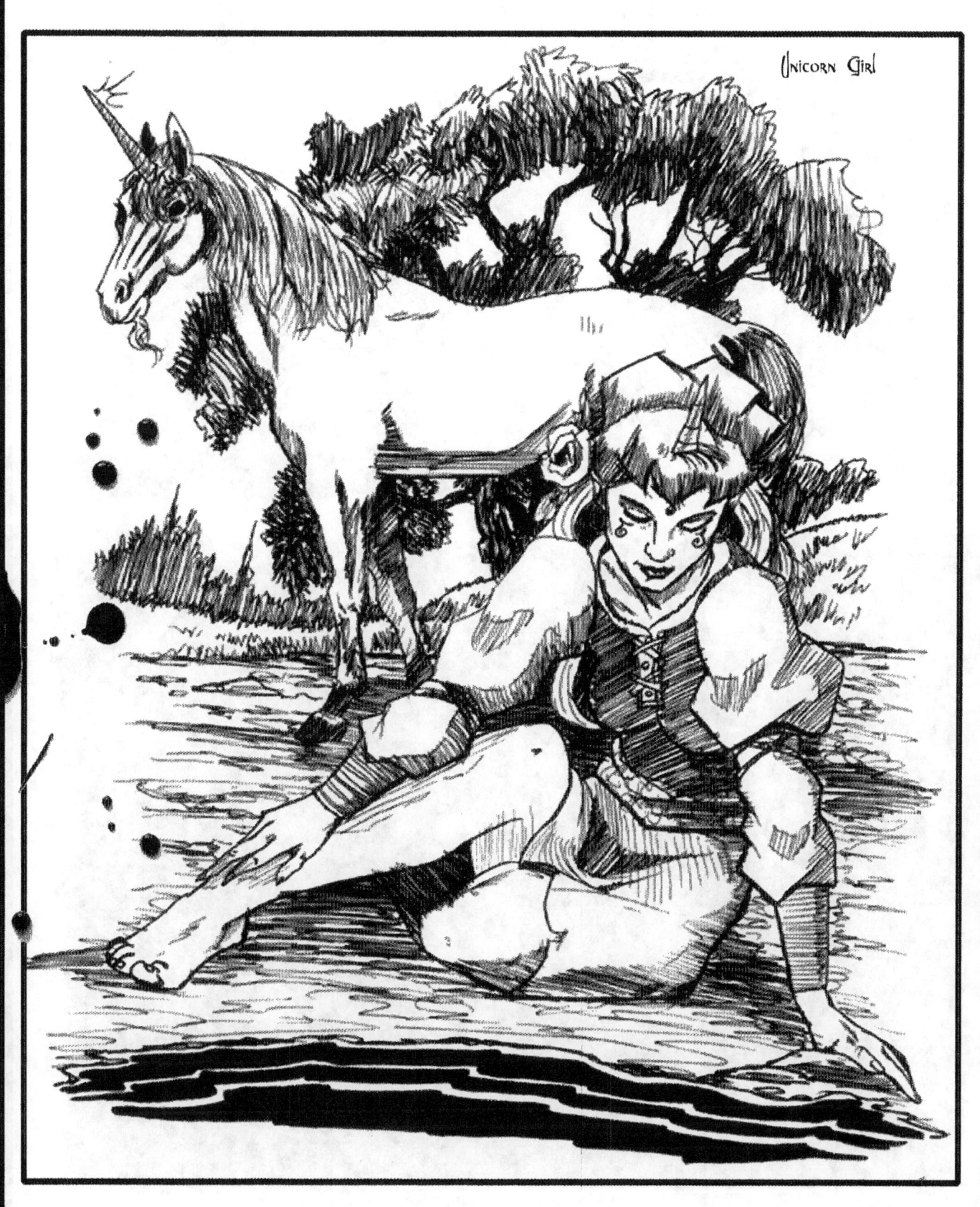

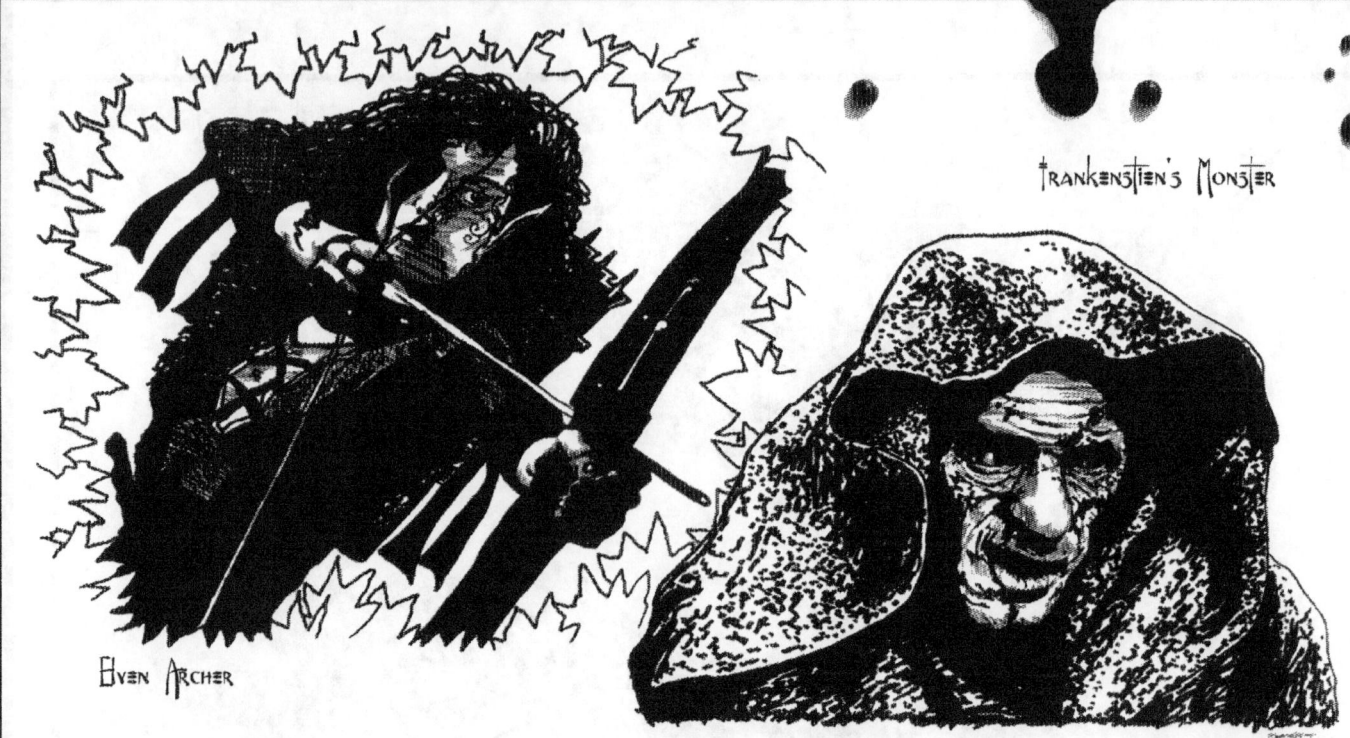

Elven Archer

Frankenstien's Monster

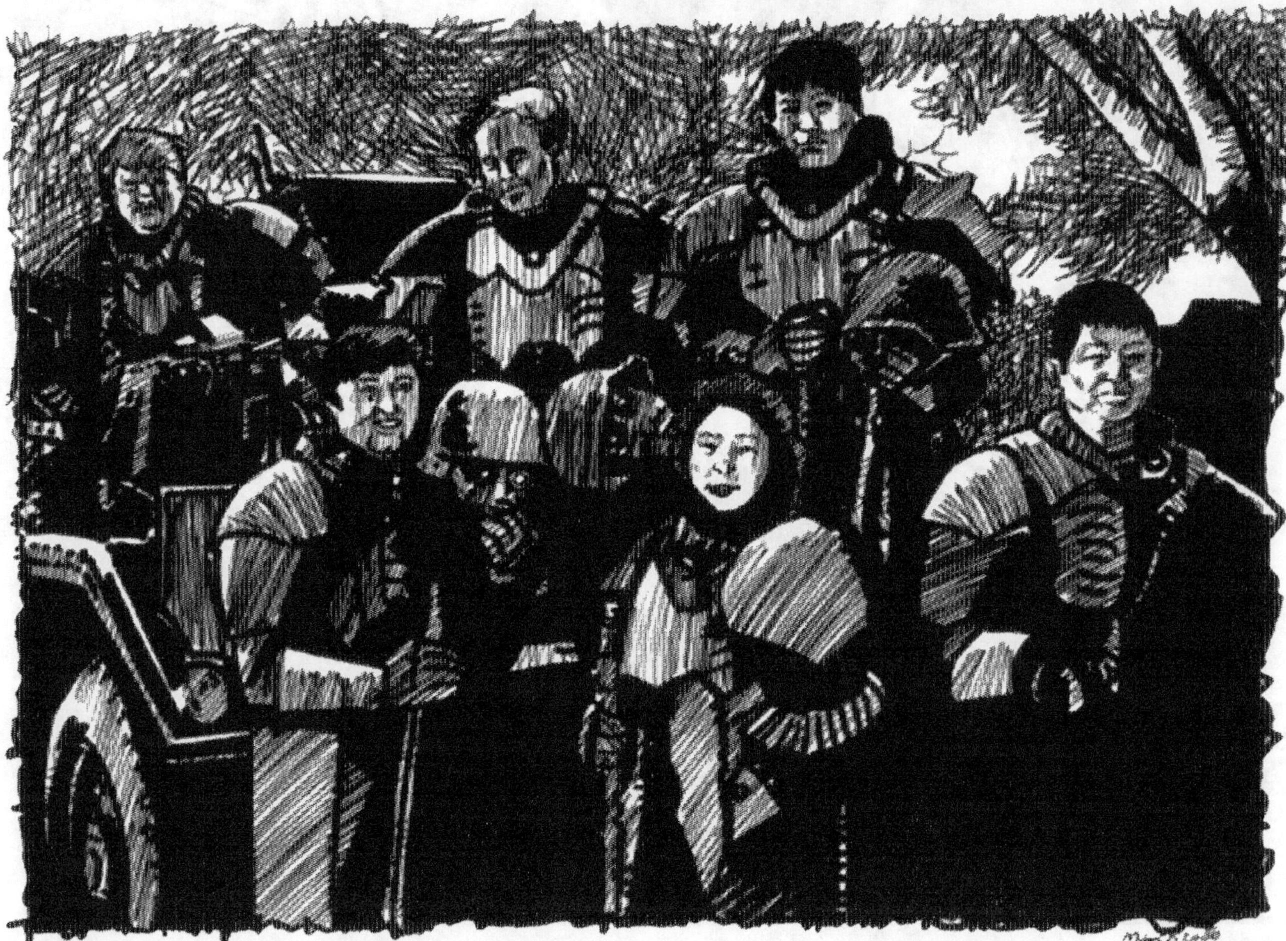

Wolf Pack

LADY HORROR

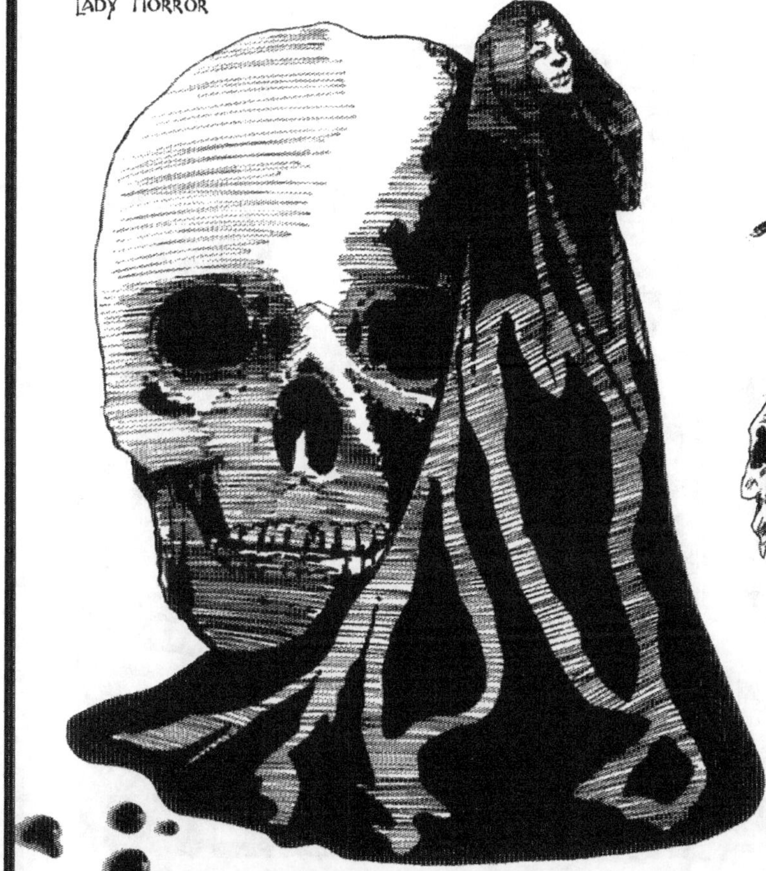

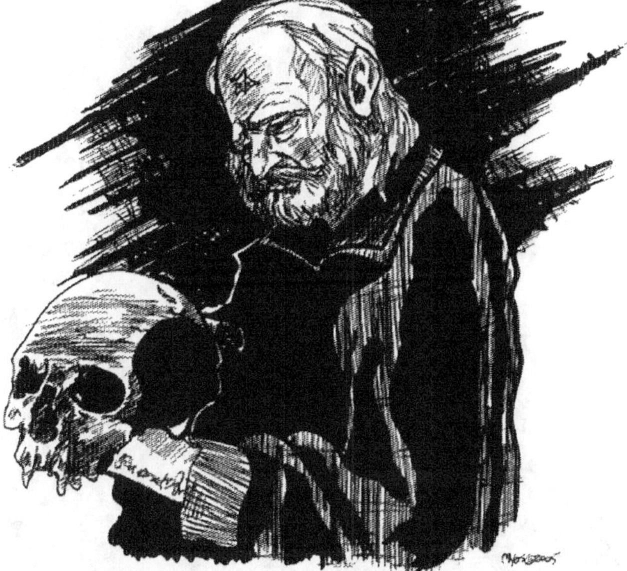

NECROMANCER

LUNAR CONFLICT

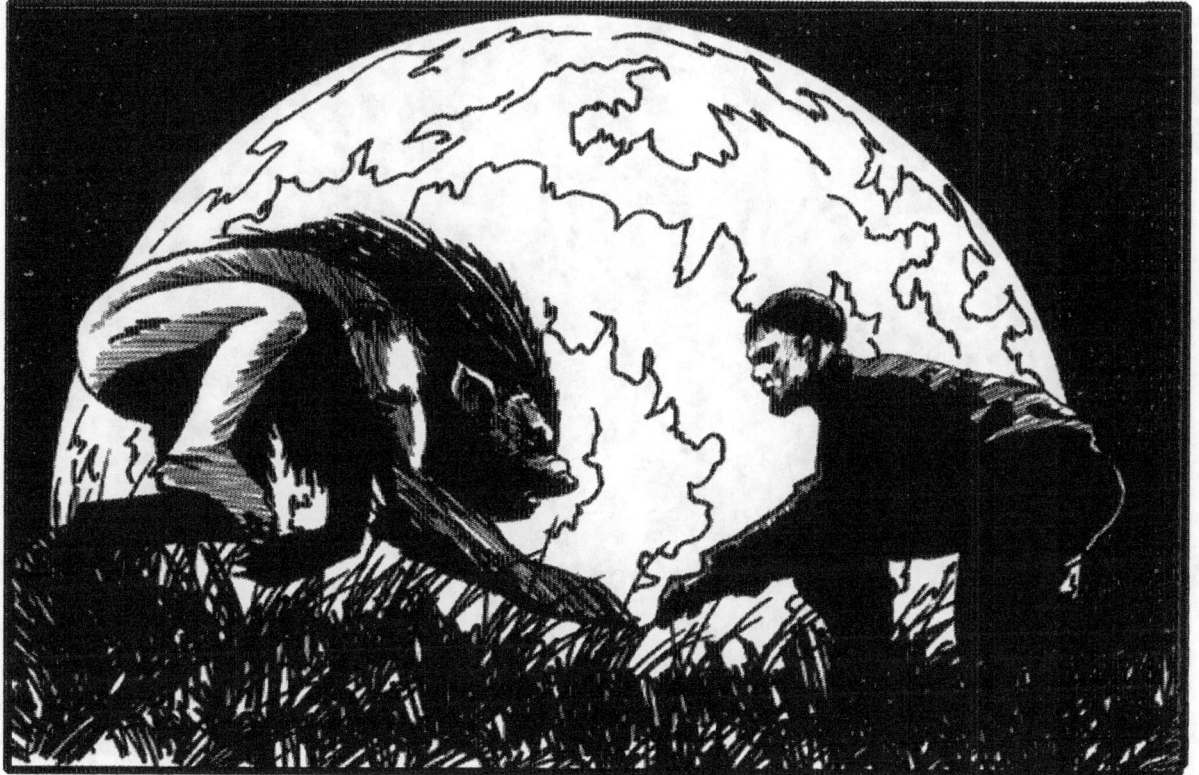

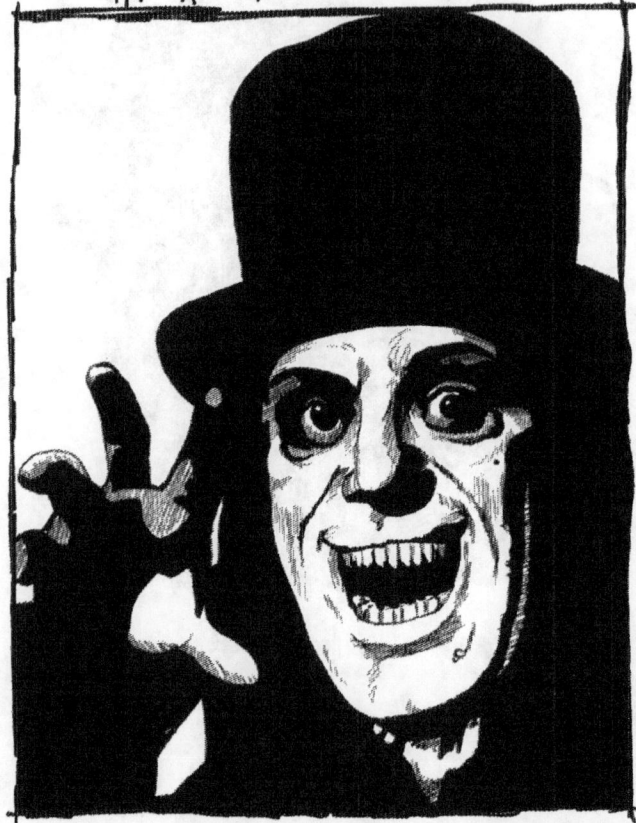

London After Midnight

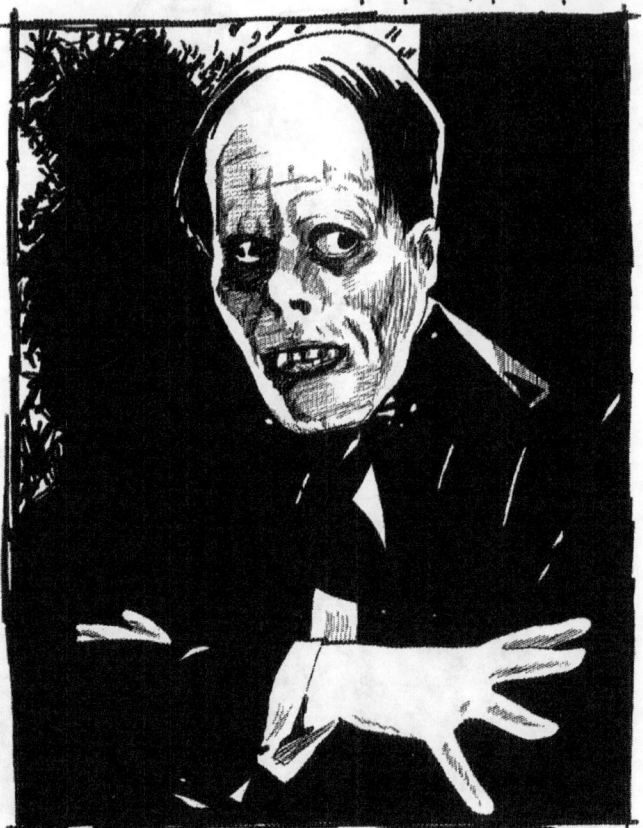

Phantom of the Opera

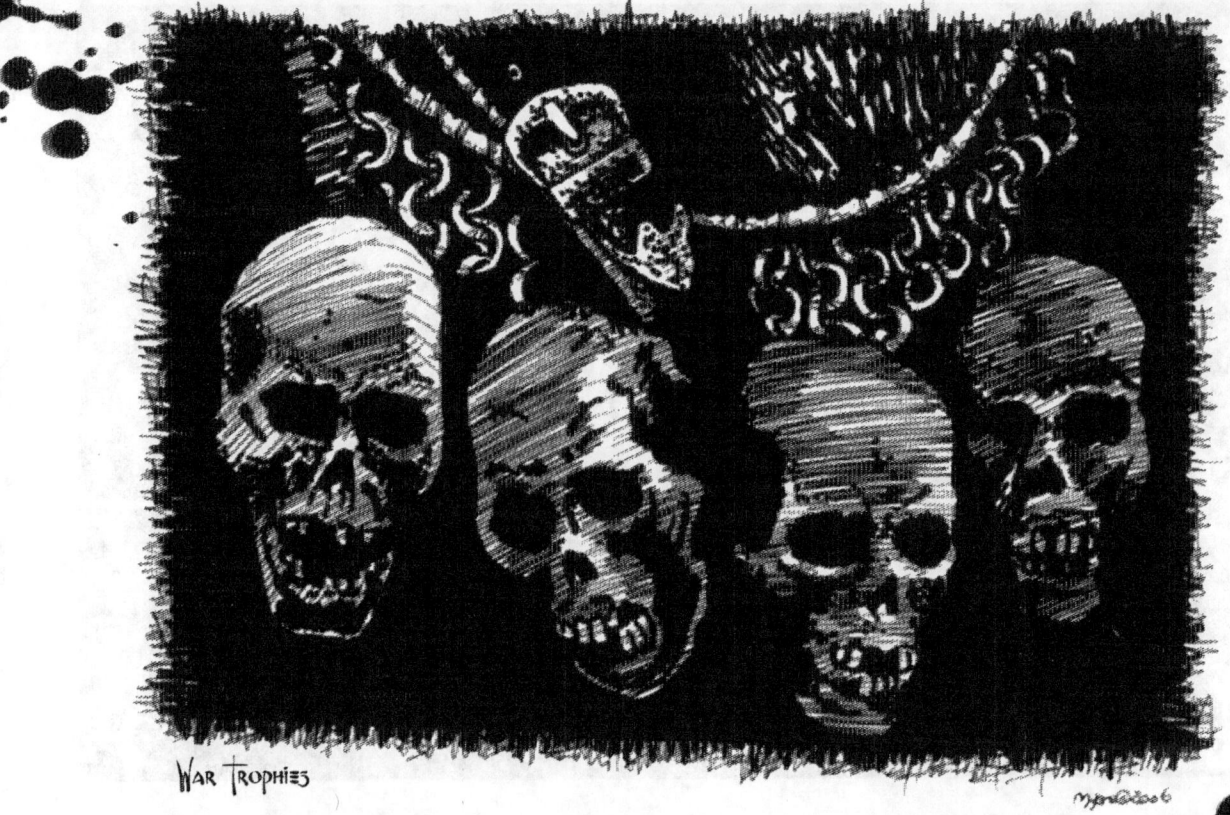

War Trophies

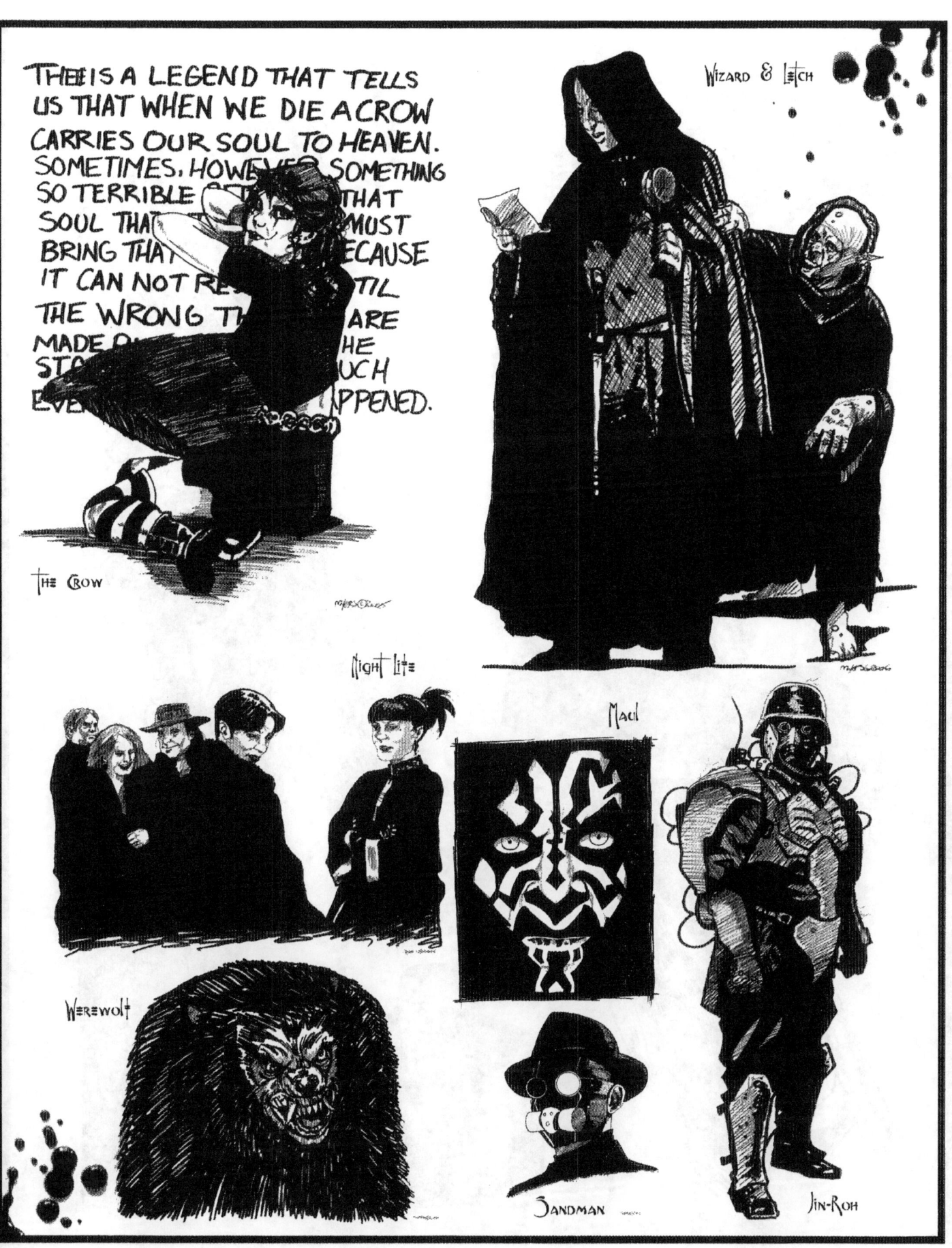

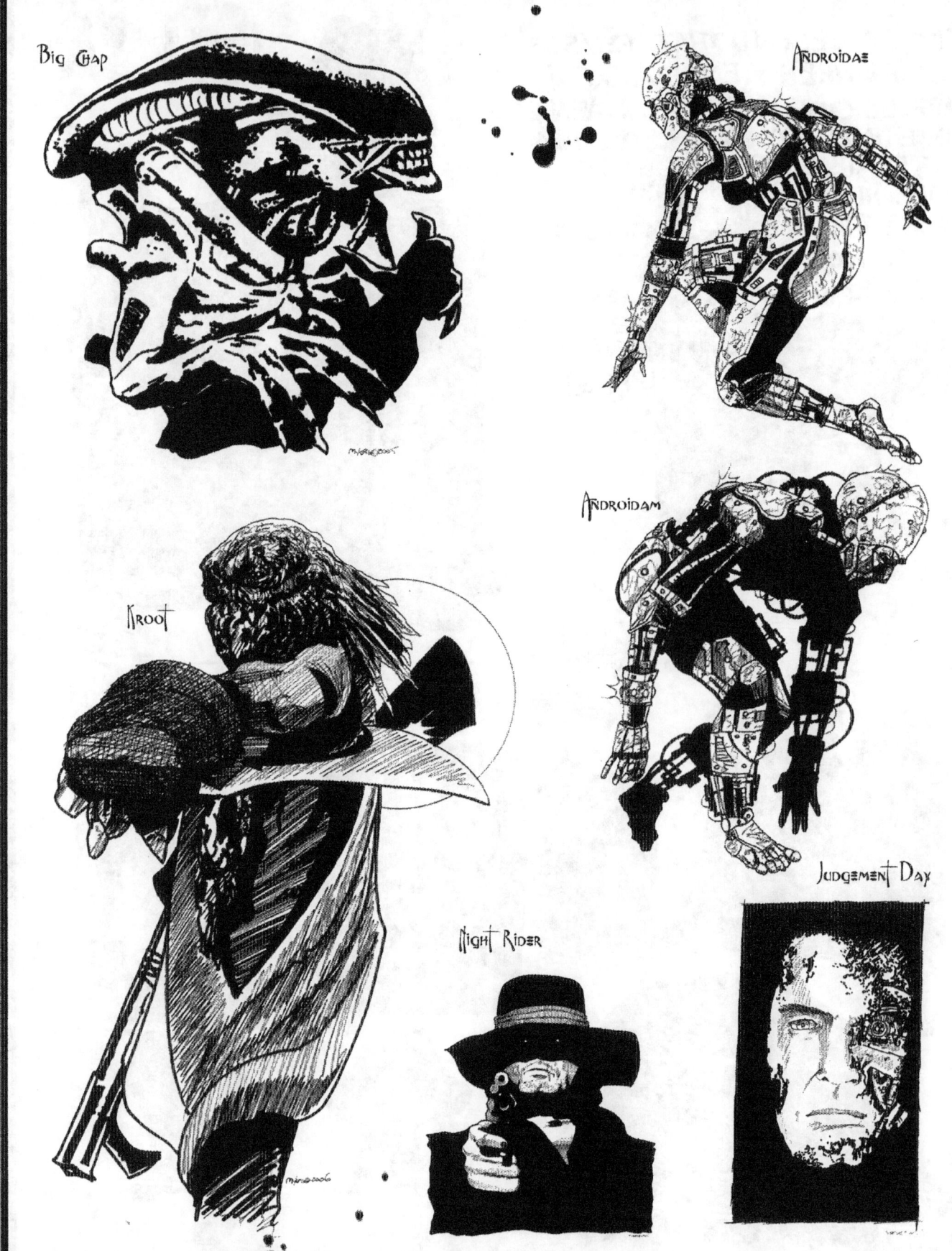

Big Chap

Androidae

Androidam

Kroot

Night Rider

Judgement Day

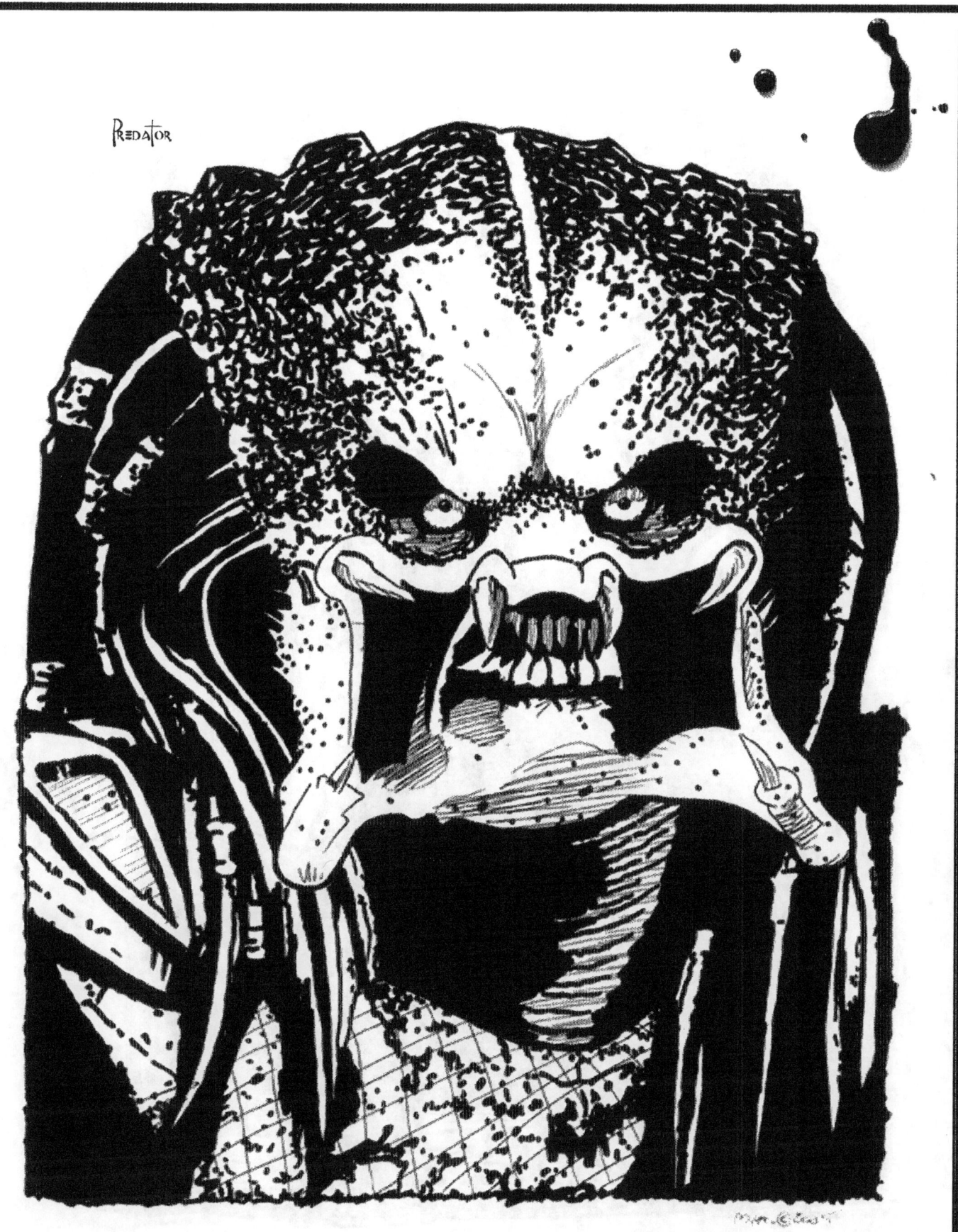

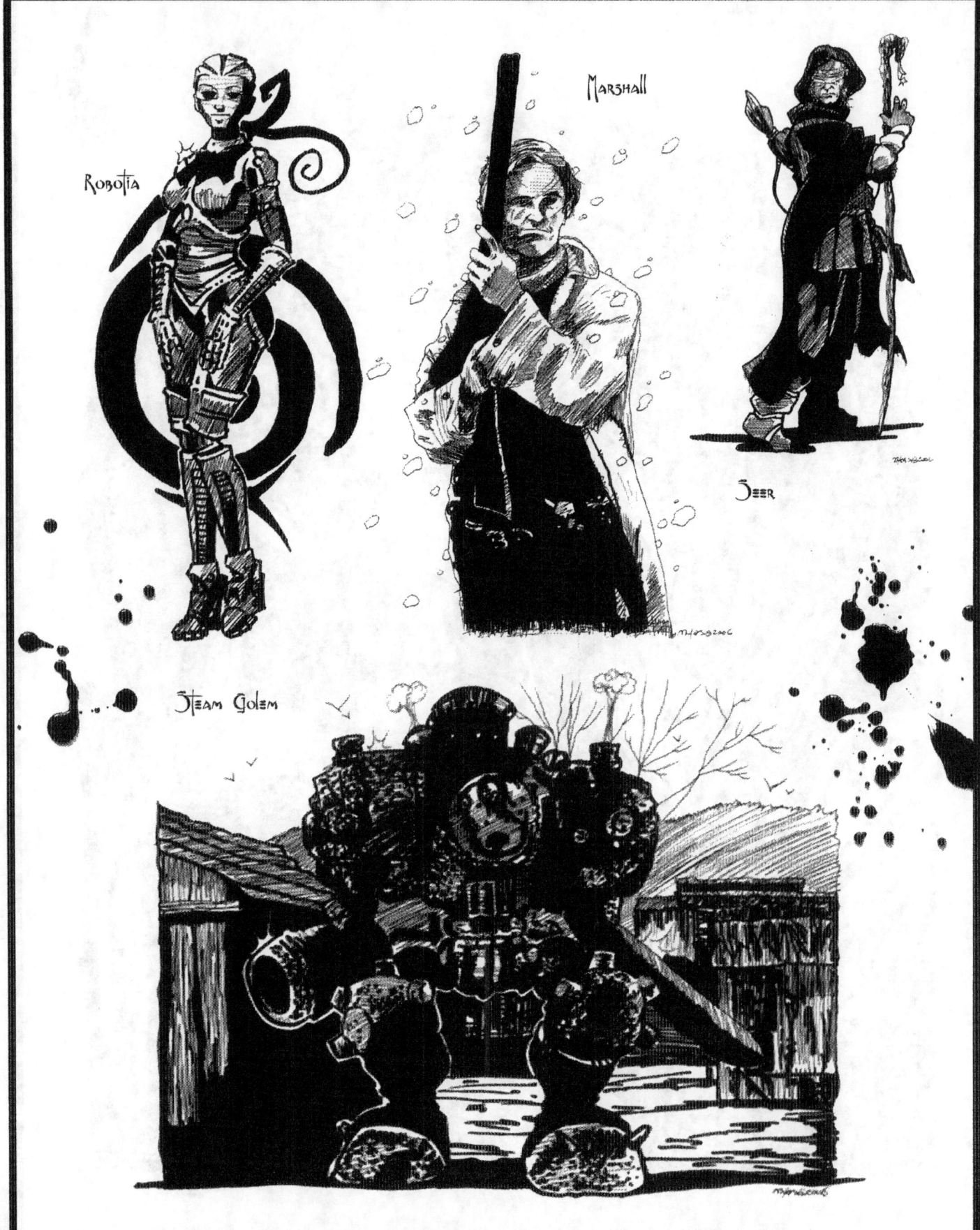

Robotia

Marshall

Seer

Steam Golem

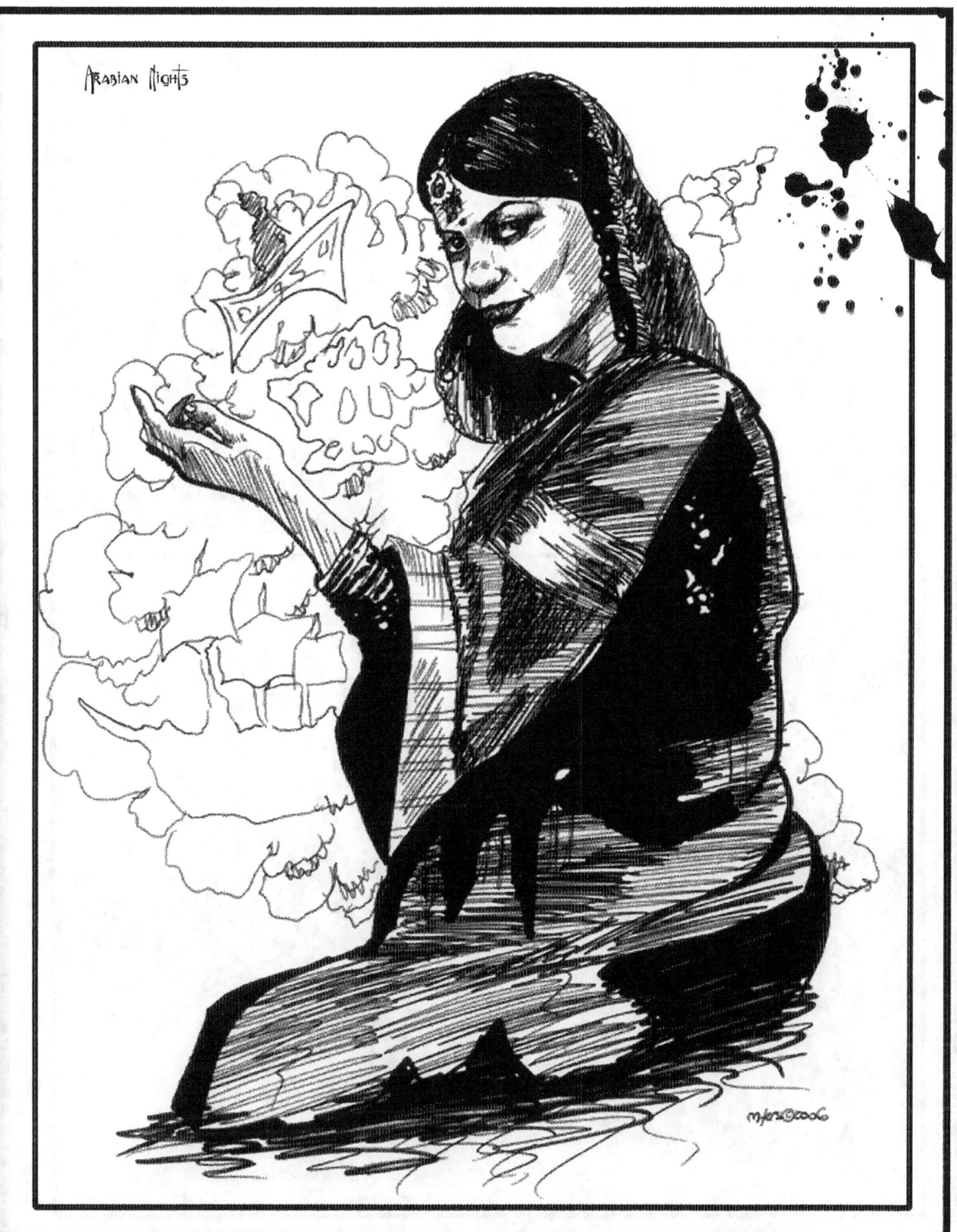
ARABIAN NIGHTS

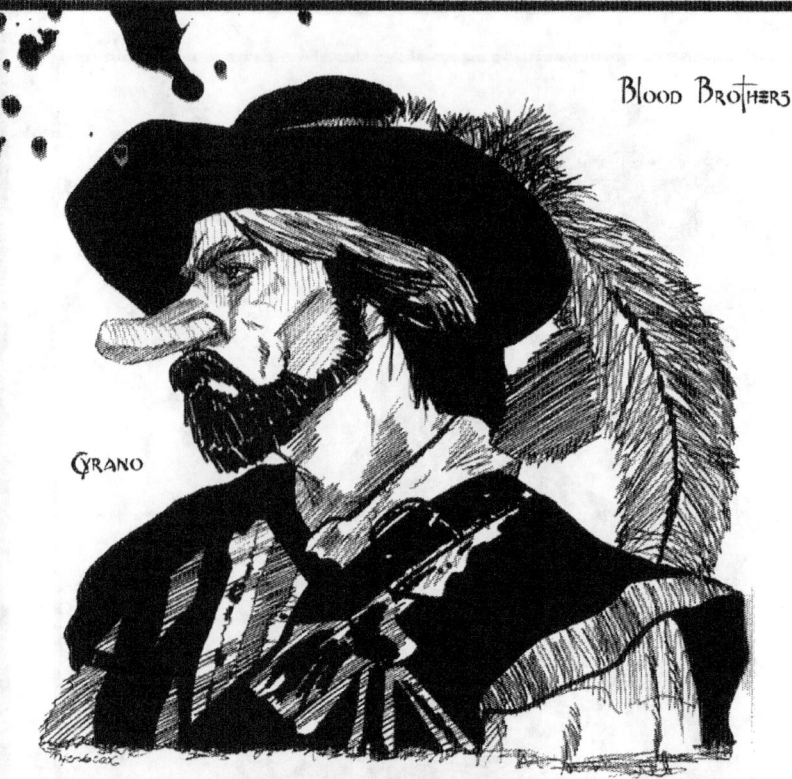

BLOOD BROTHERS

CYRANO

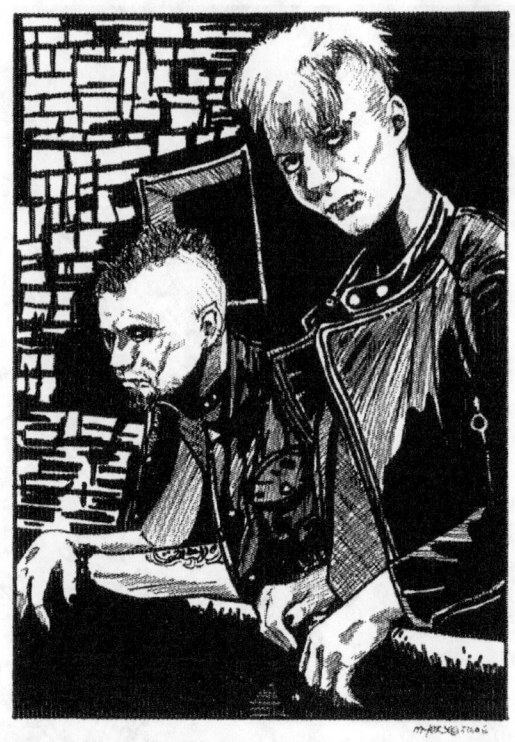

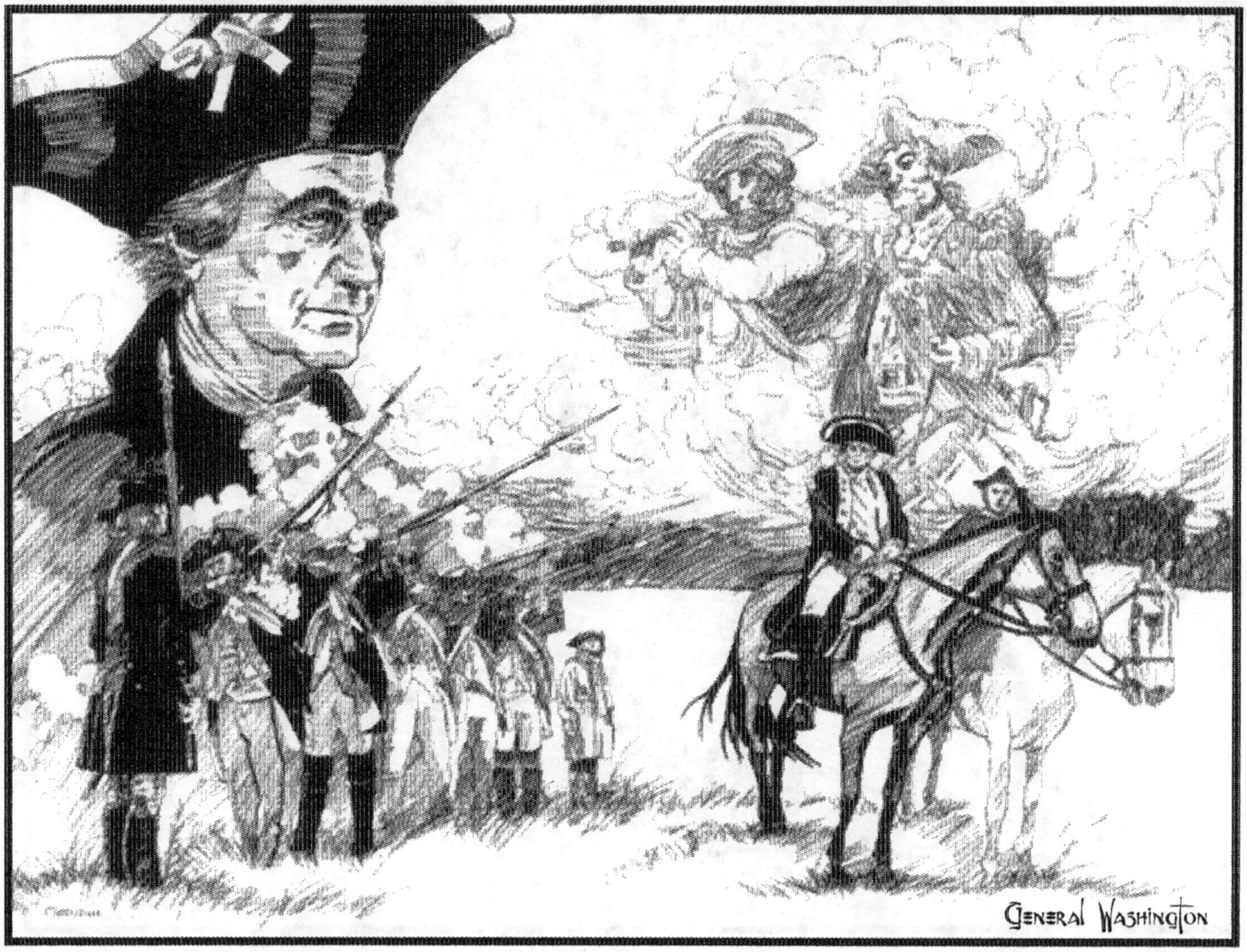

GENERAL WASHINGTON

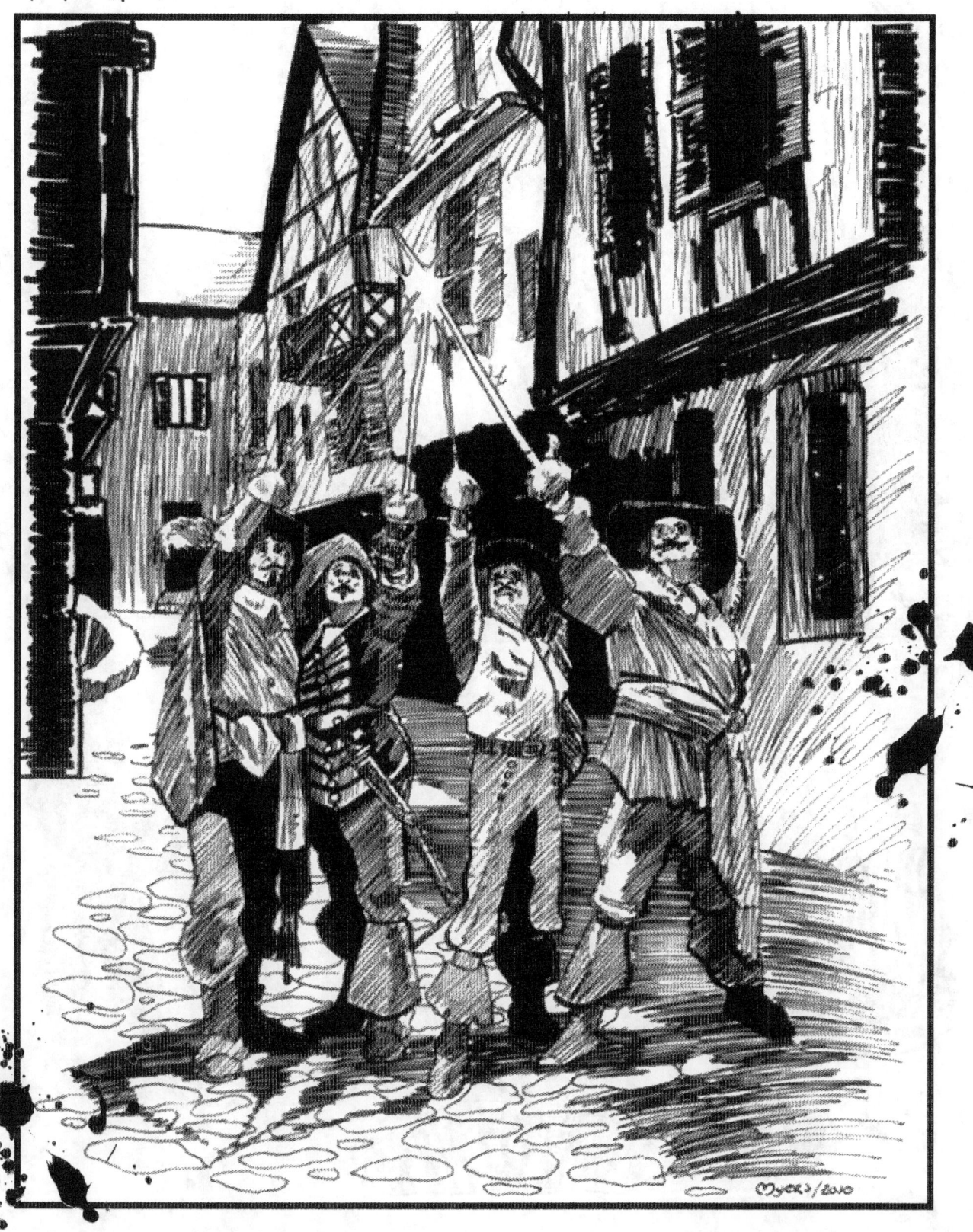

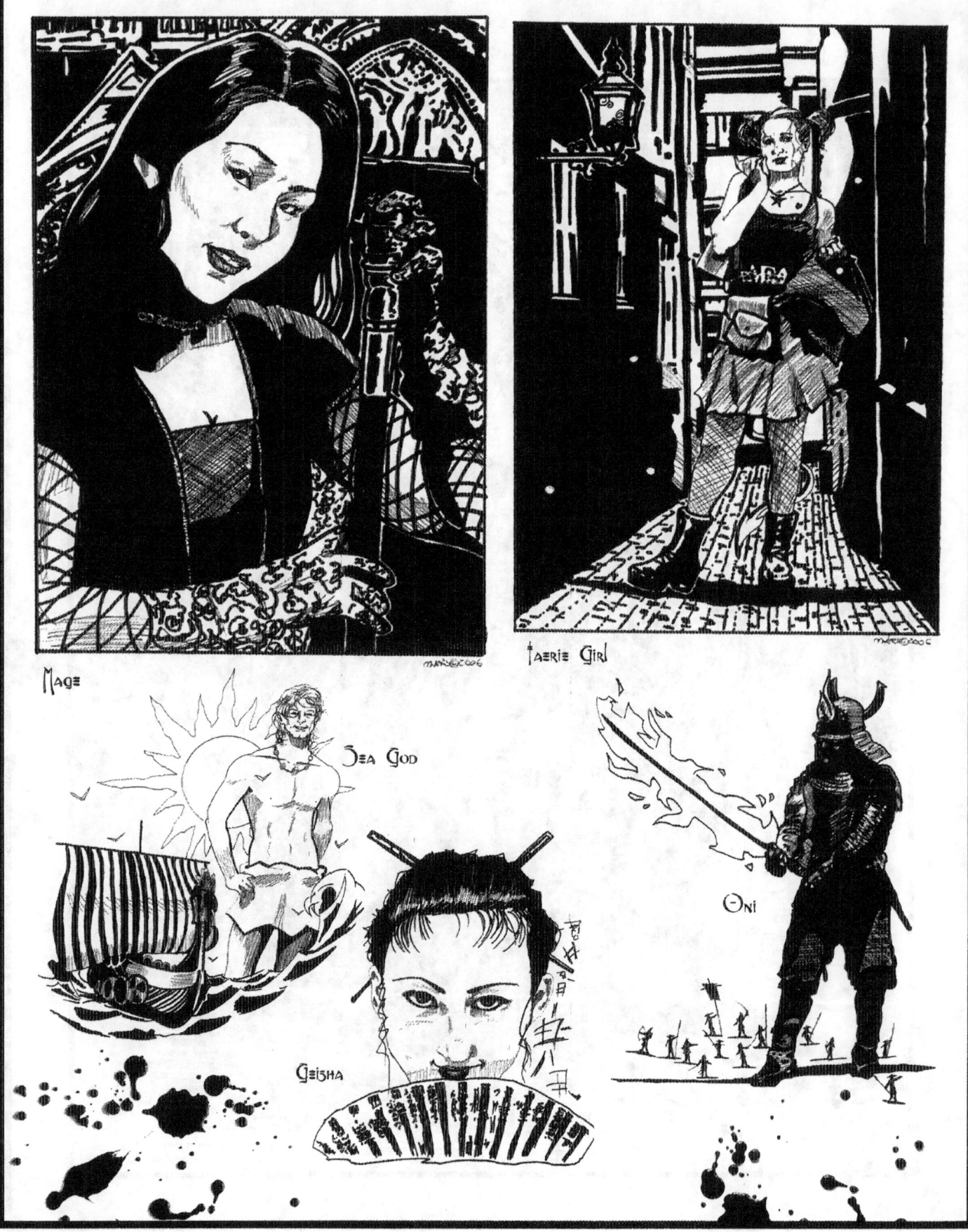

Mage

Faerie Girl

Sea God

Geisha

Oni

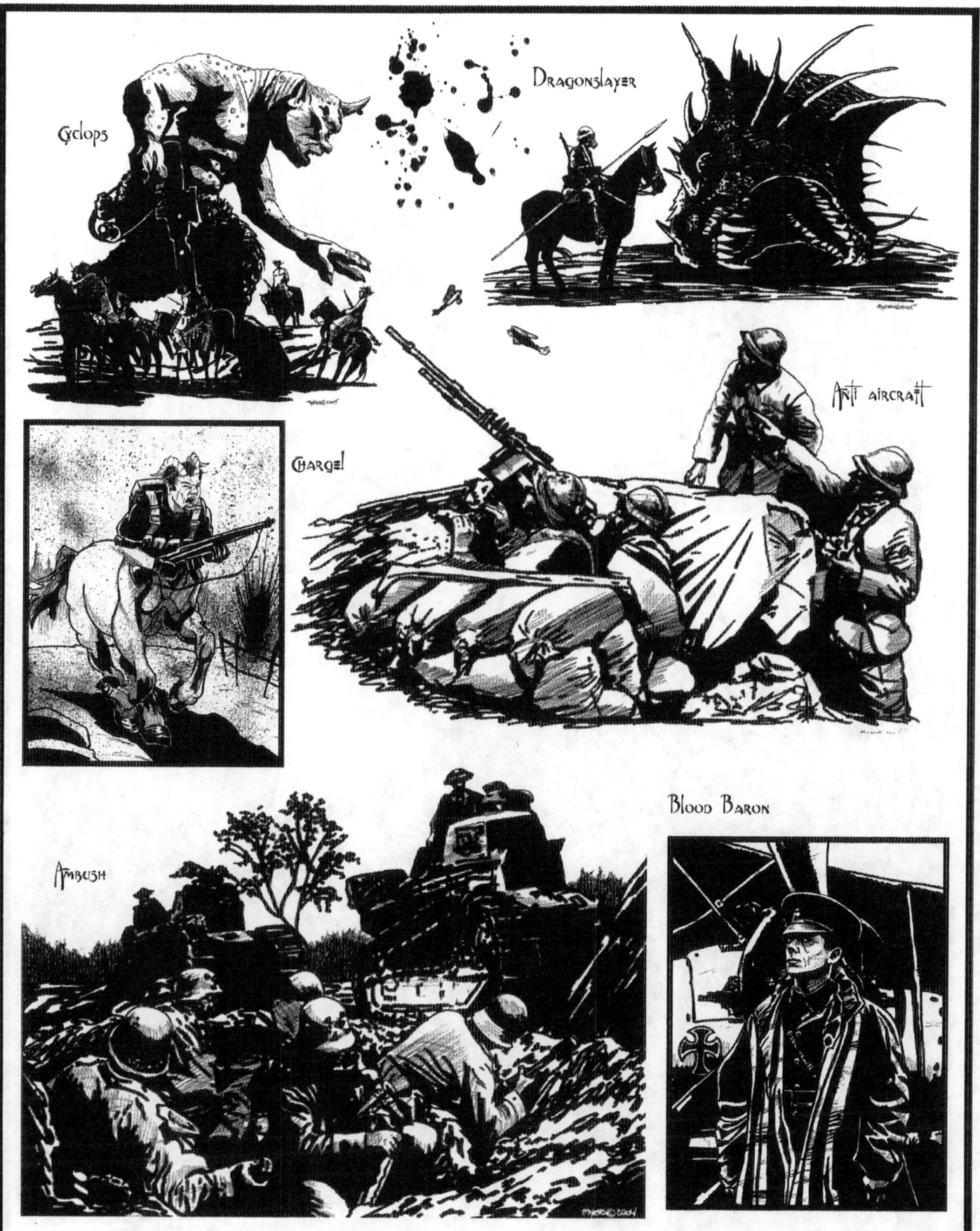

Cyclops

Dragonslayer

Charge!

Anti aircraft

Ambush

Blood Baron

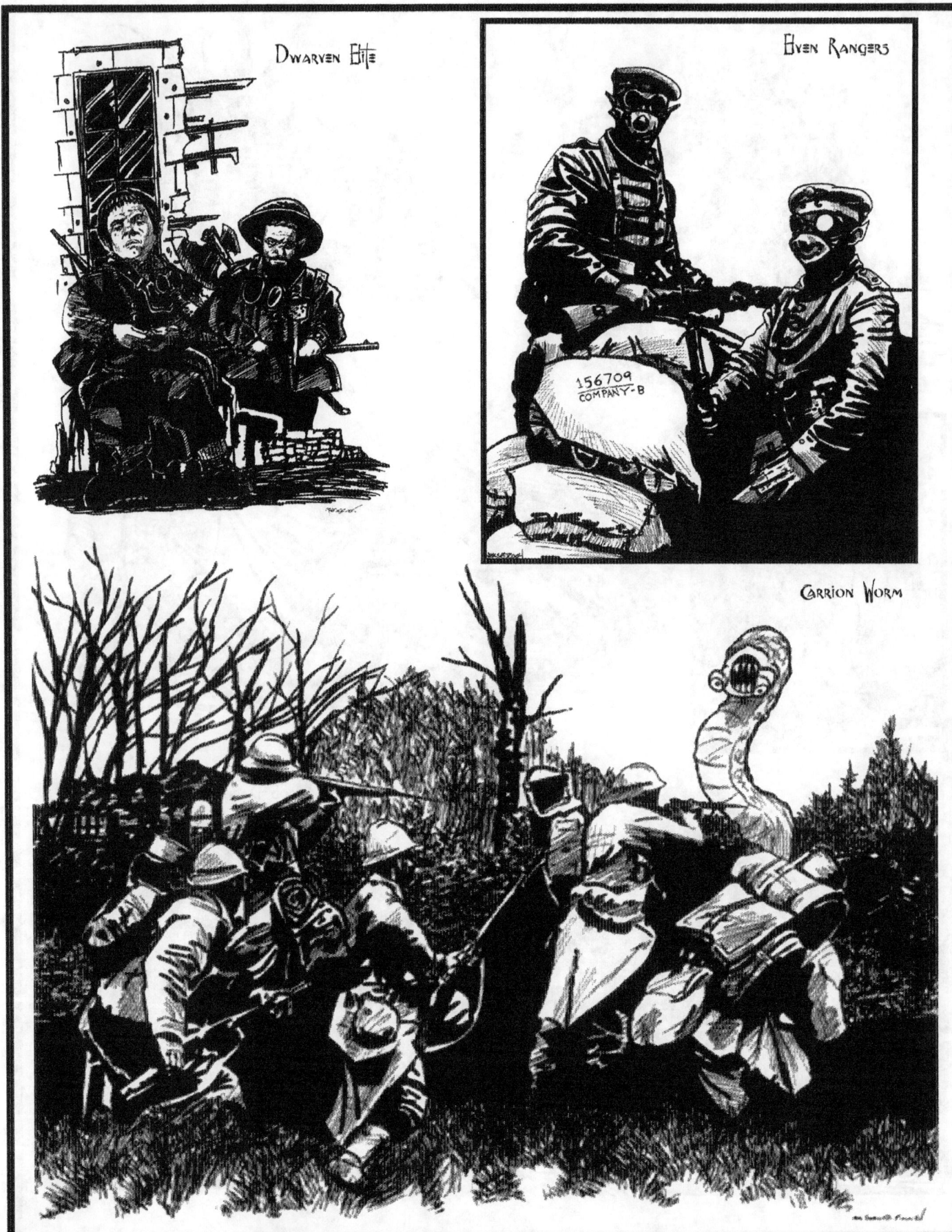

Dwarven Elite

Elven Rangers

156709
COMPANY-B

Carrion Worm

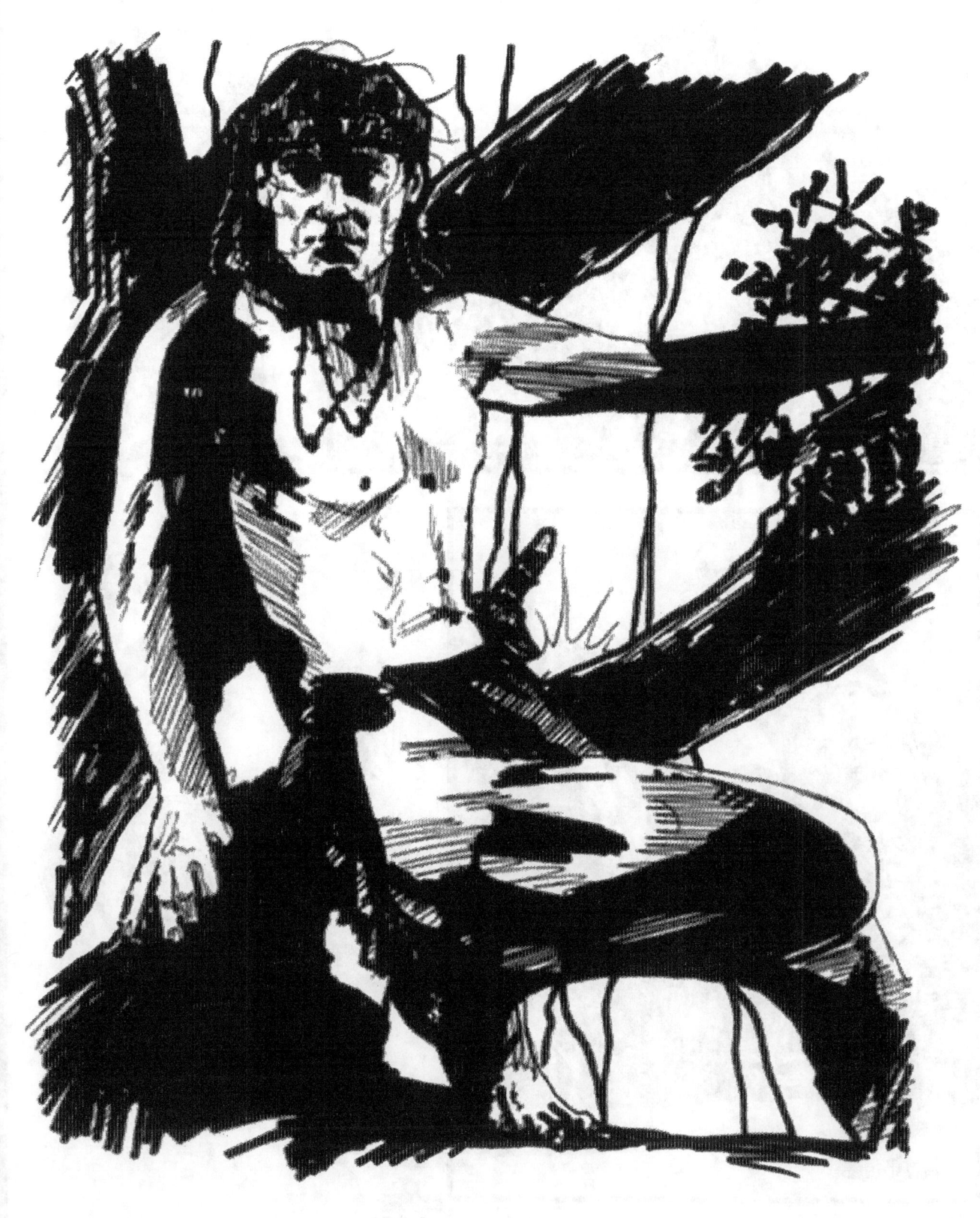

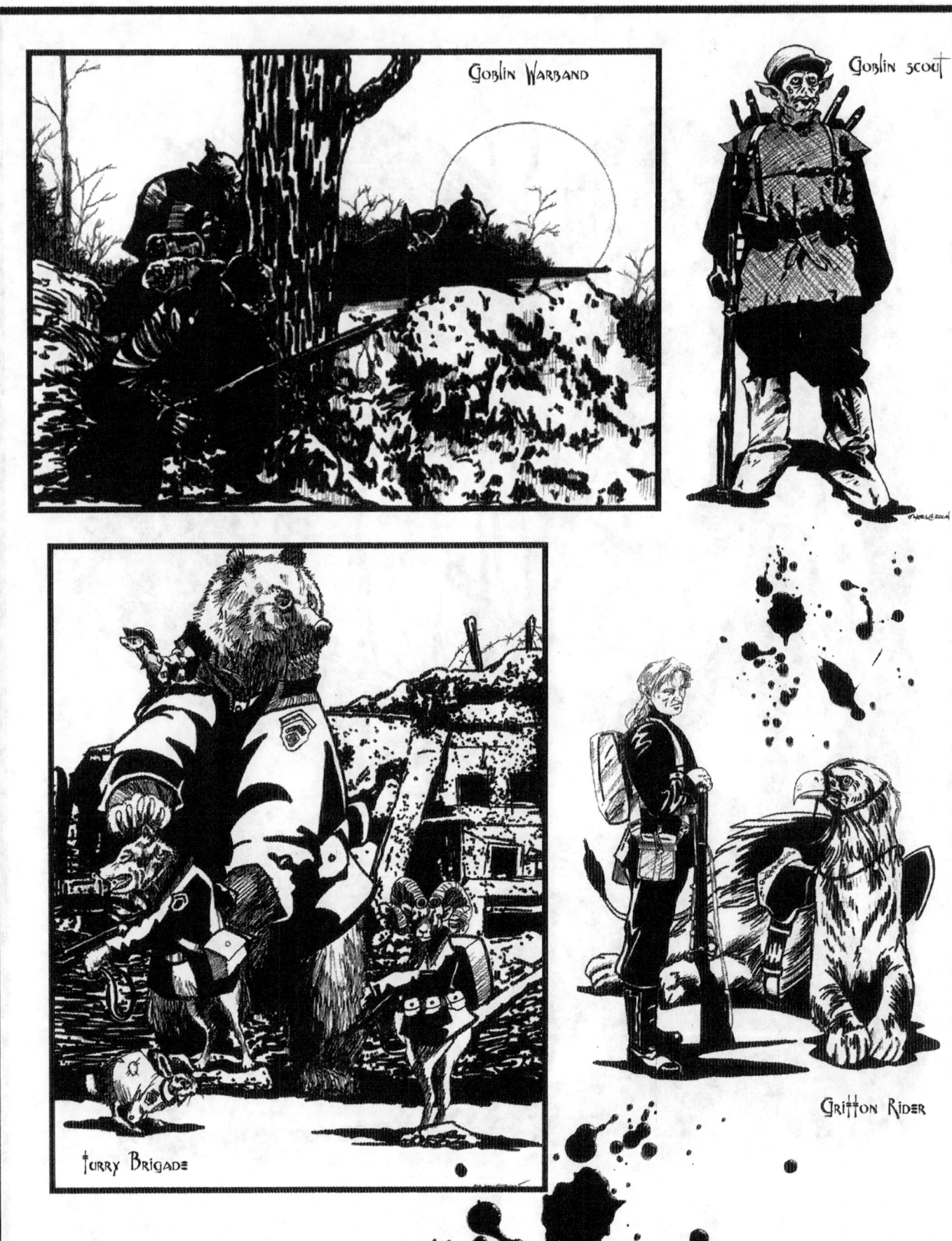

GOBLIN WARBAND

GOBLIN SCOUT

fURRY BRIGADE

GRIffON RIDER

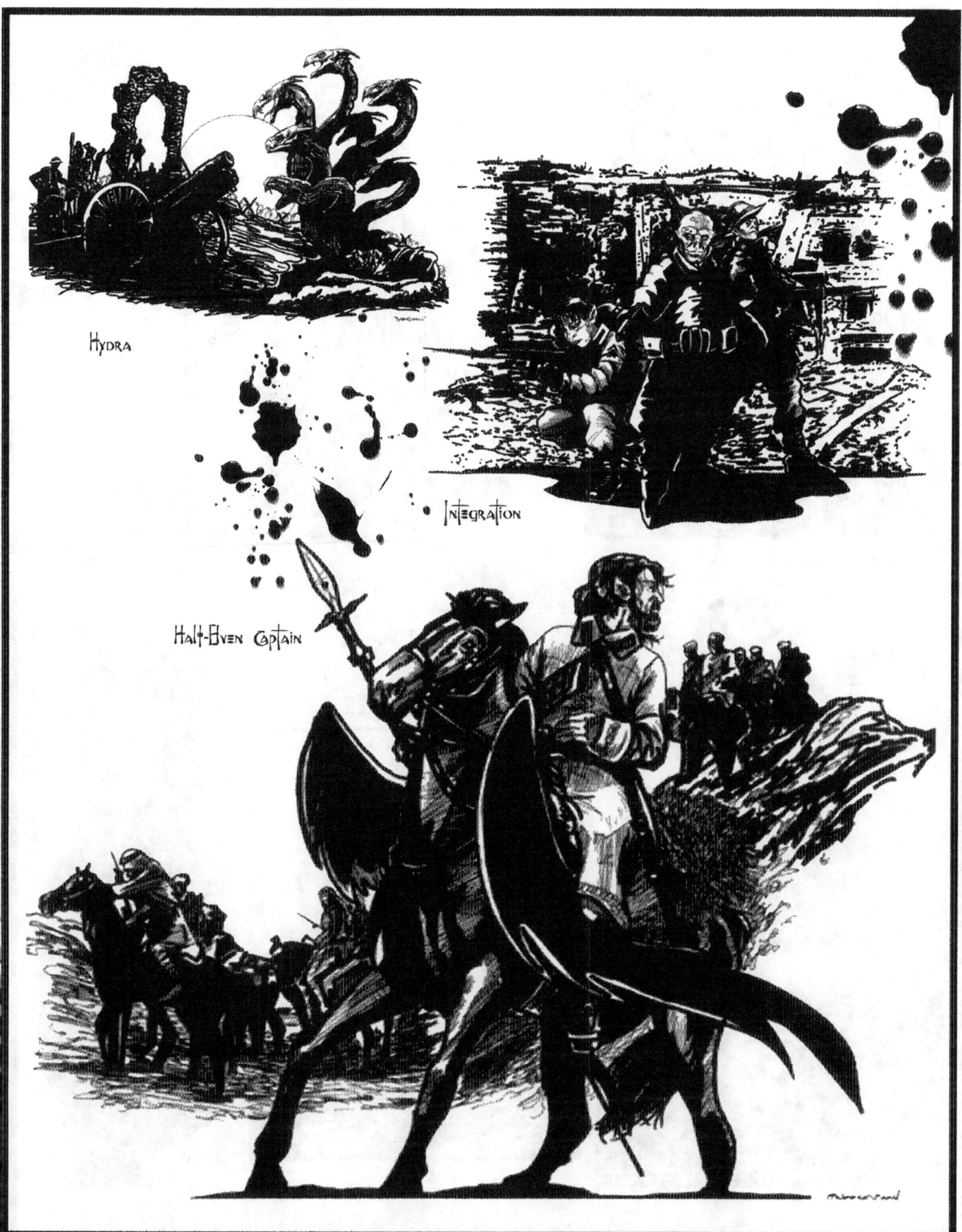

Hydra

Integration

Half-Elven Captain

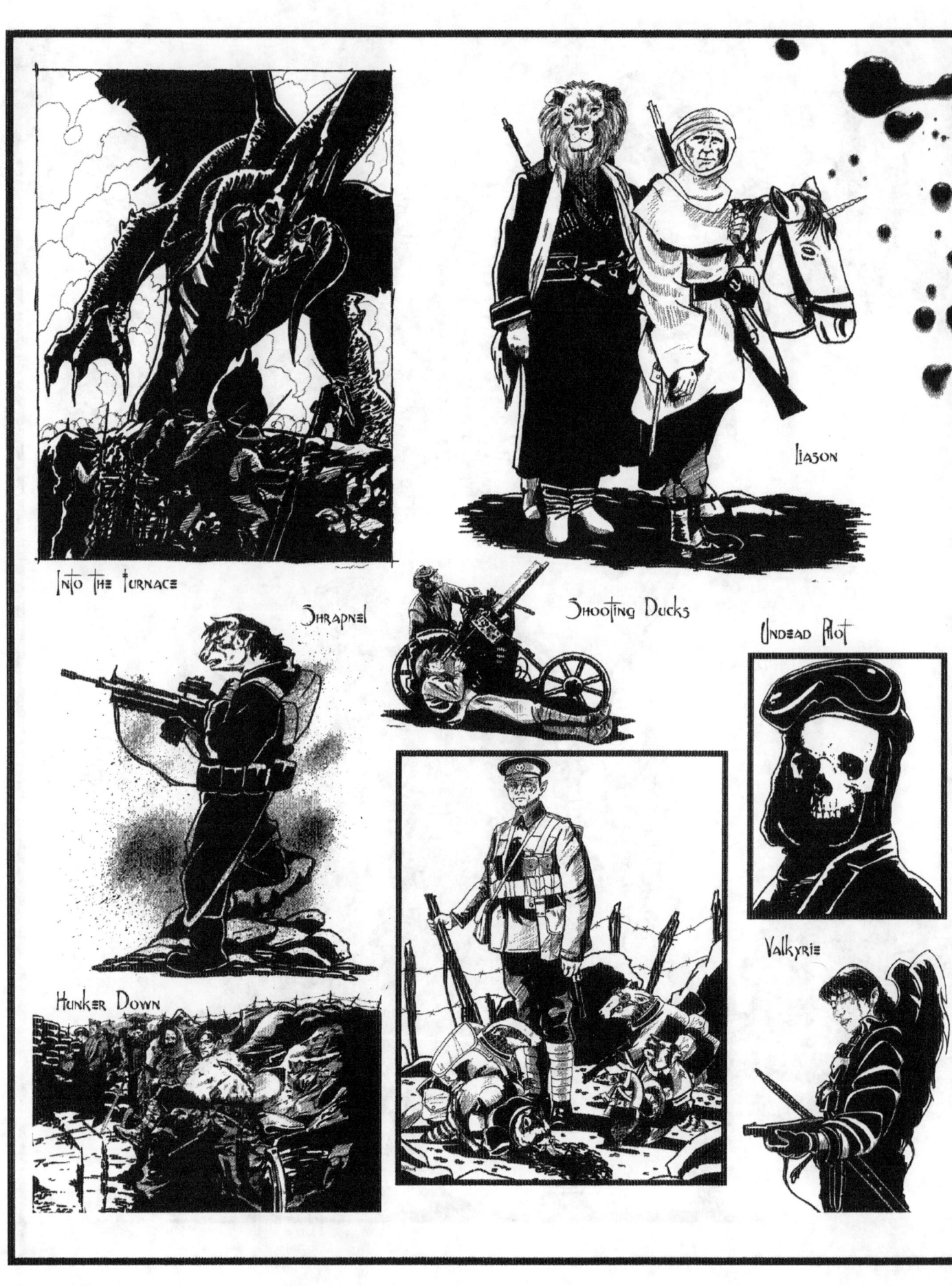

Into the Furnace

Liason

Shrapnel

Shooting Ducks

Undead Riot

Hunker Down

Valkyrie

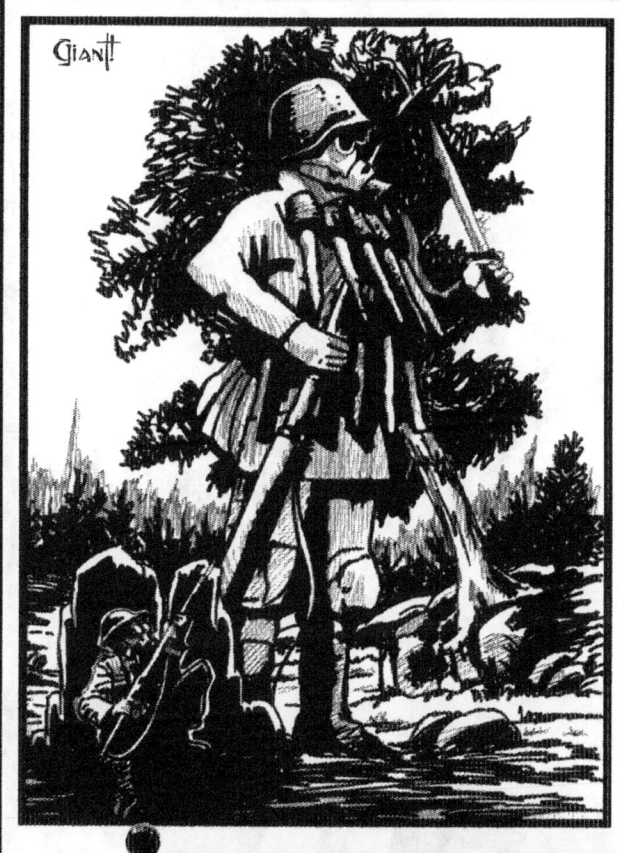

Giant!

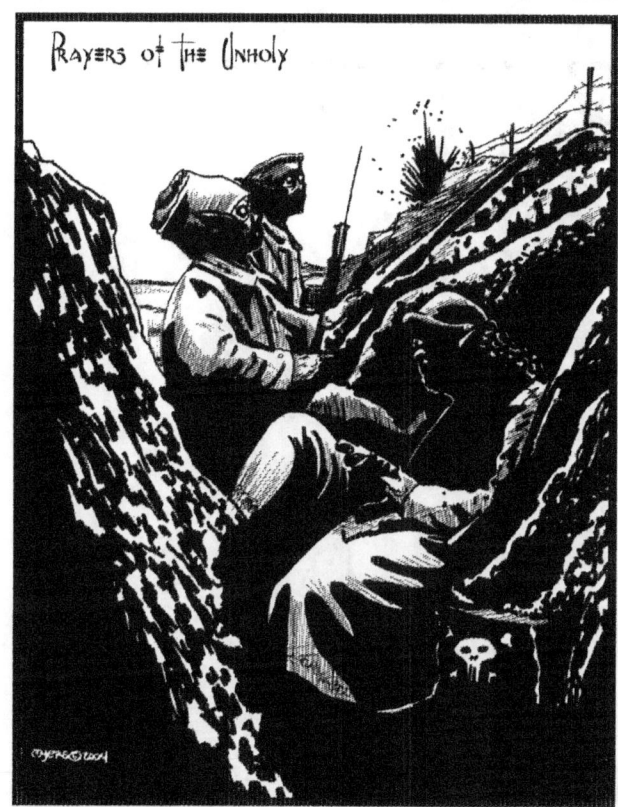

Prayers of the Unholy

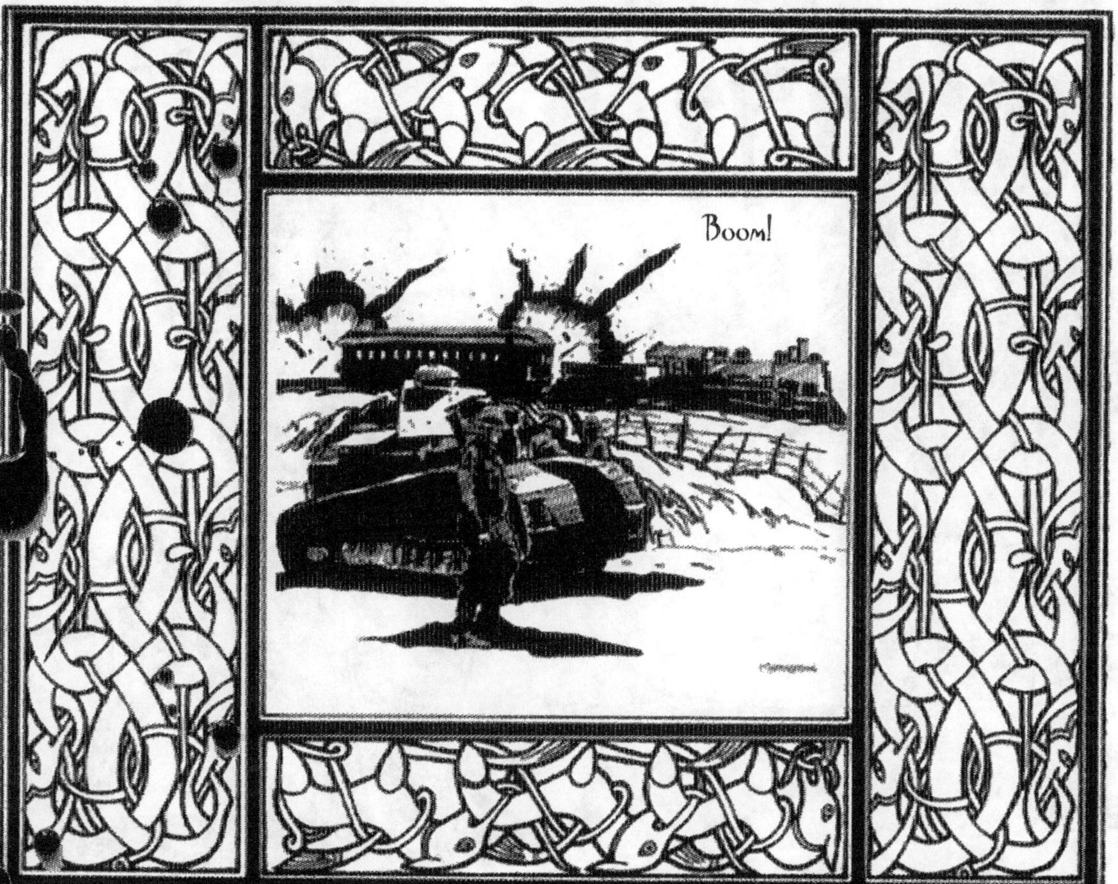

Boom!

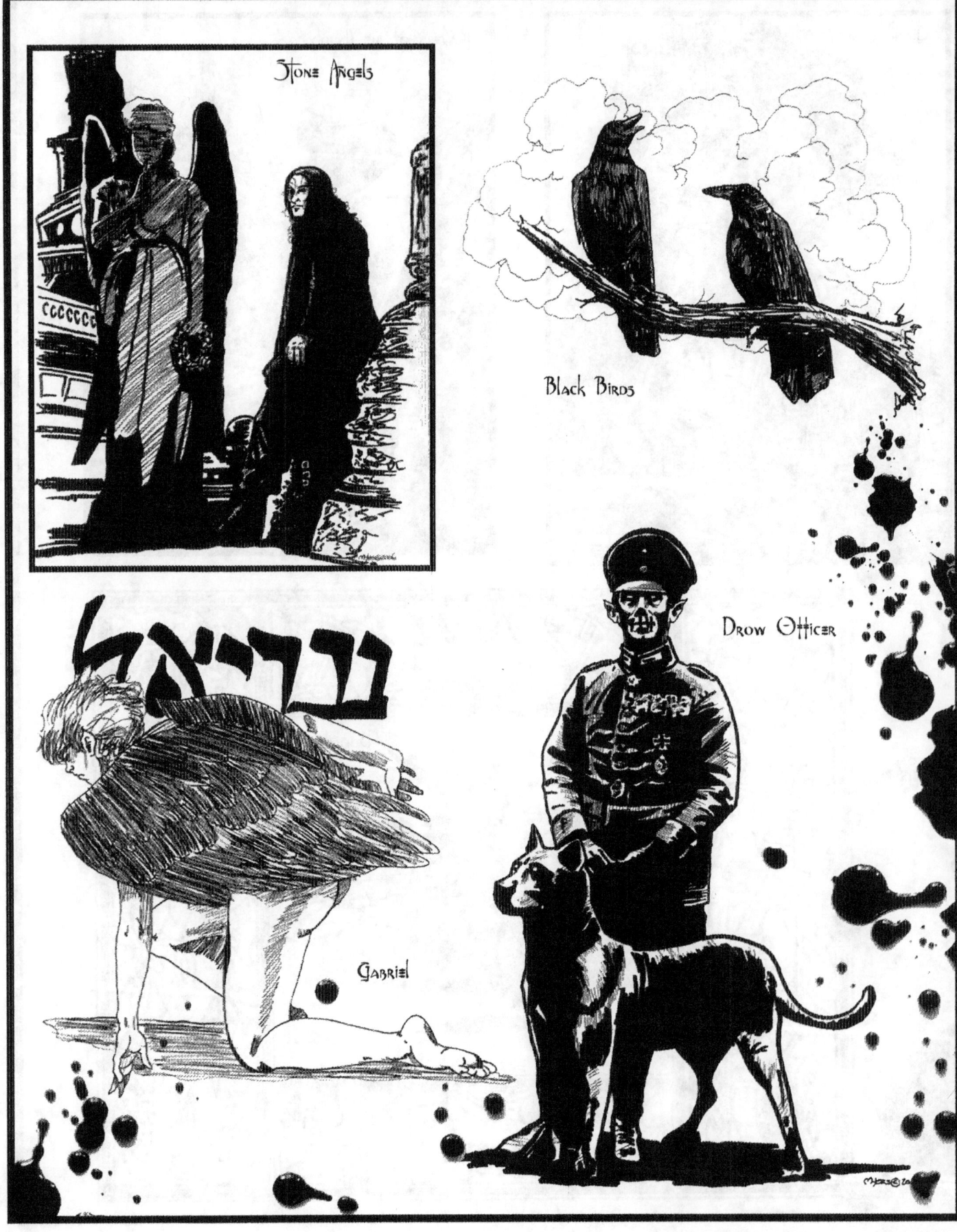

Stone Angels

Black Birds

בריאל

Gabriel

Drow Officer

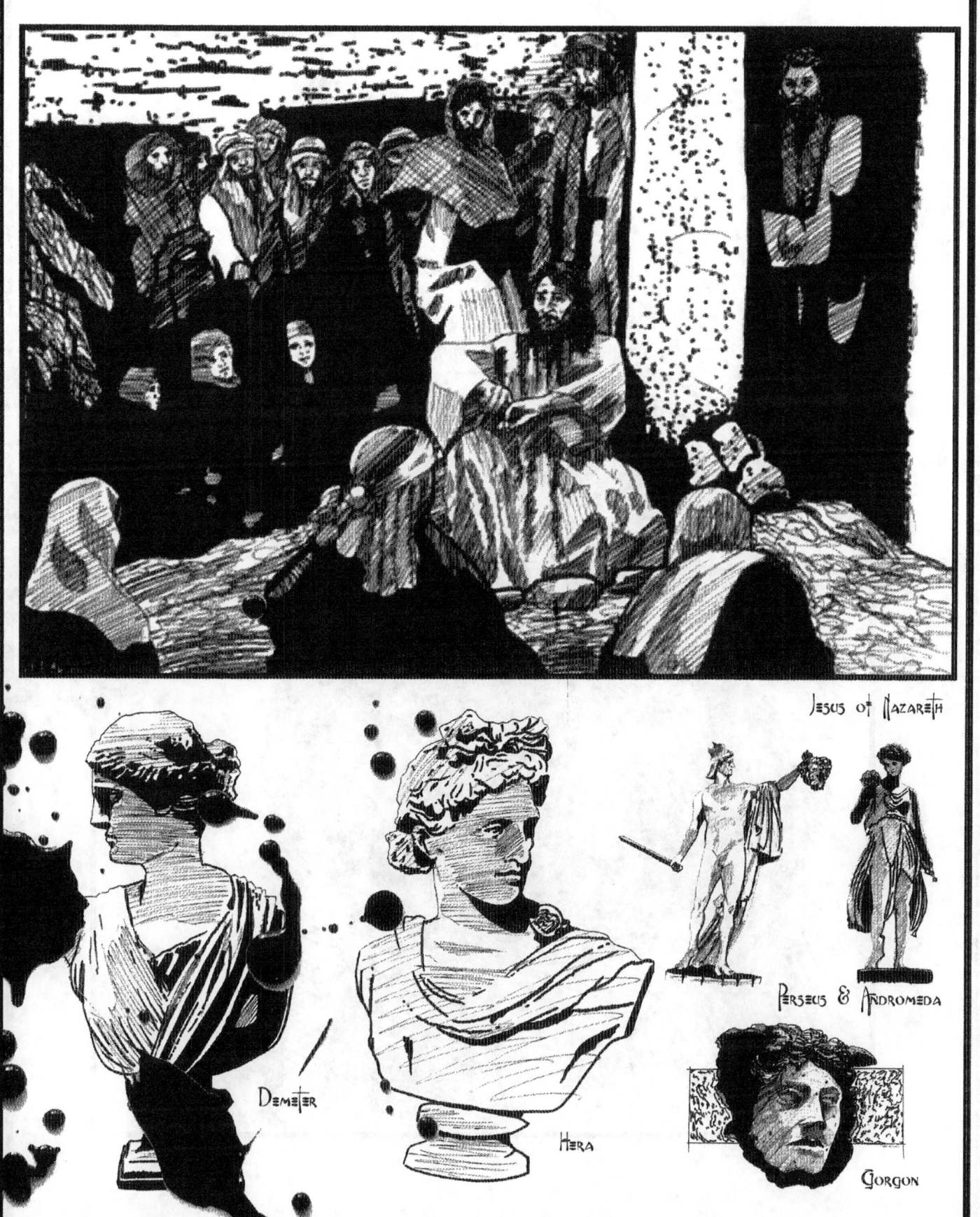

Jesus of Nazareth

Demeter

Hera

Perseus & Andromeda

Gorgon

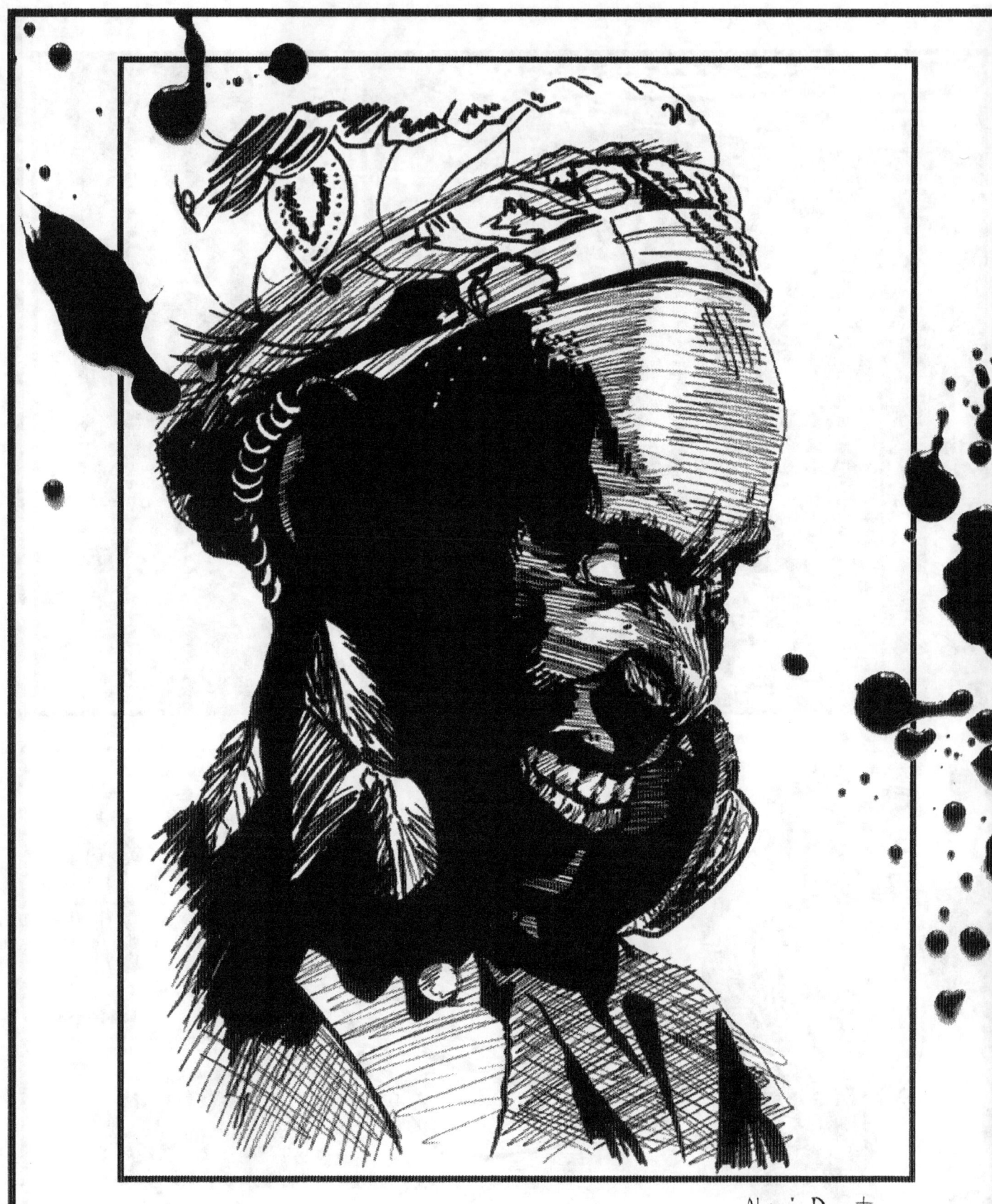

Africa's Daughter

Vengeful Angel

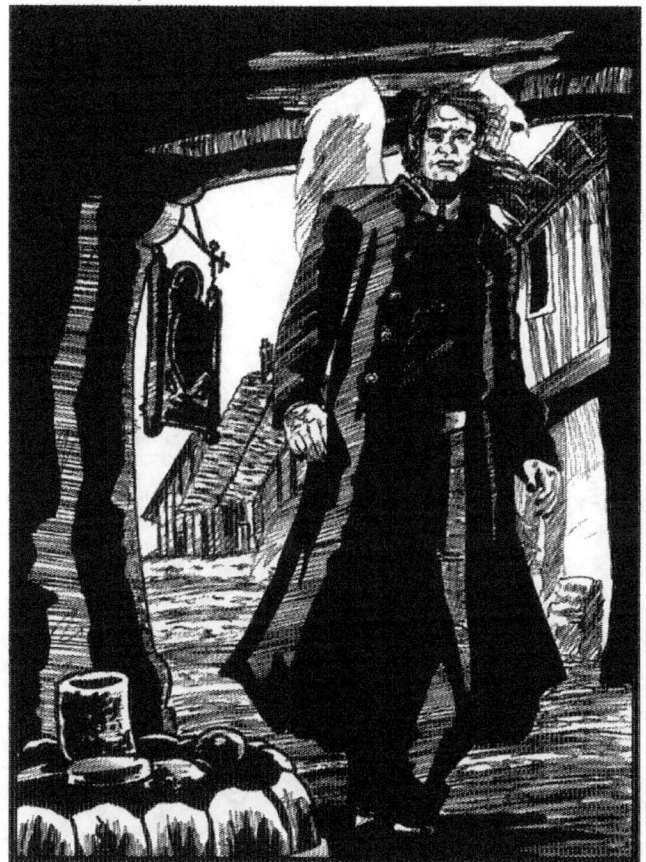

Unlikely Friends

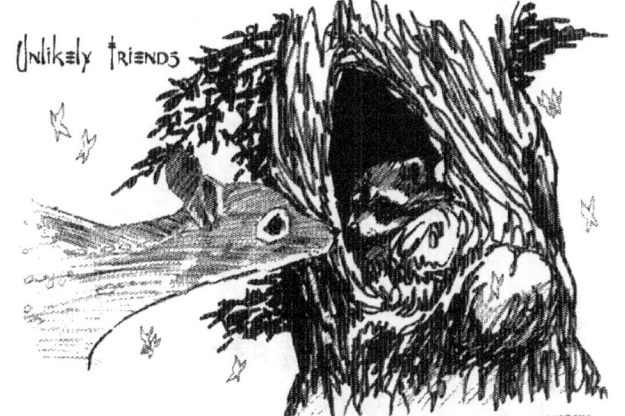

Owl

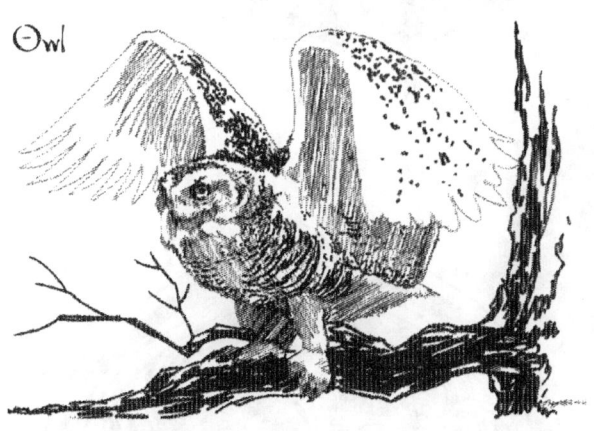

Night Wolf

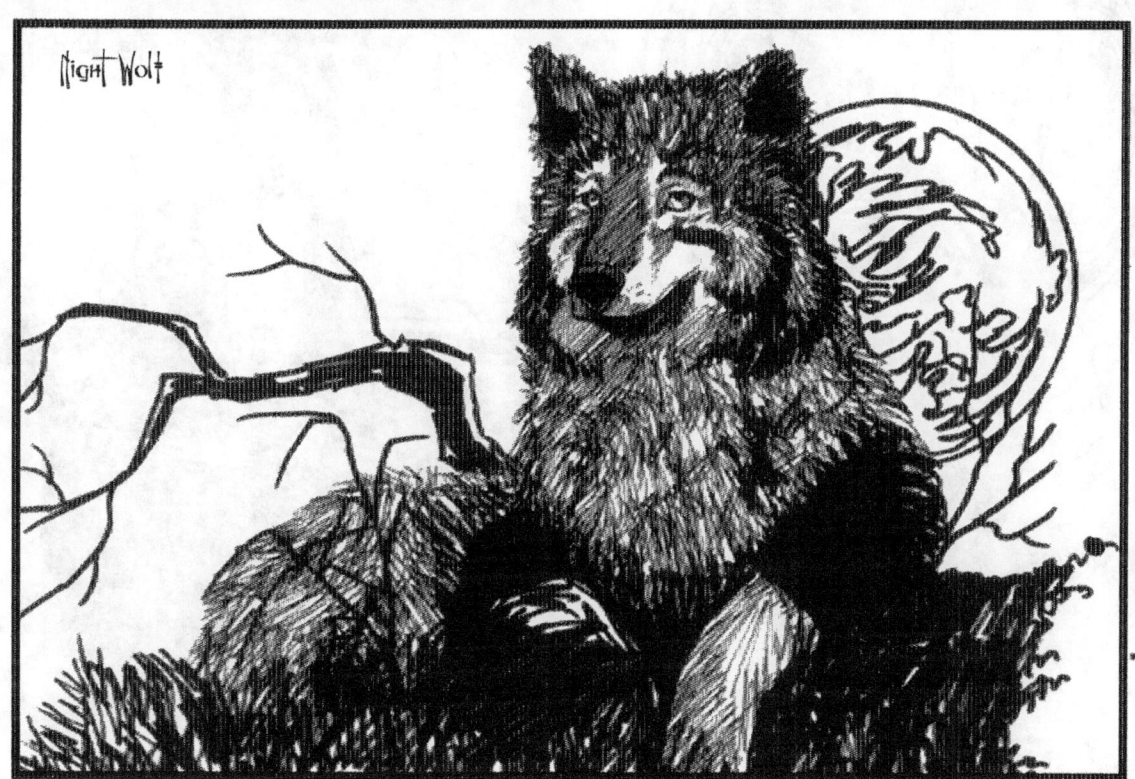

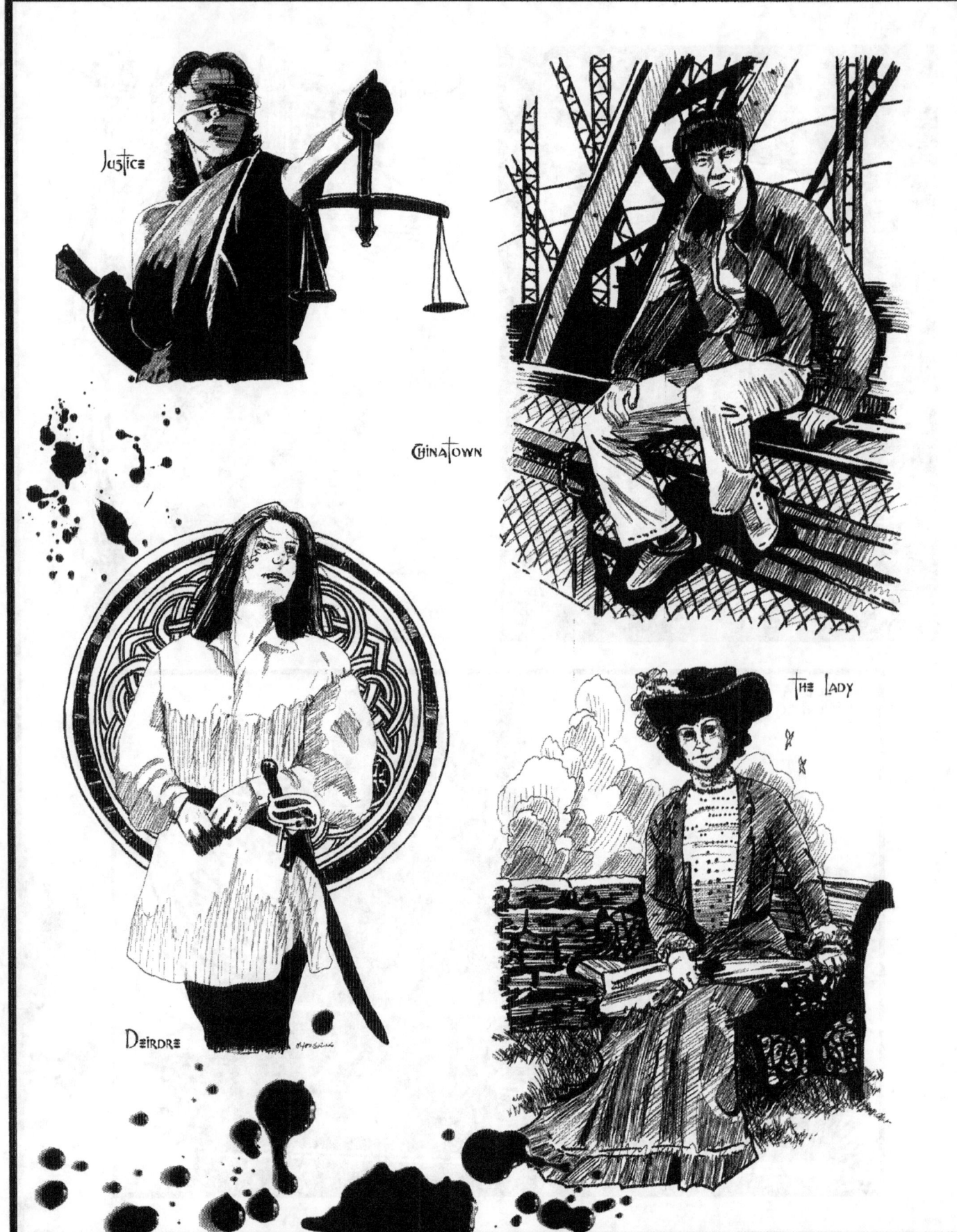

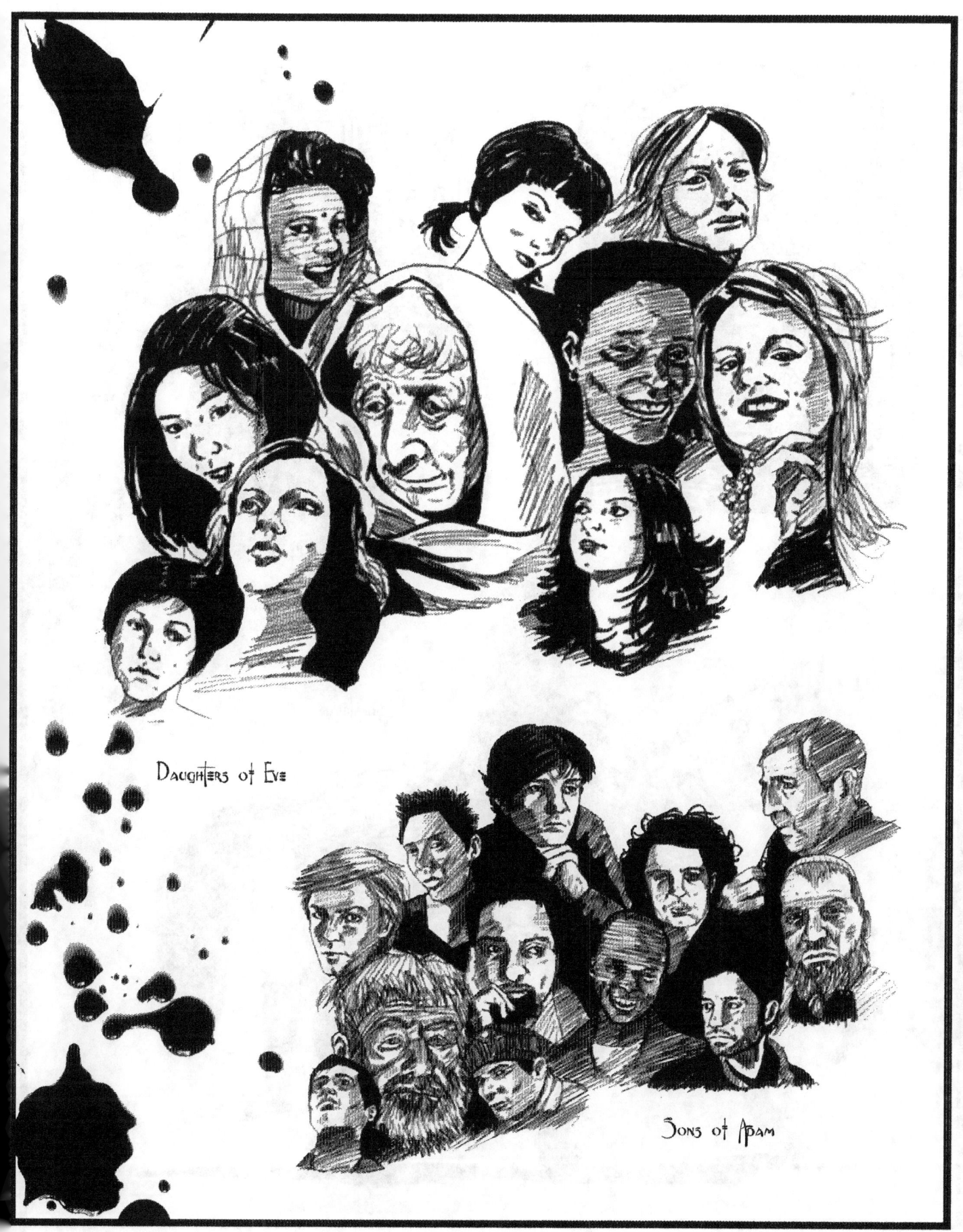

Daughters of Eve

Sons of Adam

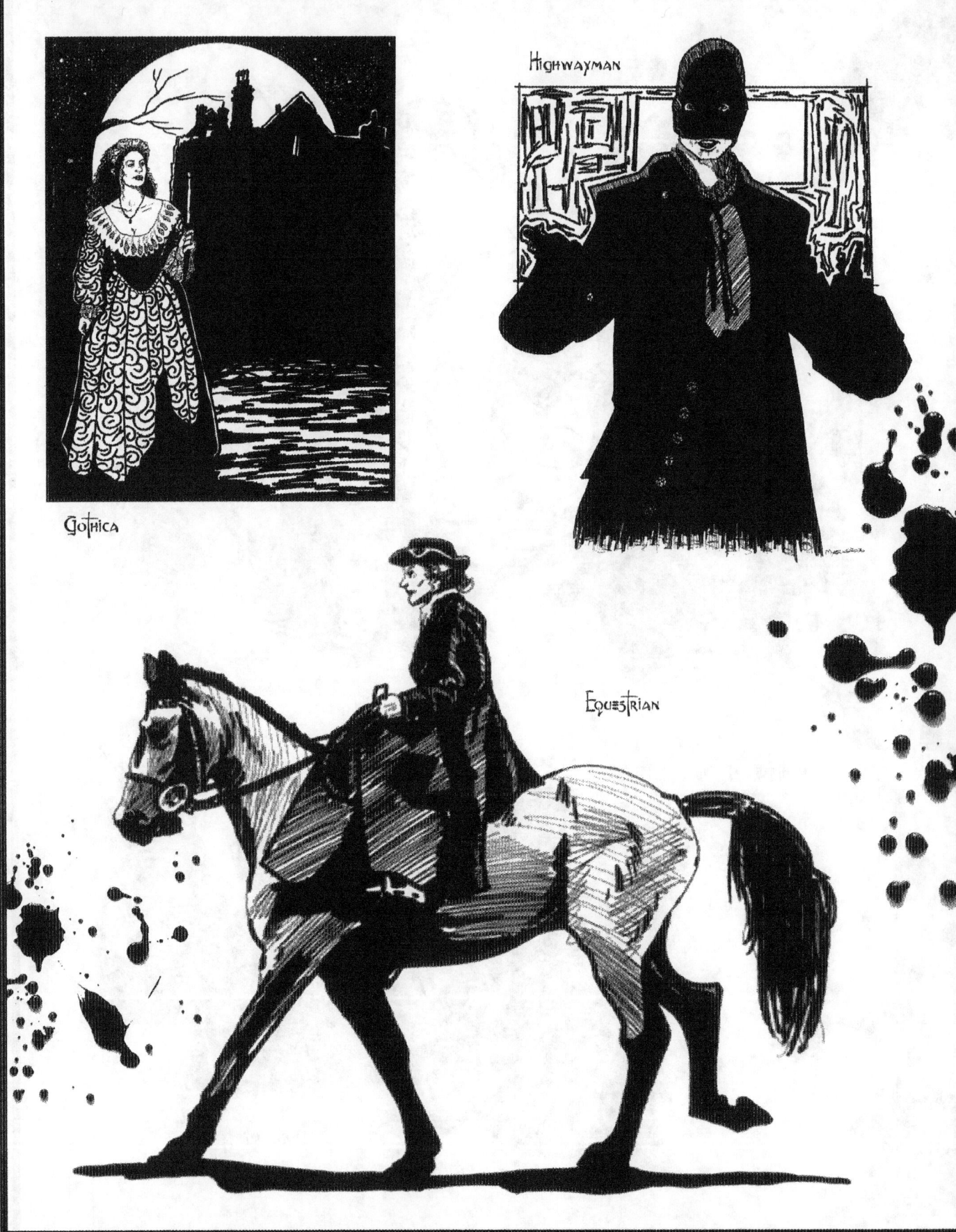

GOTHICA

HIGHWAYMAN

EQUESTRIAN

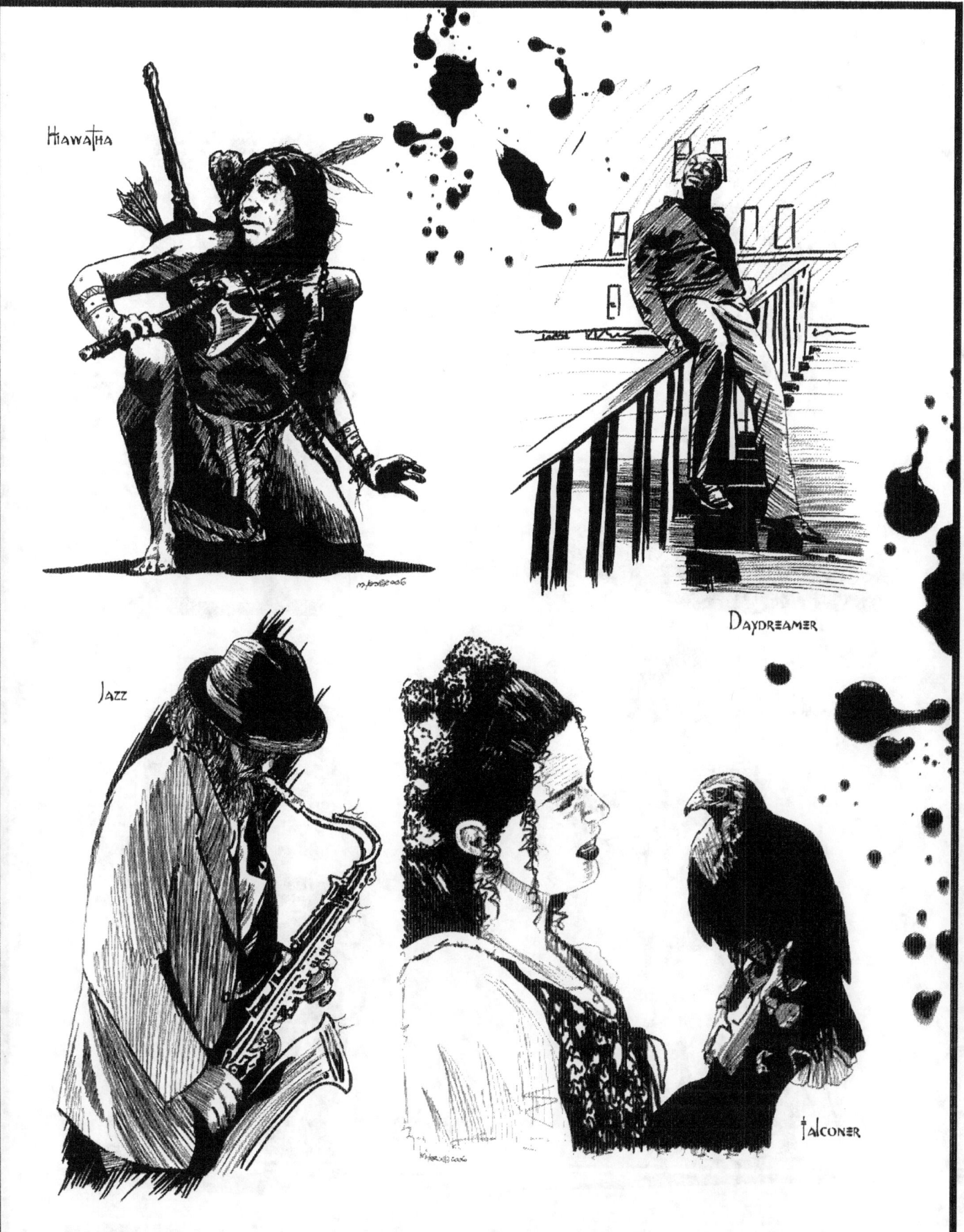

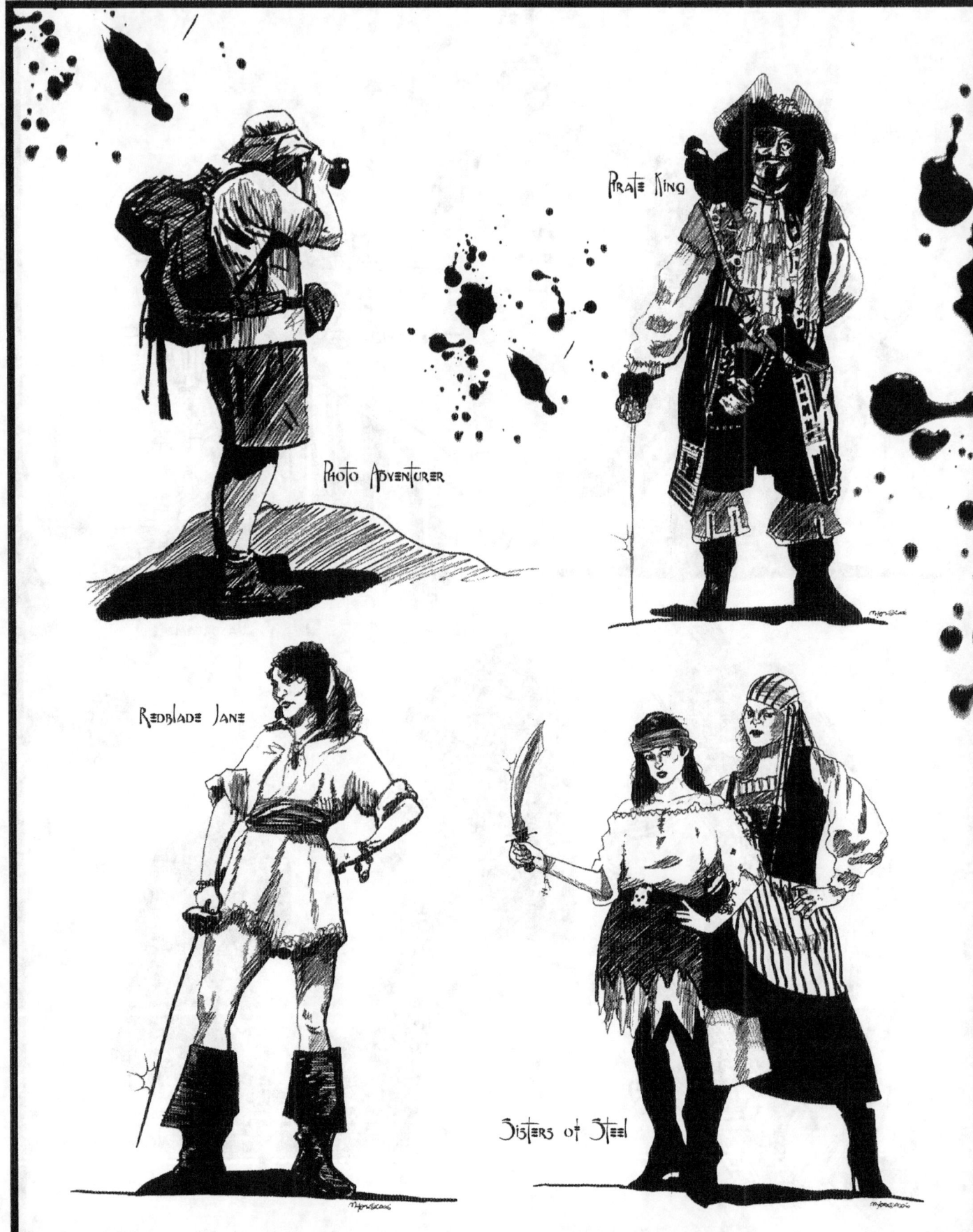

Photo Adventurer

Pirate King

Redblade Jane

Sisters of Steel

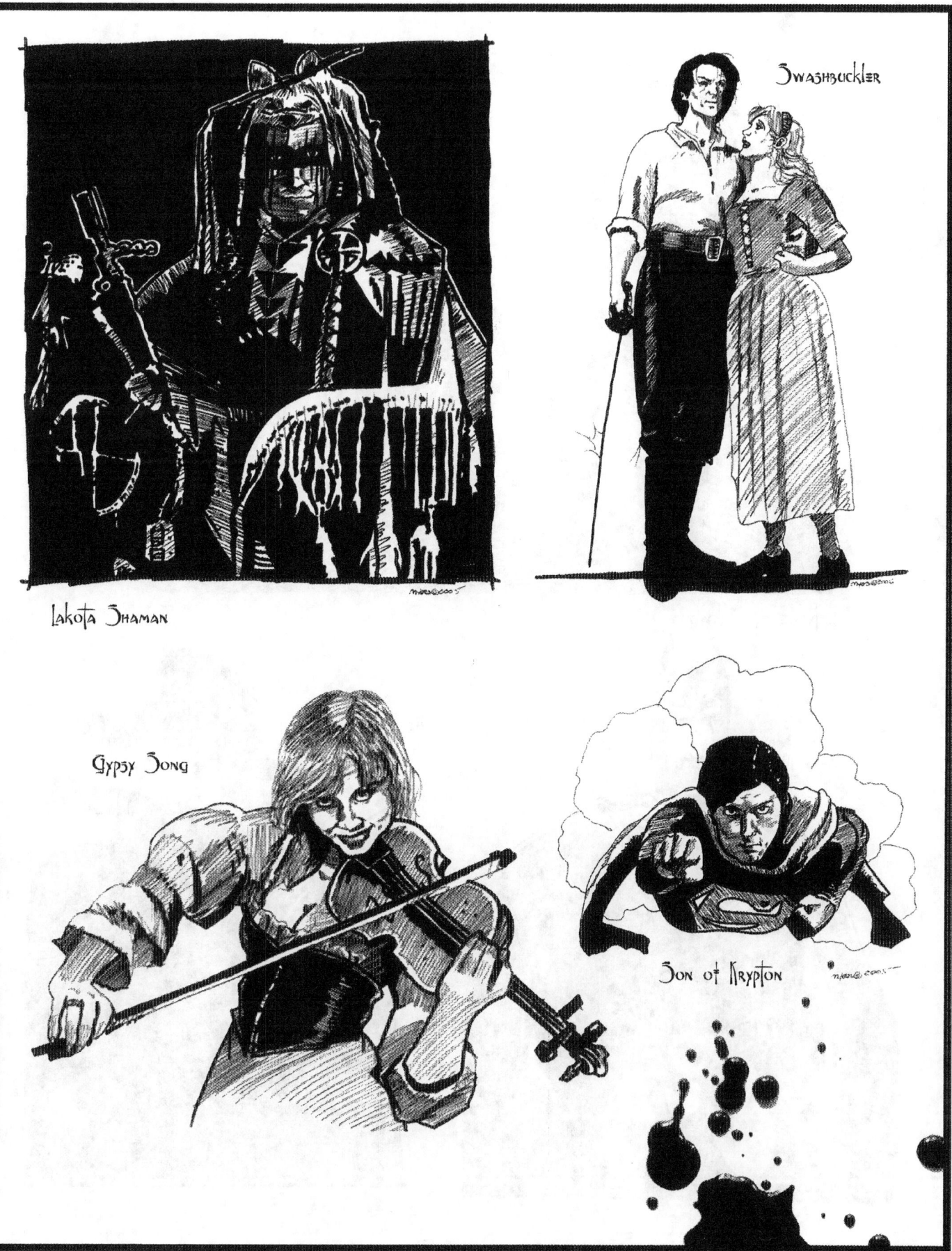

Lakota Shaman

Swashbuckler

Gypsy Song

Son of Krypton

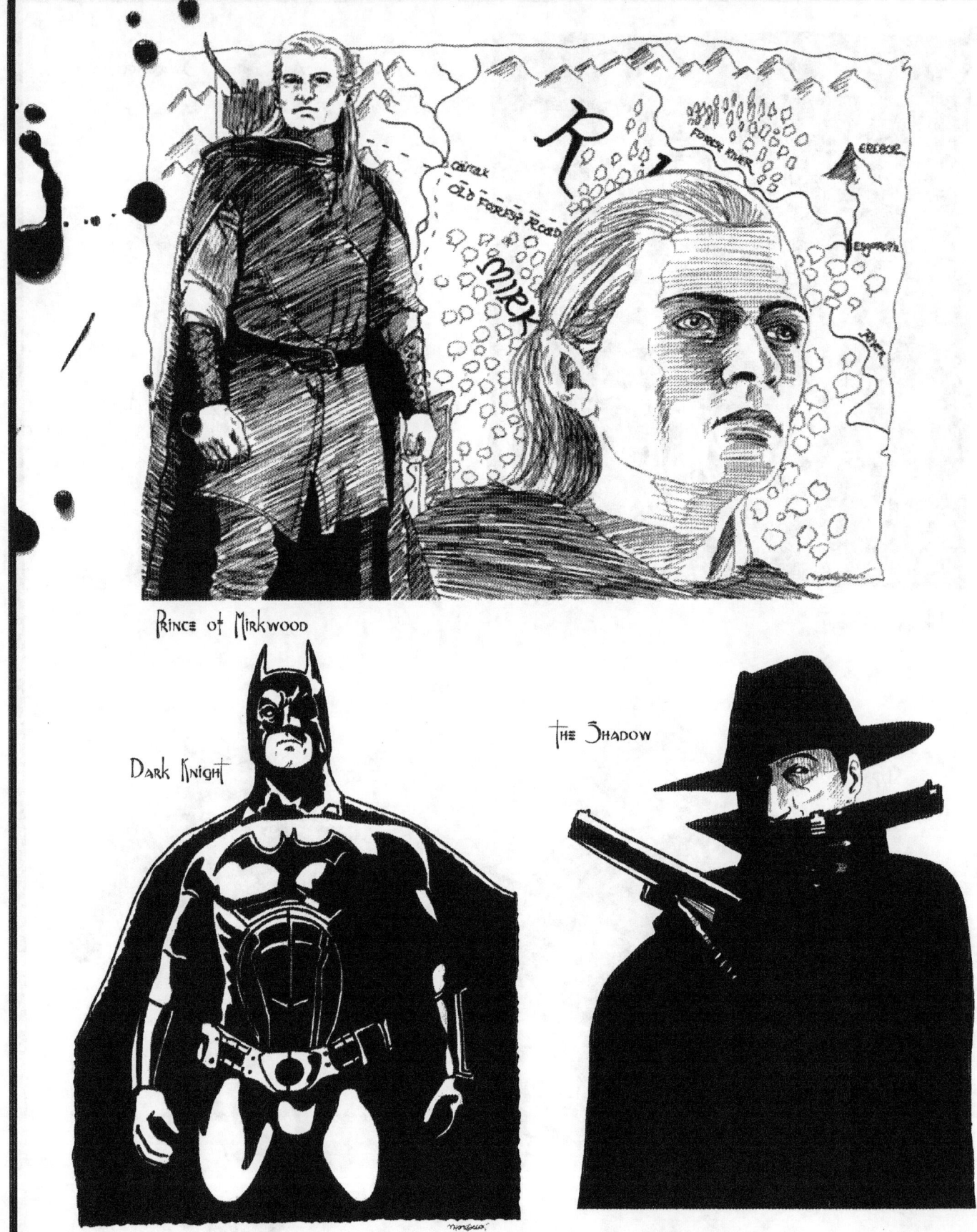

Prince of Mirkwood

Dark Knight

The Shadow

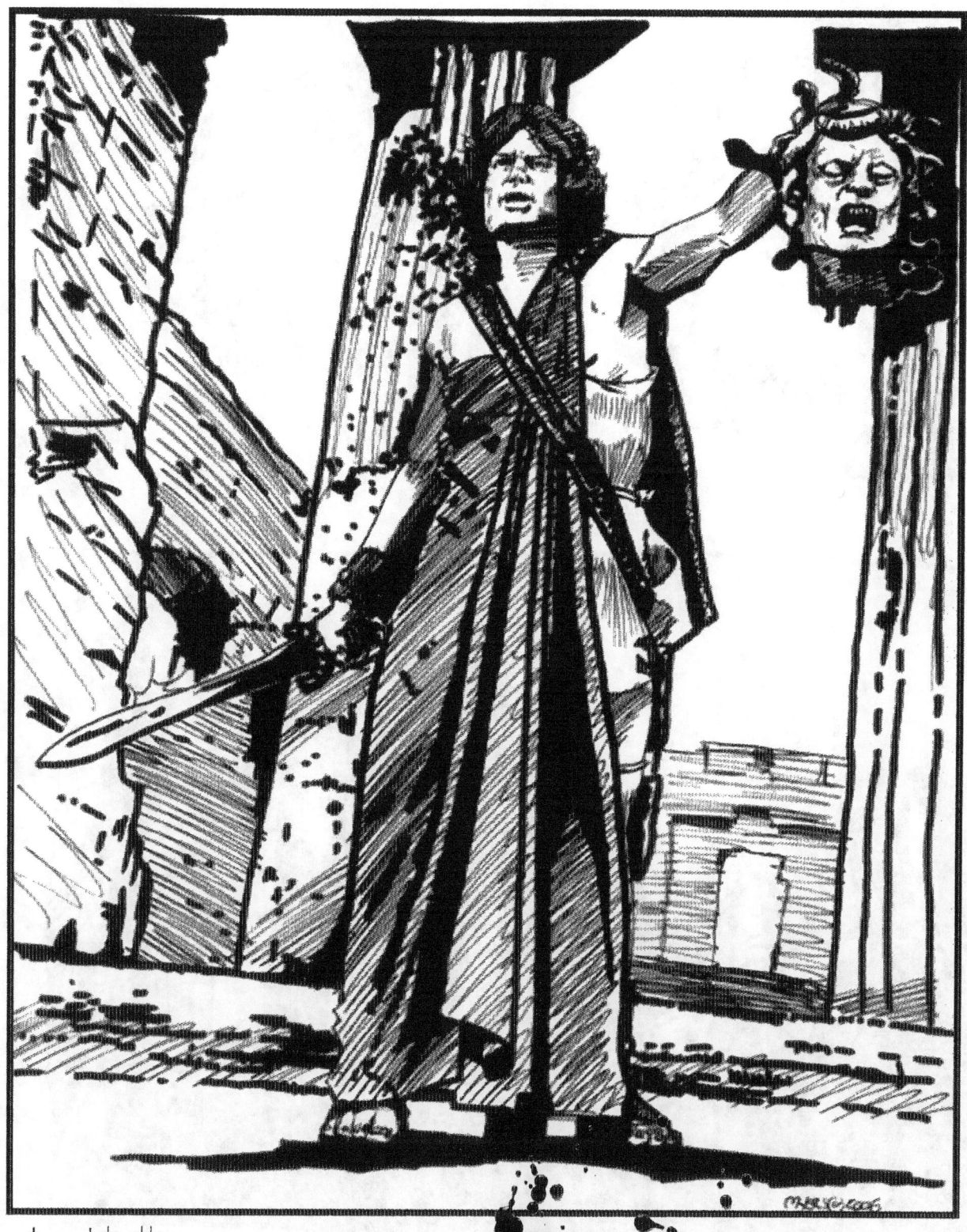

CLASH OF THE TITANS

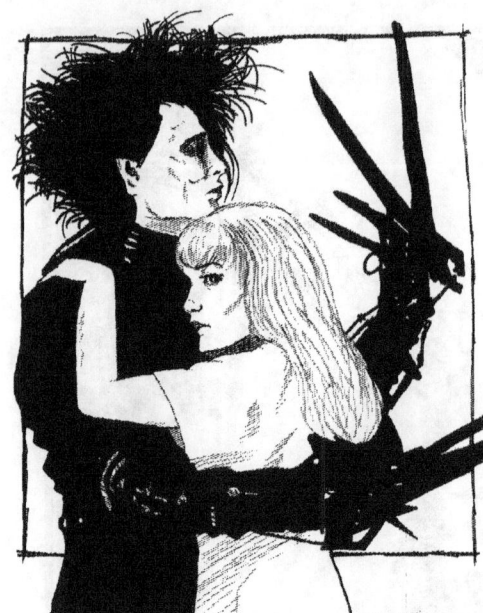
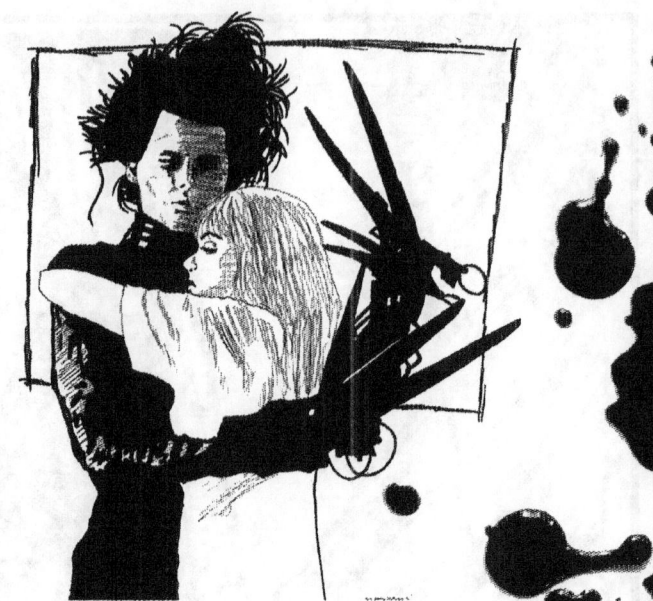

Edward Scissorhands

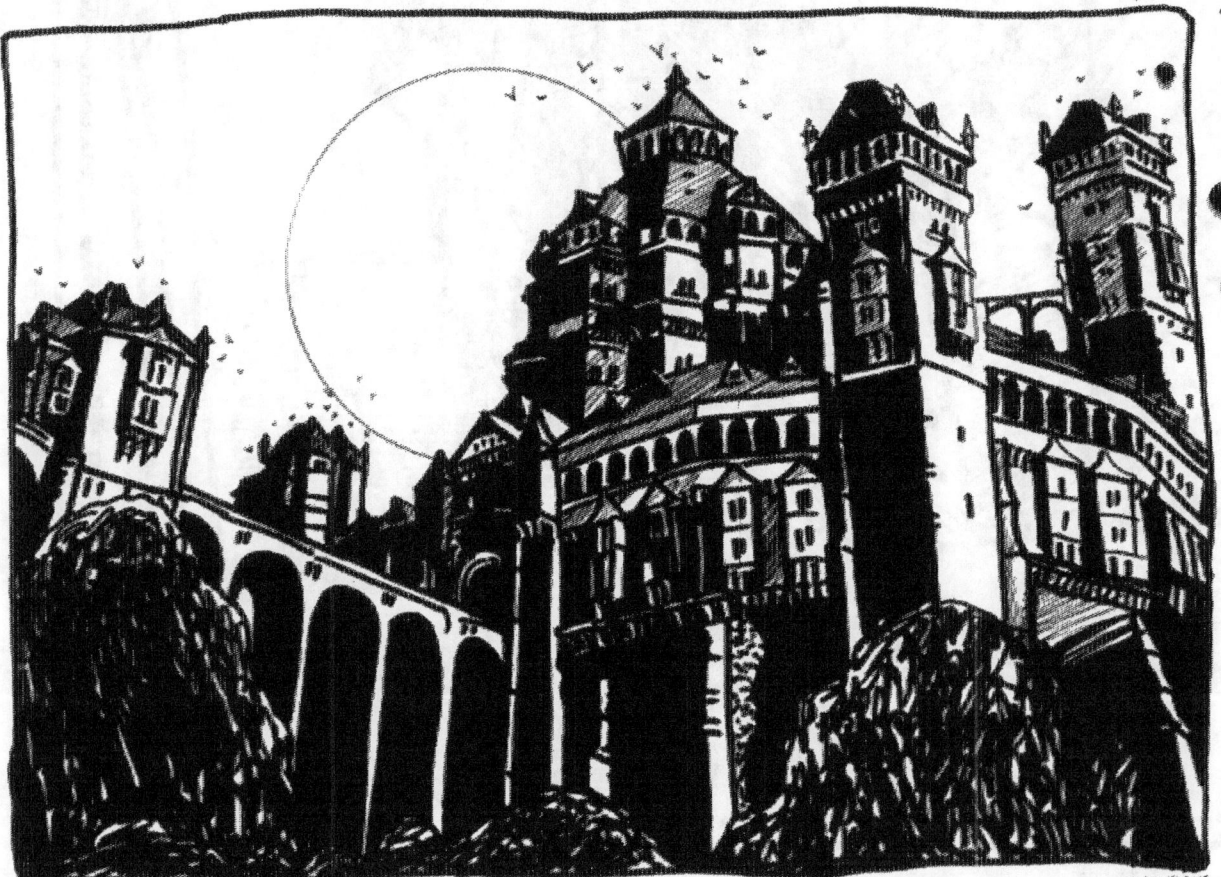

Castle Fantasy

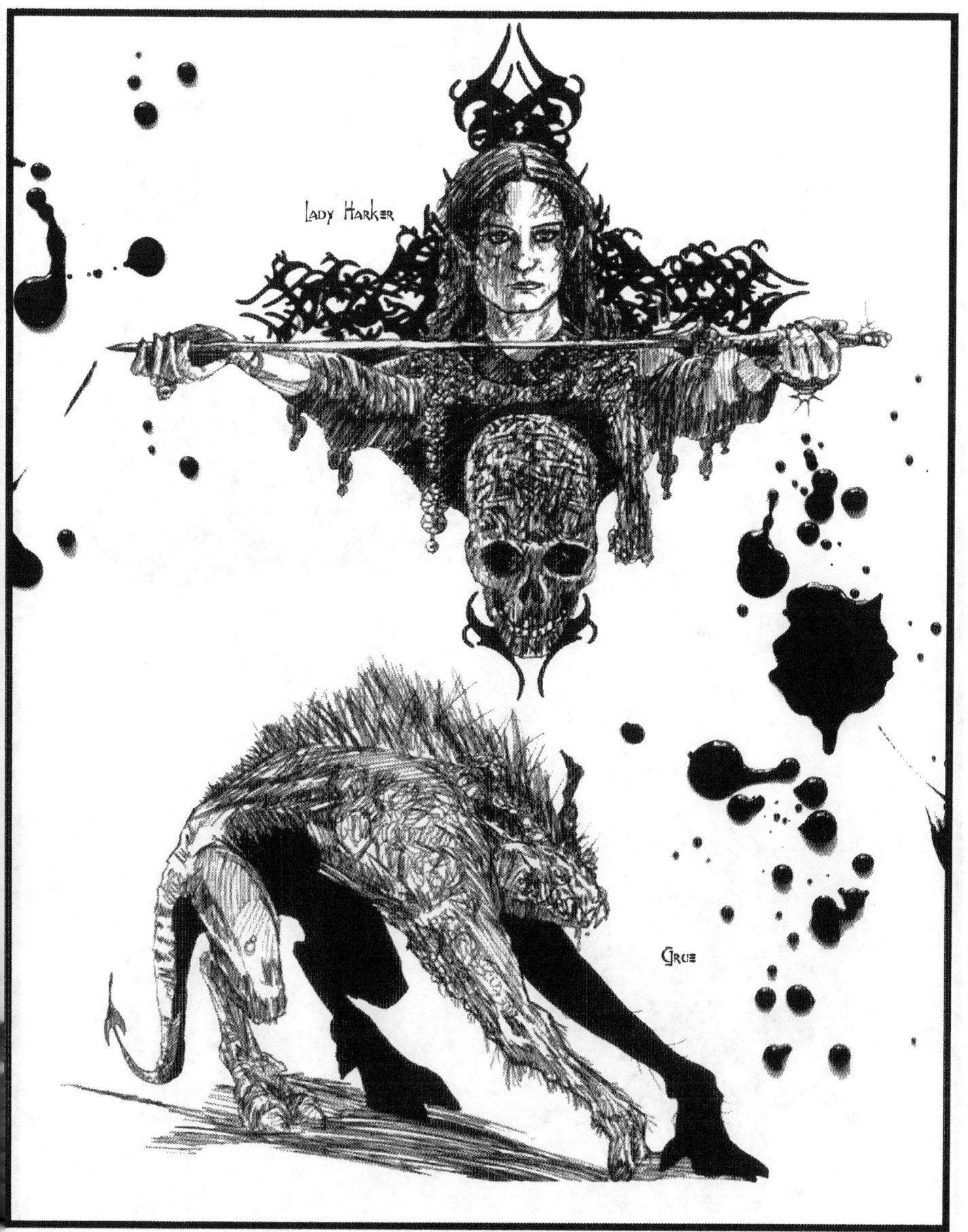

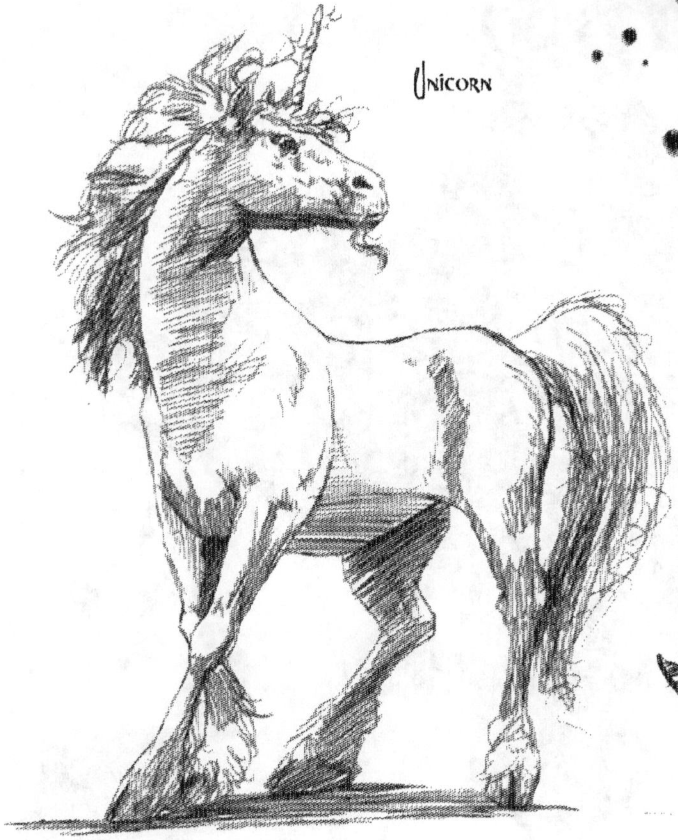

Unicorn

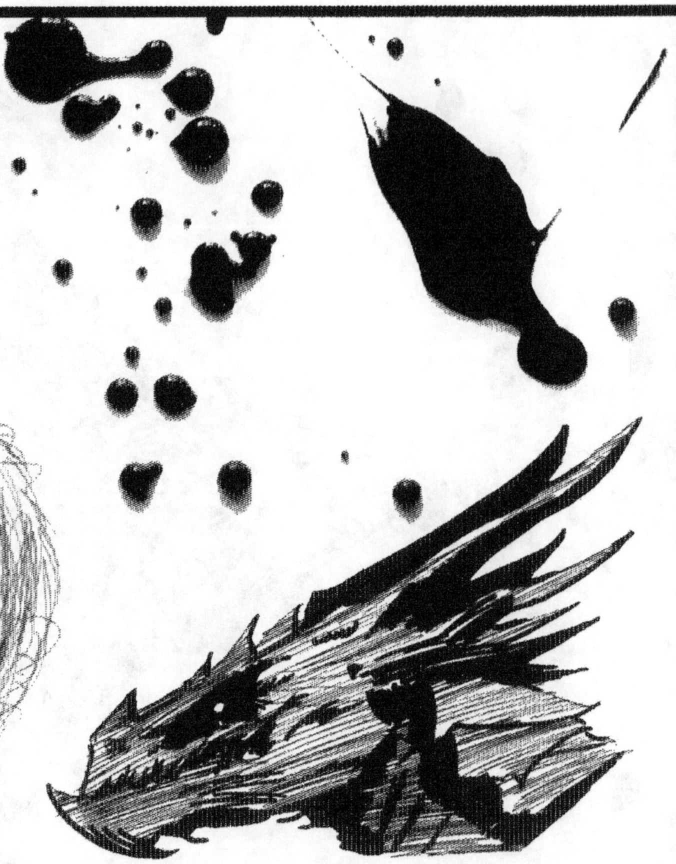

Dragonhead

Griffon

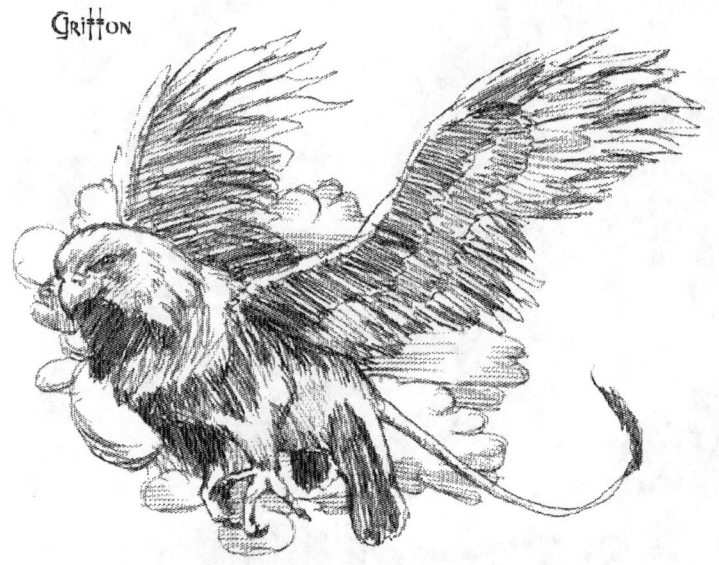

Darkling Nixies

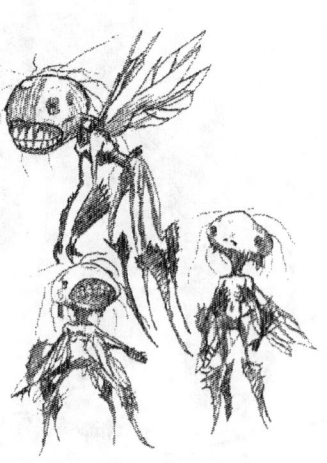

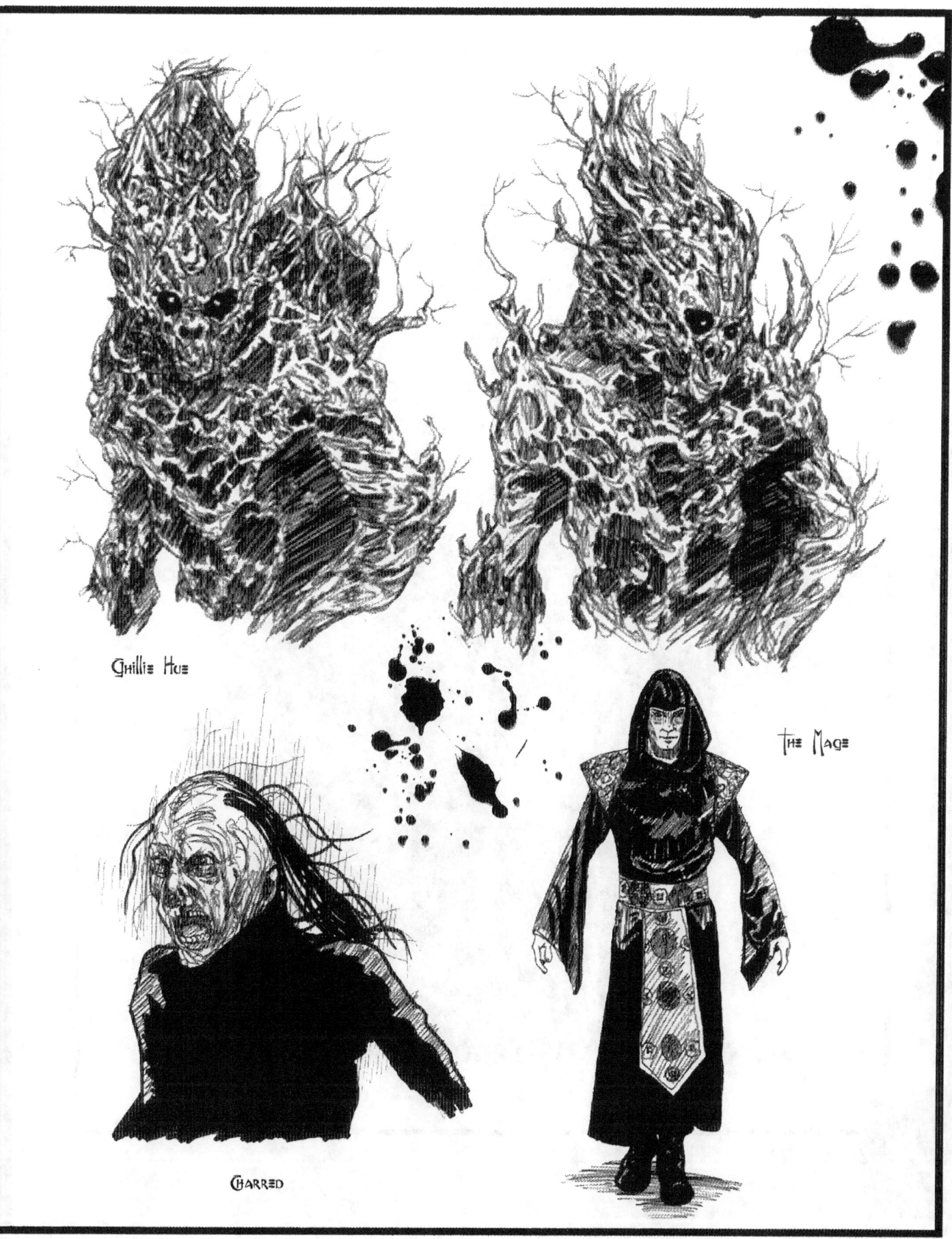

GHILLIE HUE

THE MAGE

CHARRED

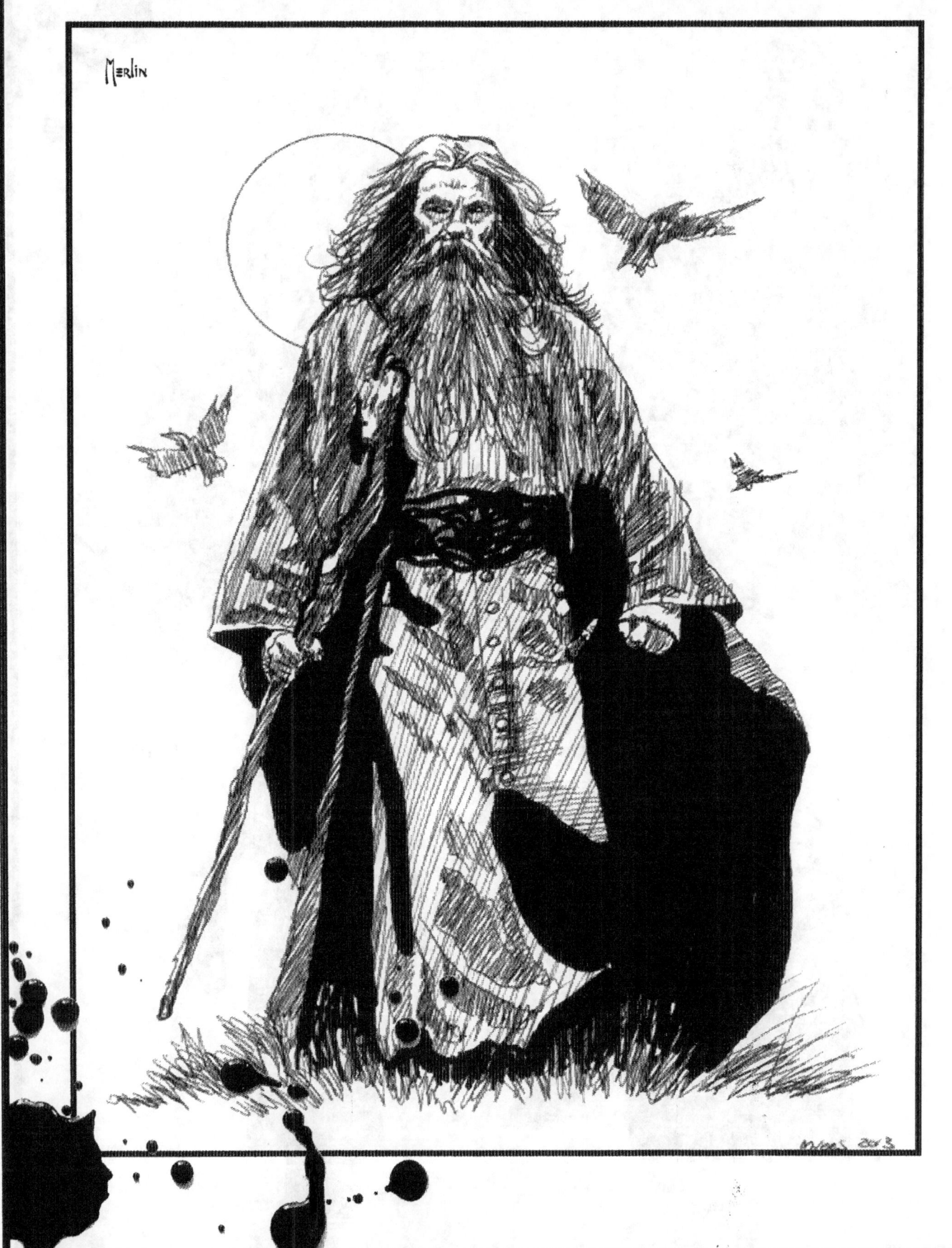
MERLIN

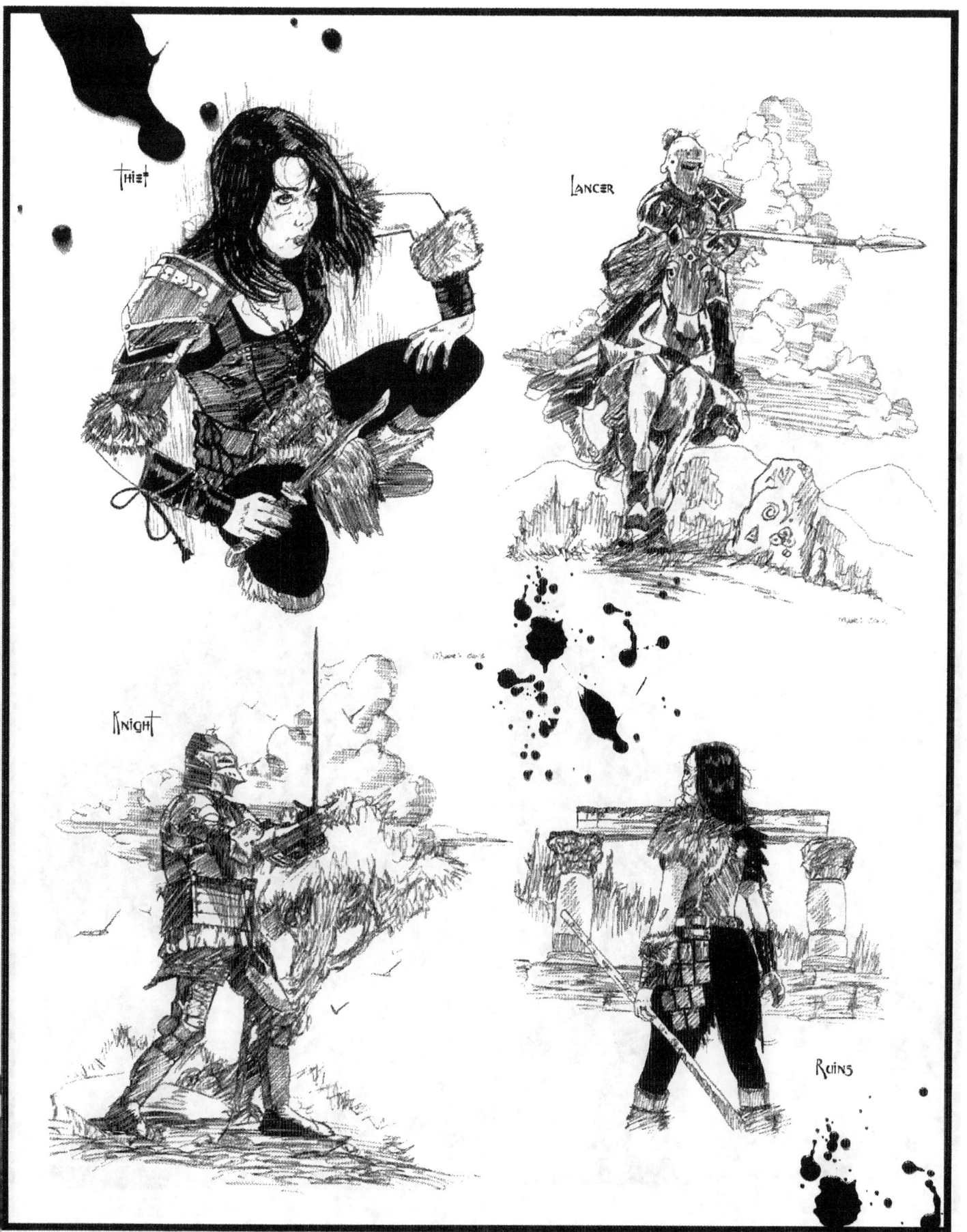

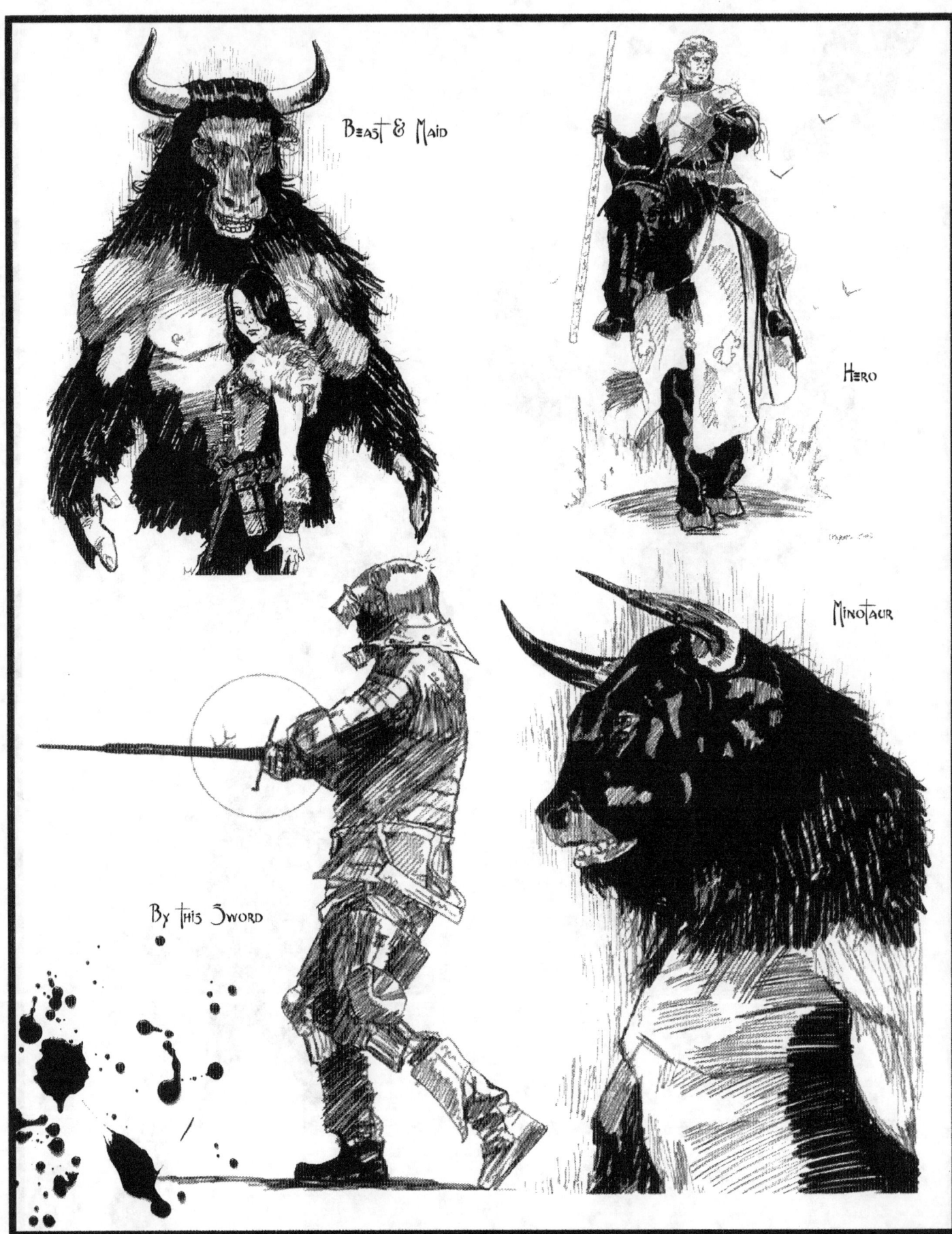

Beast & Maid

Hero

Minotaur

By this Sword

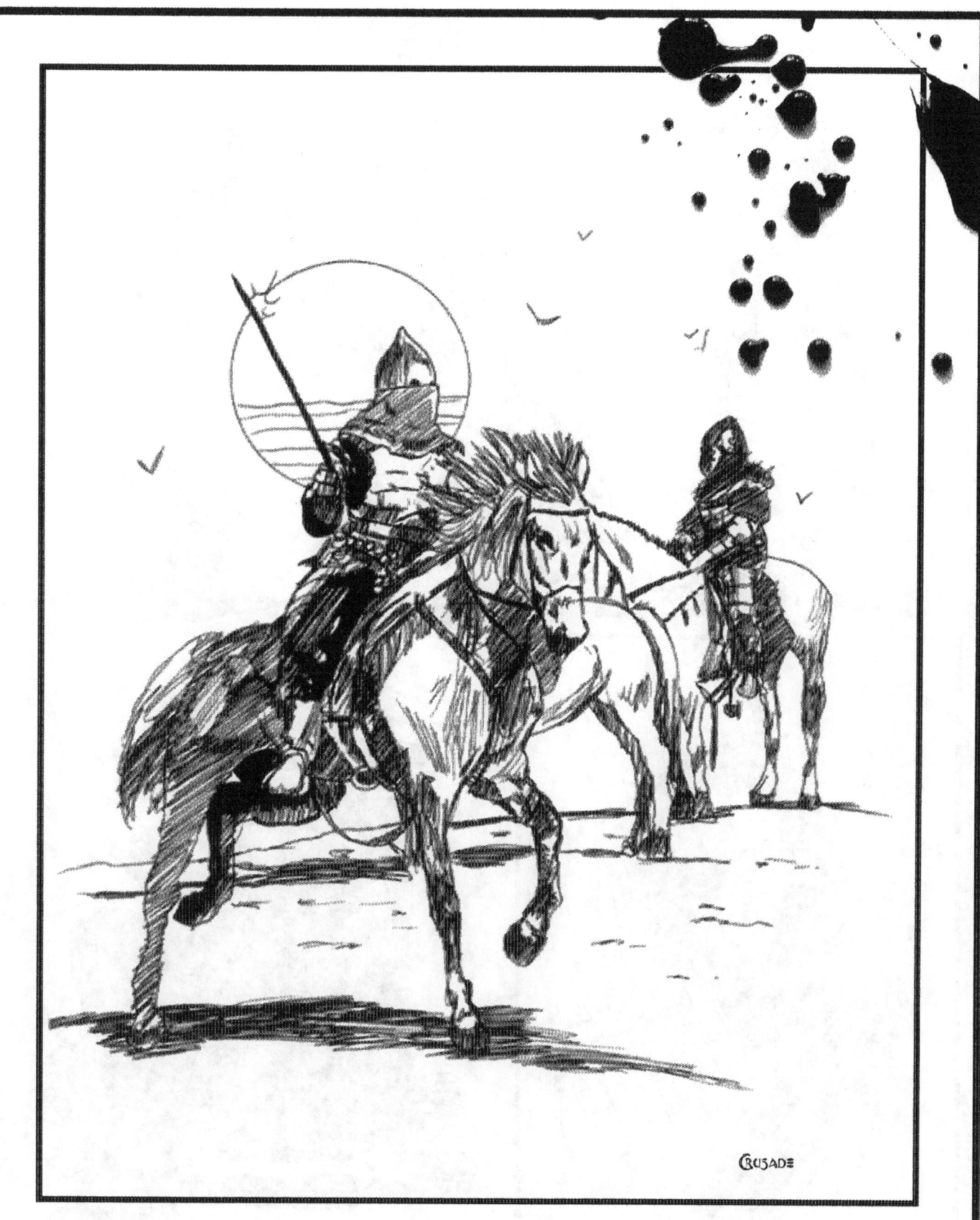

CRUSADE

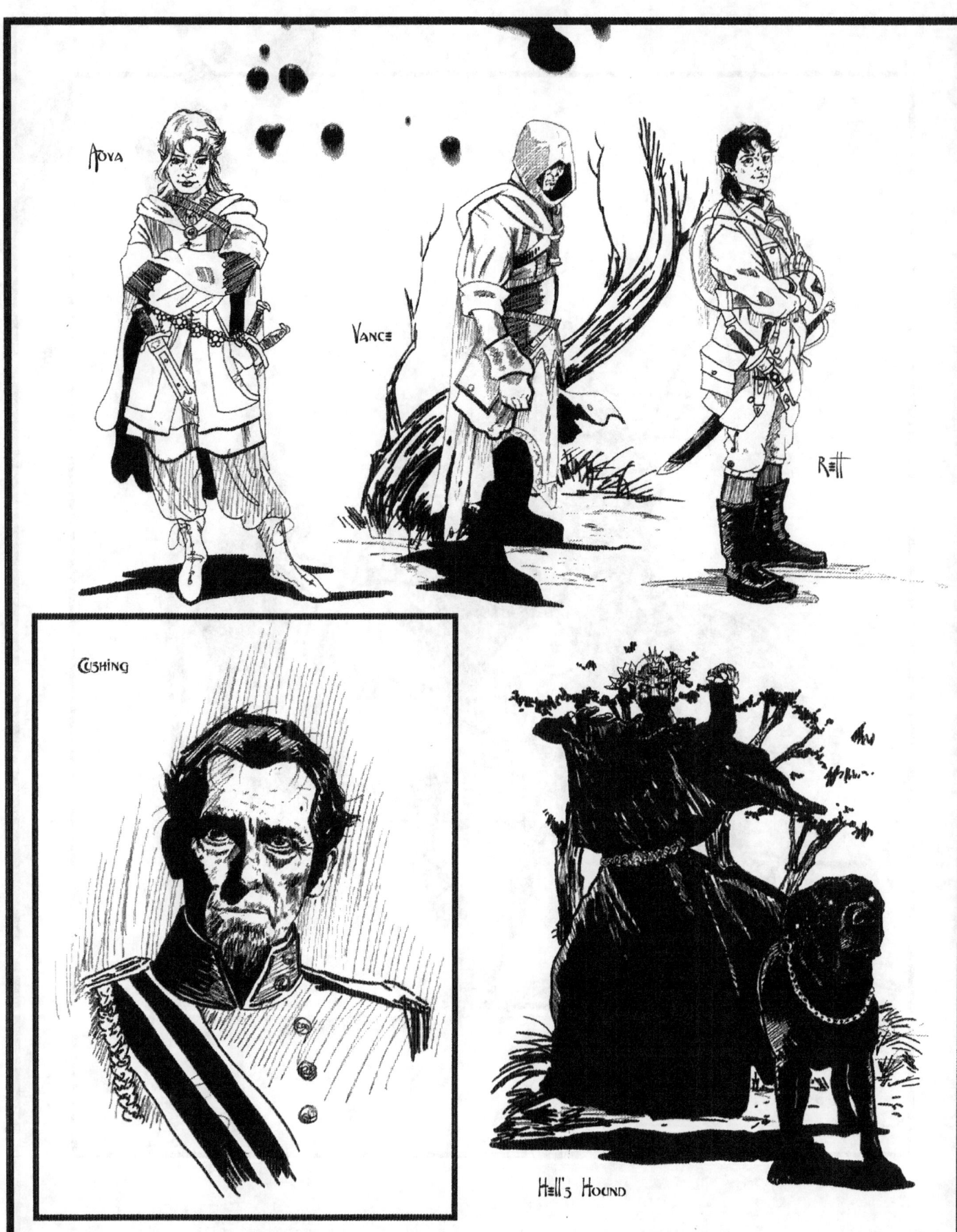

Aoya

Vance

Rett

Cushing

Hell's Hound

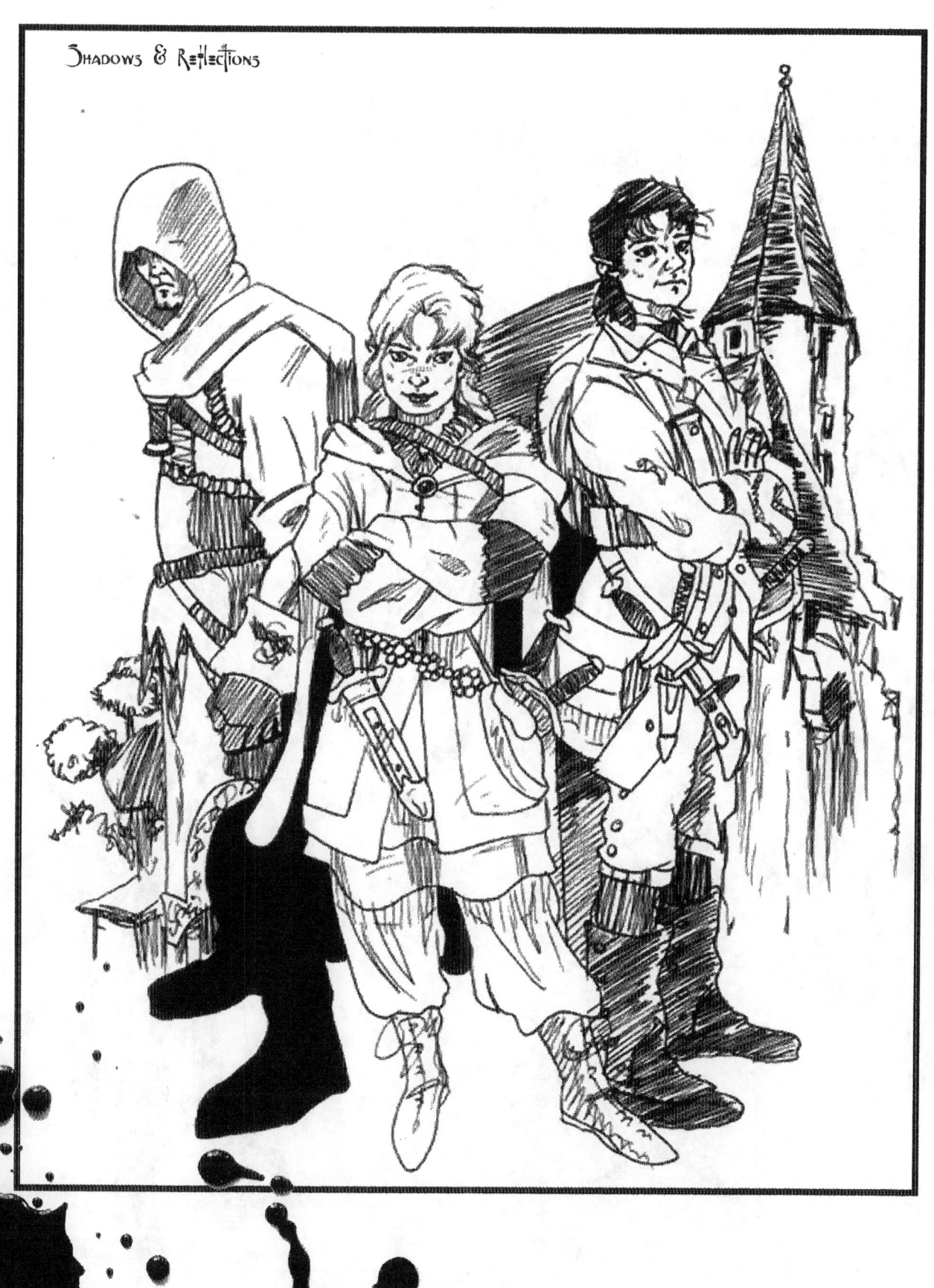

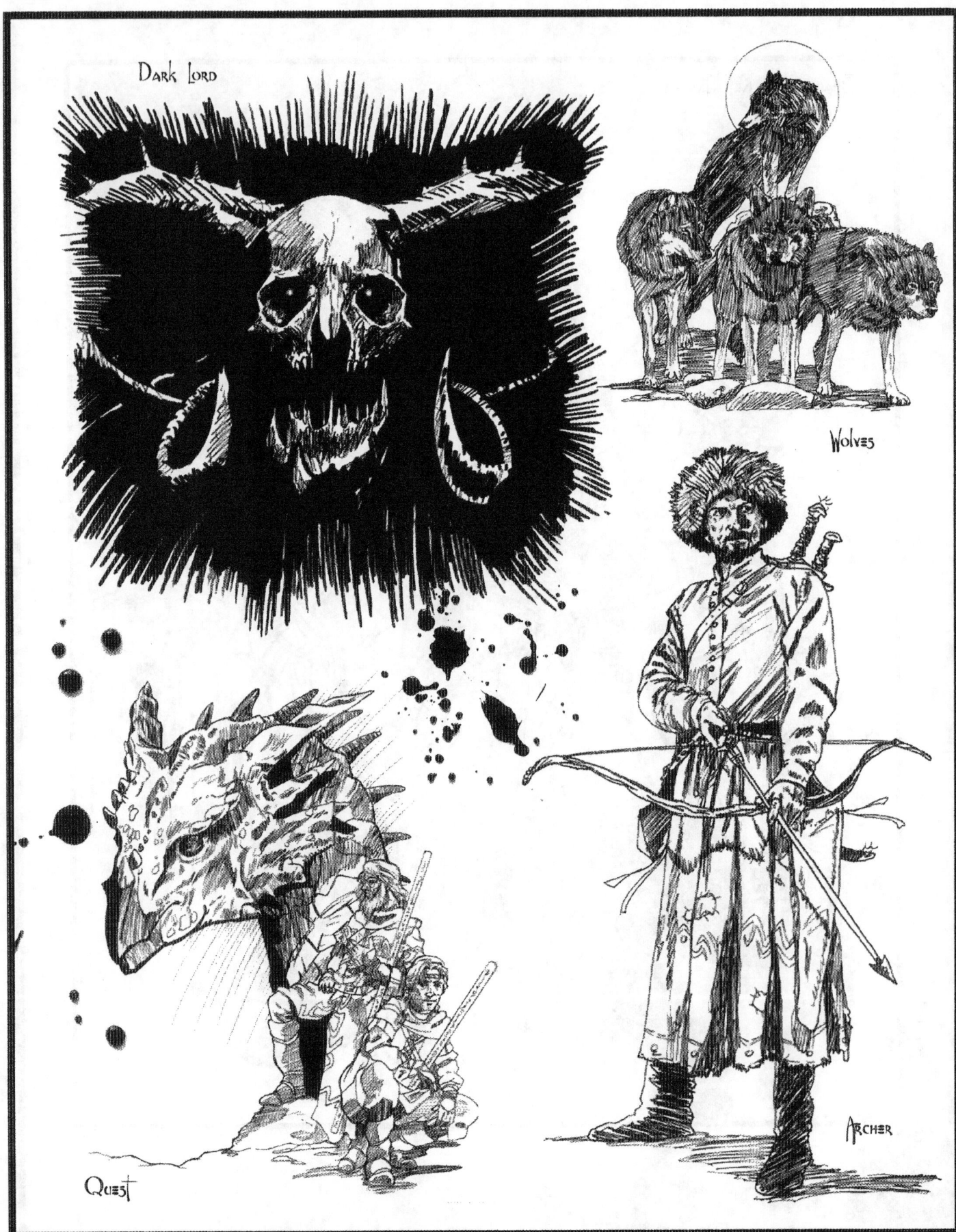

DARK LORD

WOLVES

QUEST

ARCHER

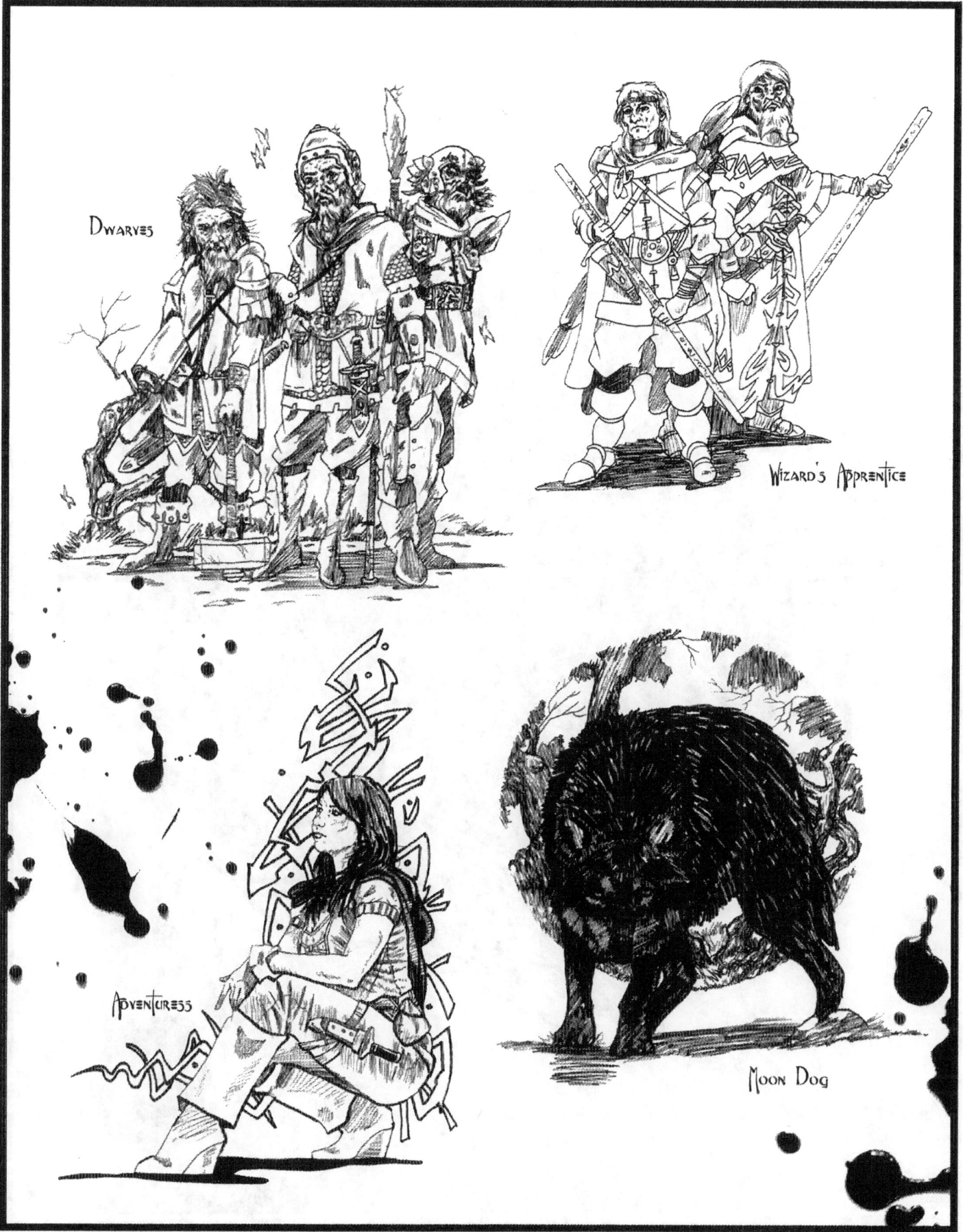

Dwarves

Wizard's Apprentice

Adventuress

Moon Dog

ANCIENT WYRM

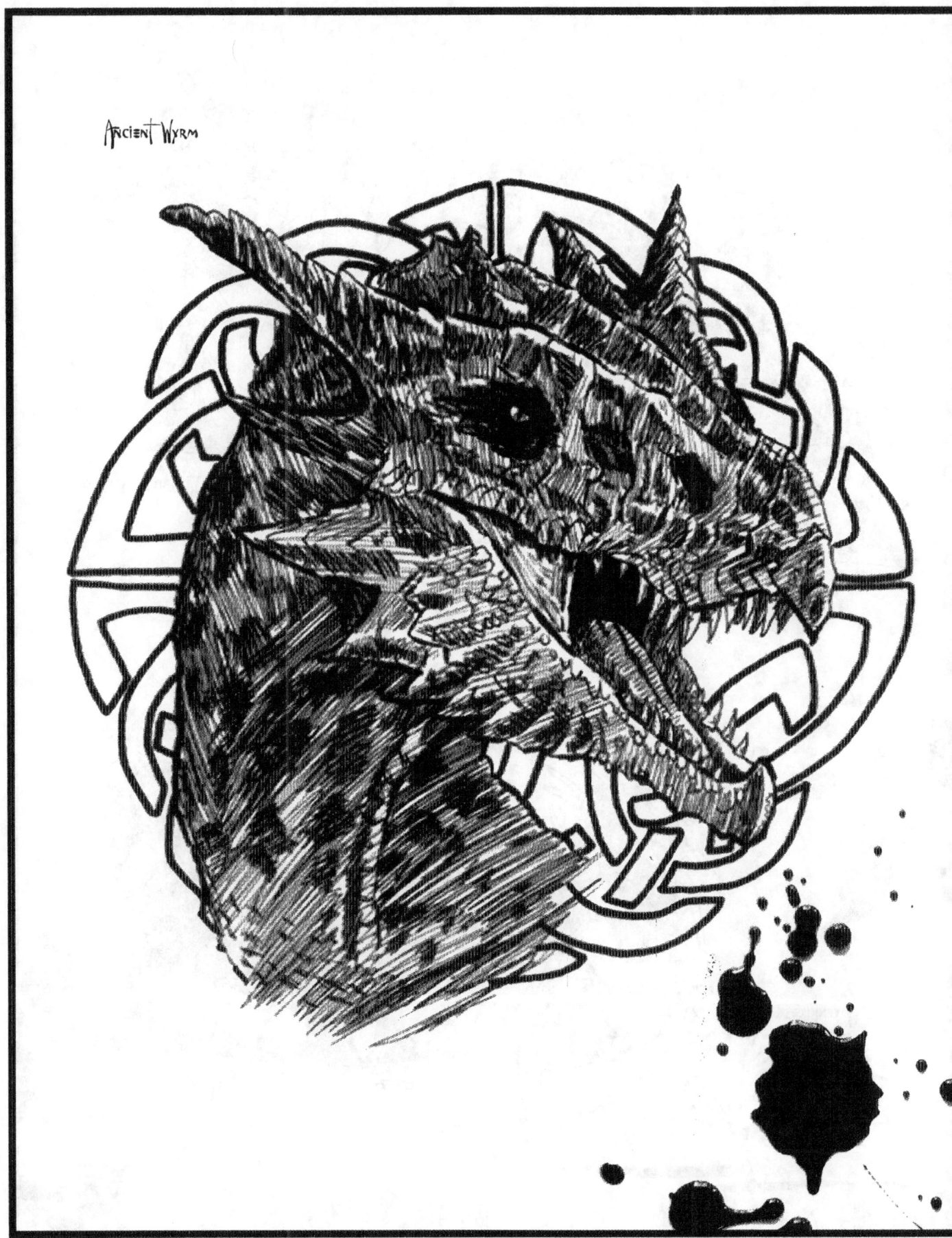

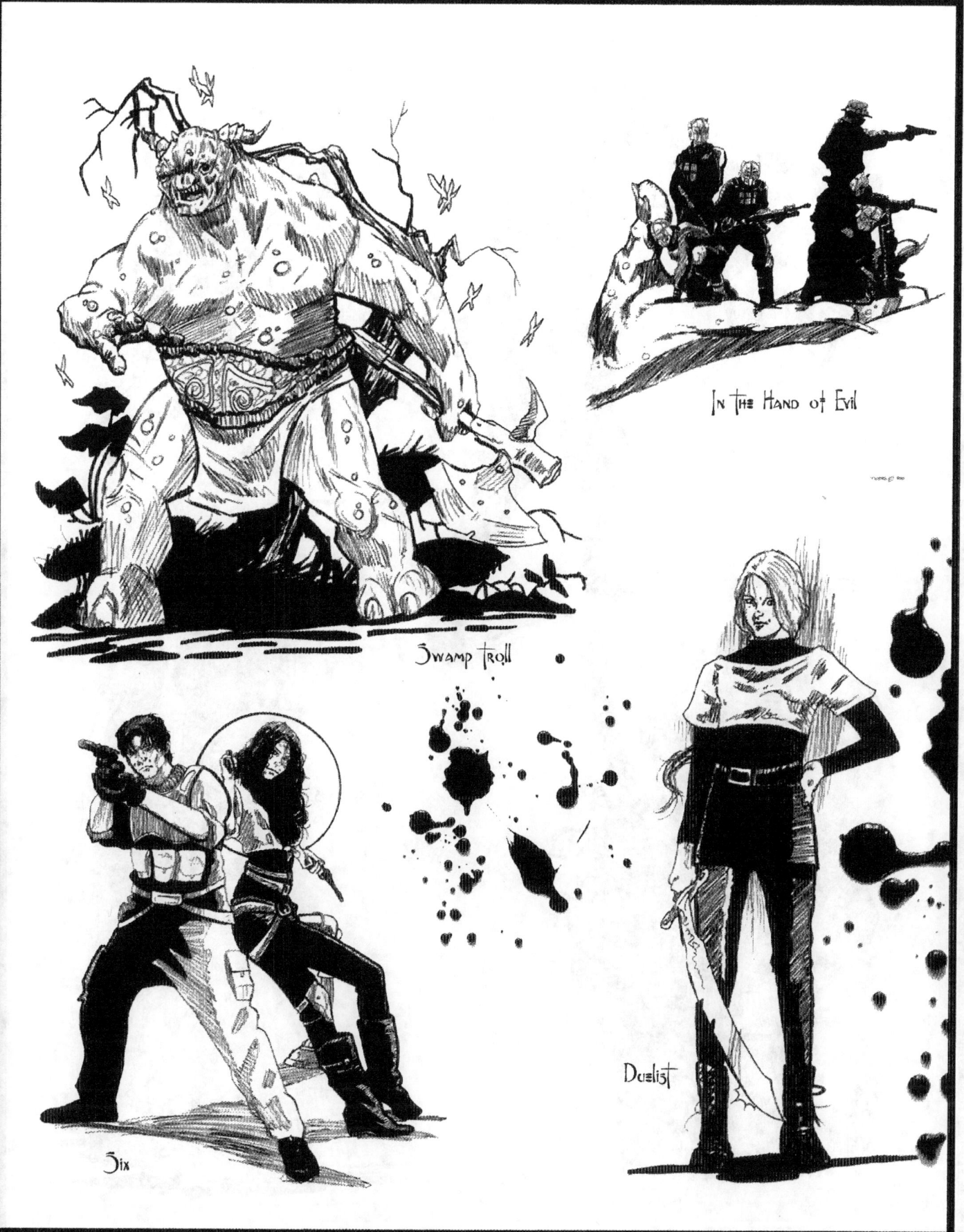

In the Hand of Evil

Swamp Troll

Six

Duelist

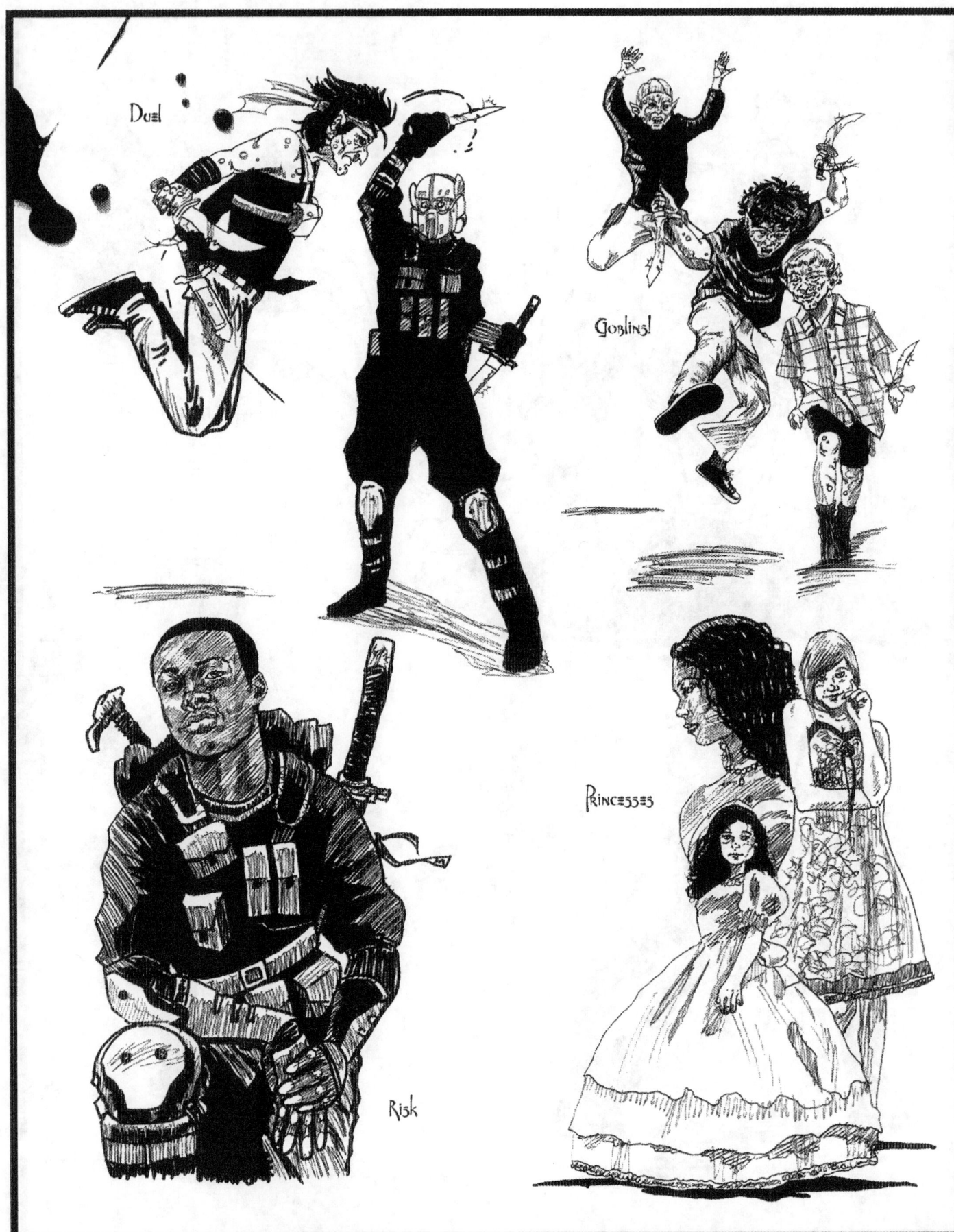

Duel

Goblins!

Risk

Princesses

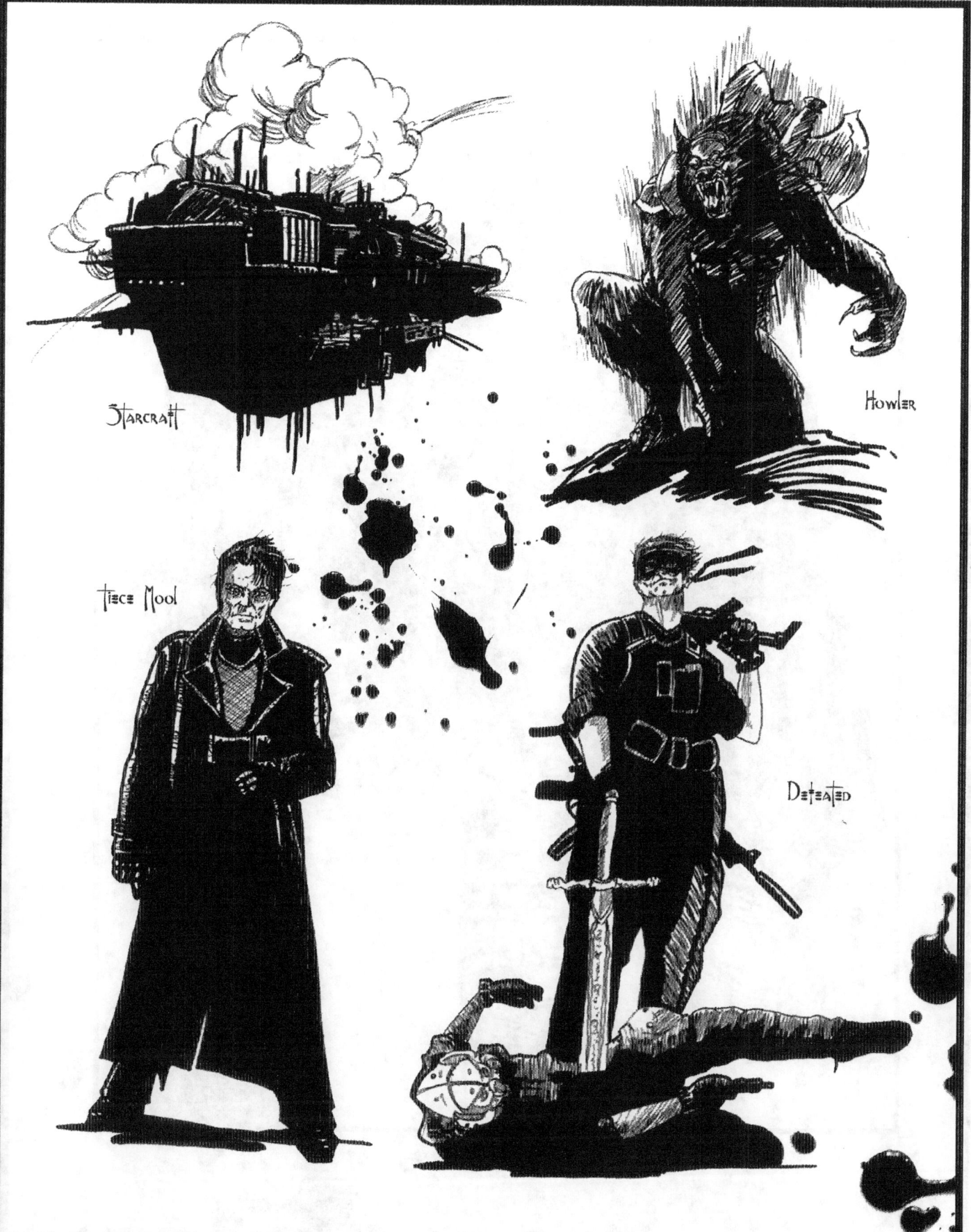

Starcraft

Howler

Tiece Mool

Defeated

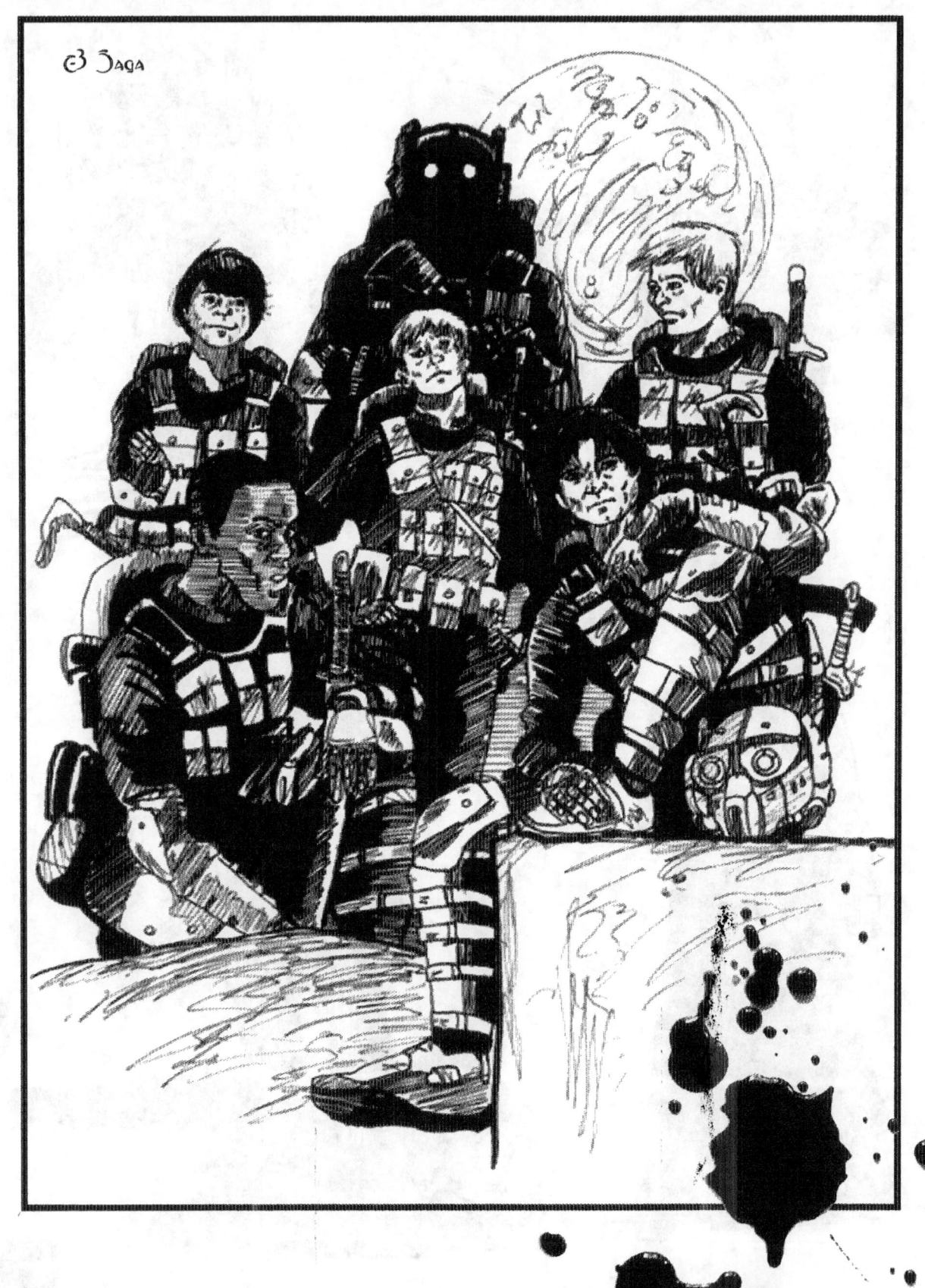

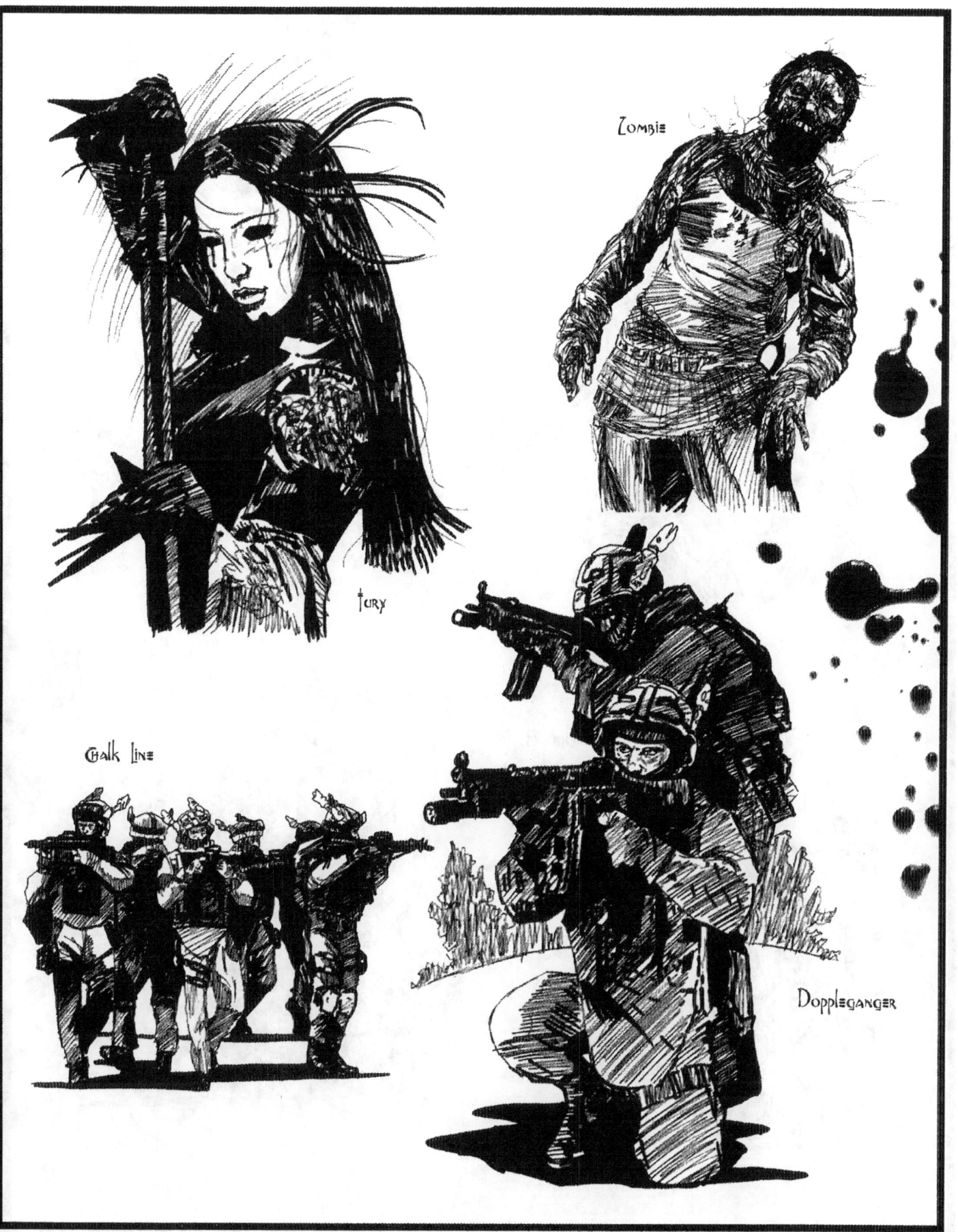

Zombie

Fury

Chalk Line

Doppleganger

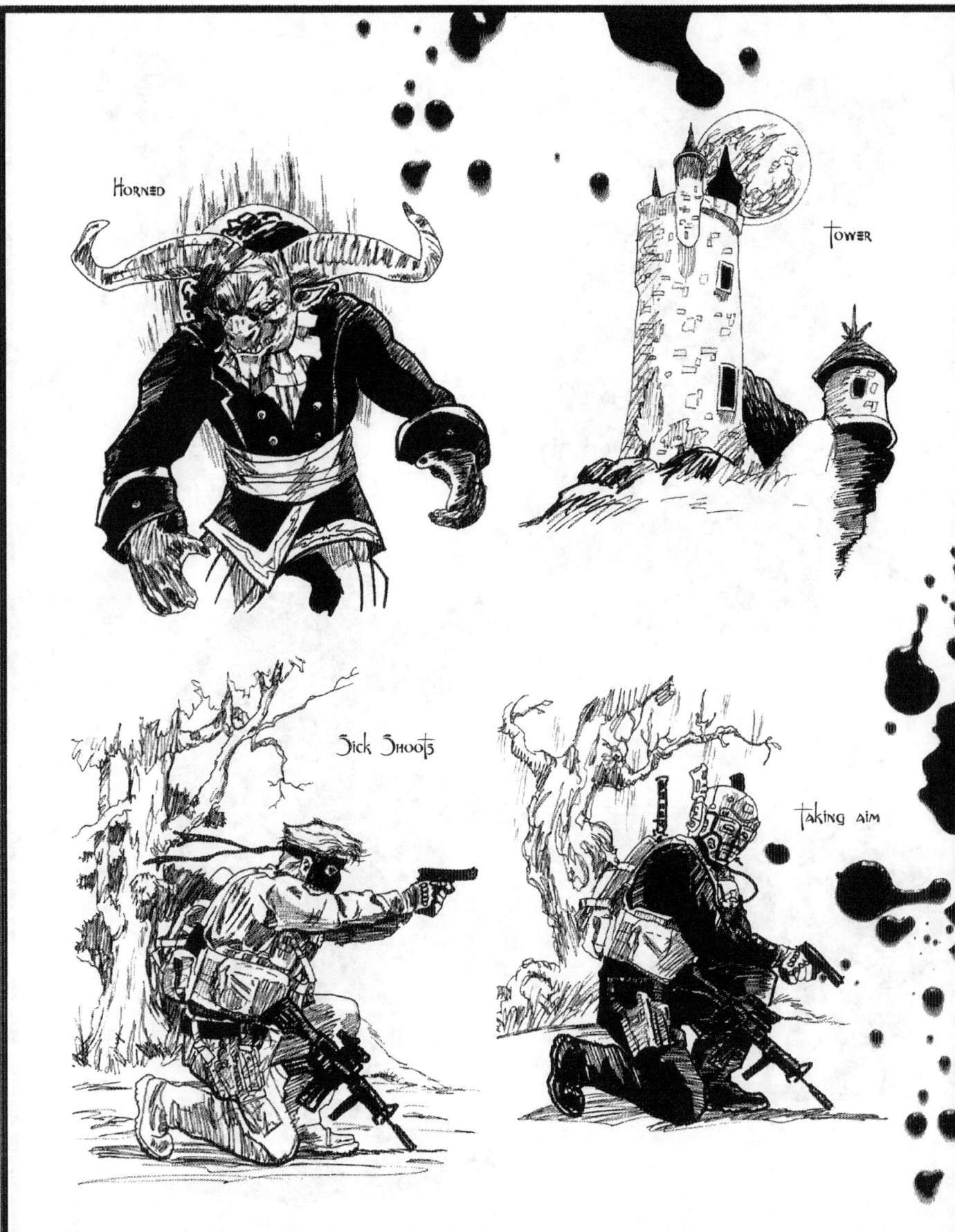

Horned

Tower

Sick Shoots

taking aim

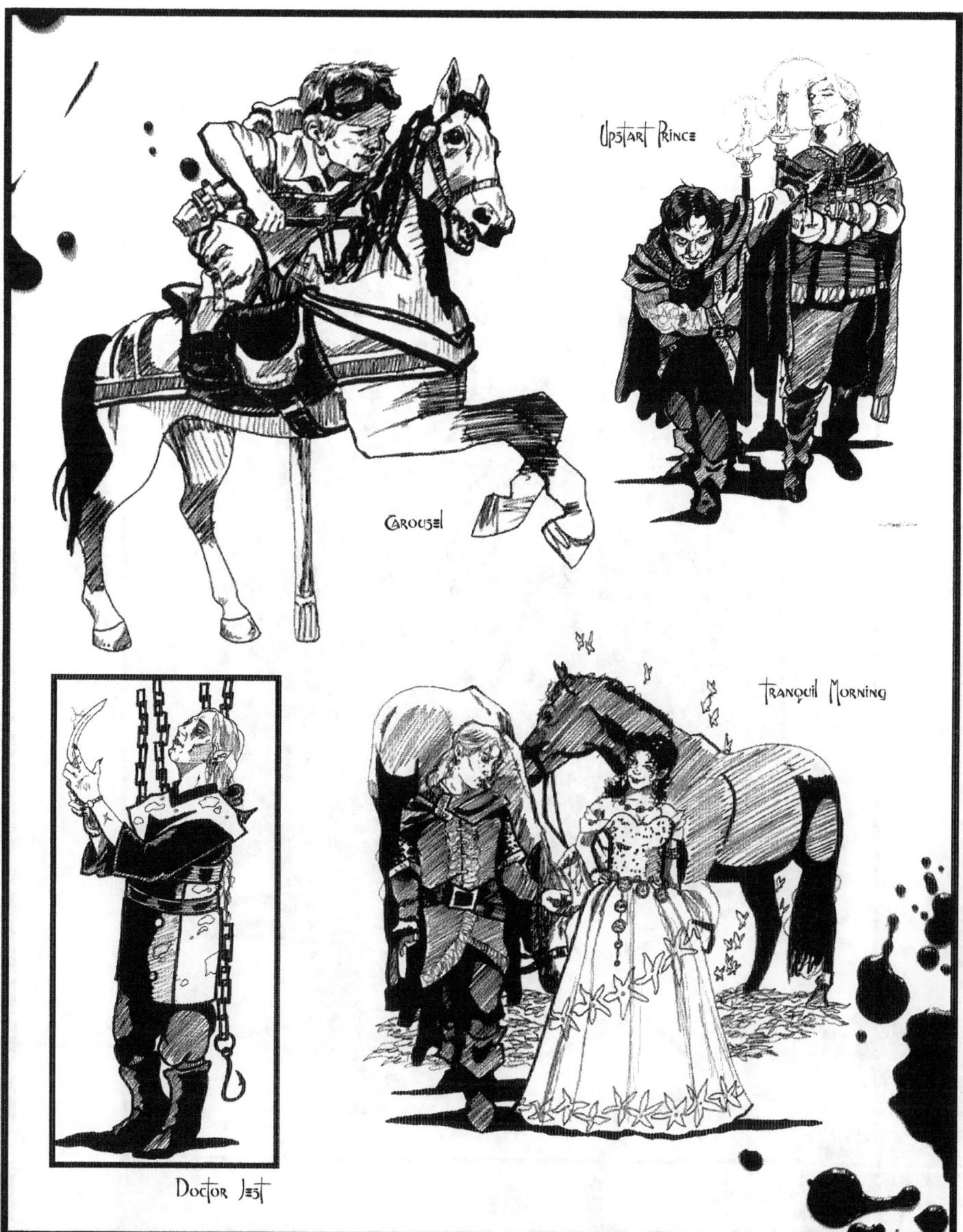

Upstart Prince

Carousel

Tranquil Morning

Doctor Jest

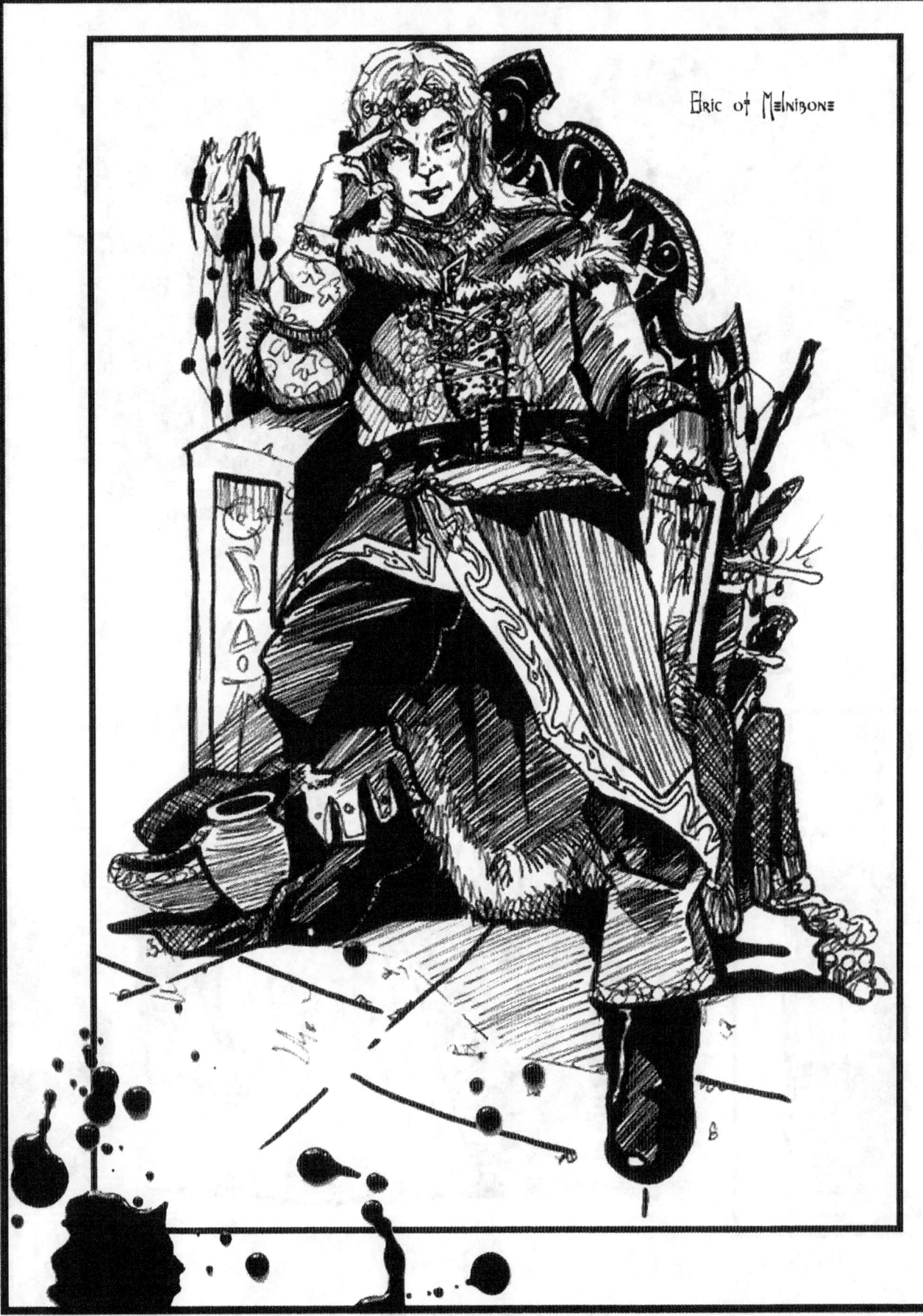

Elric of Melnibone

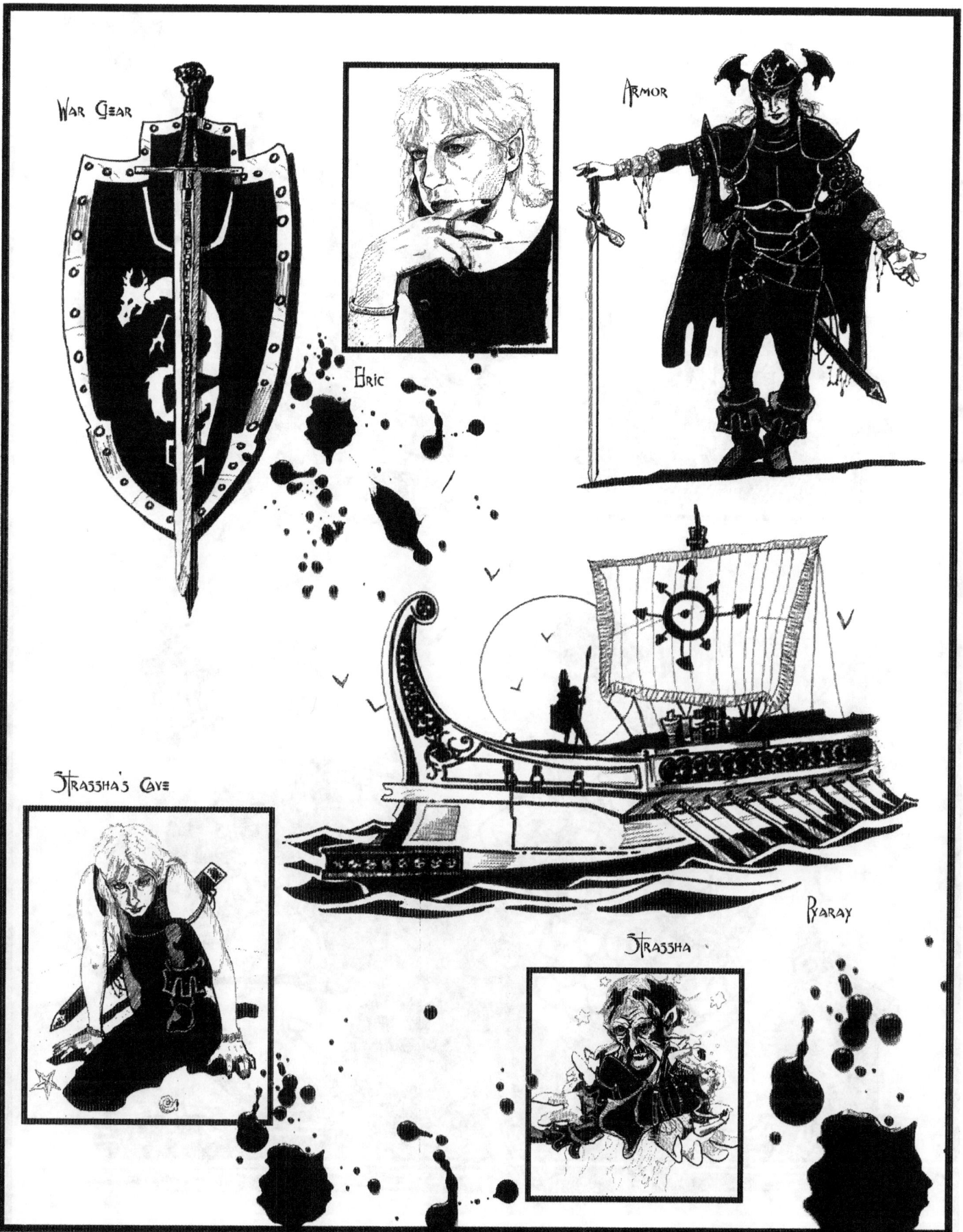

WAR GEAR

ERIC

ARMOR

STRASSHA'S CAVE

PYARAY

STRASSHA

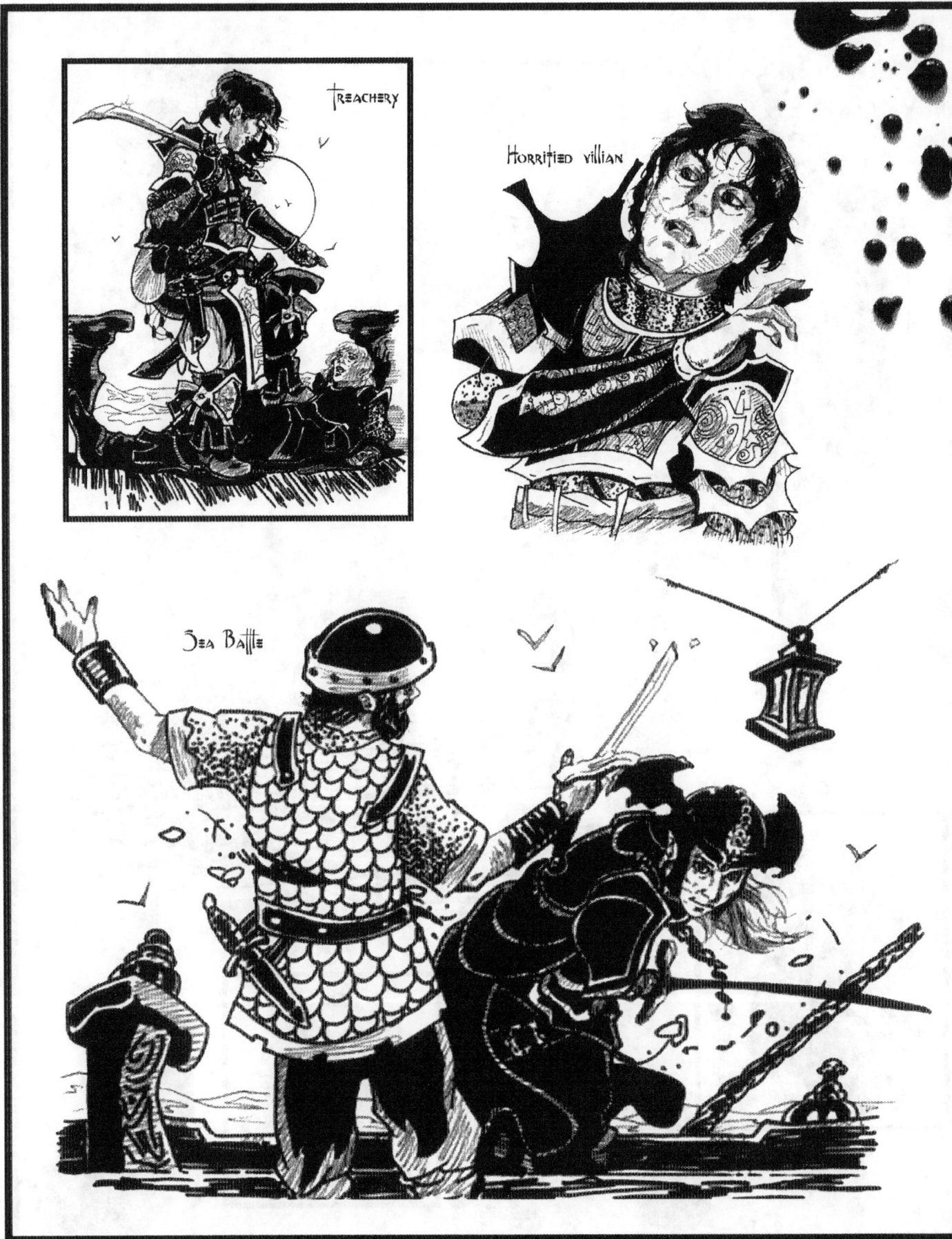

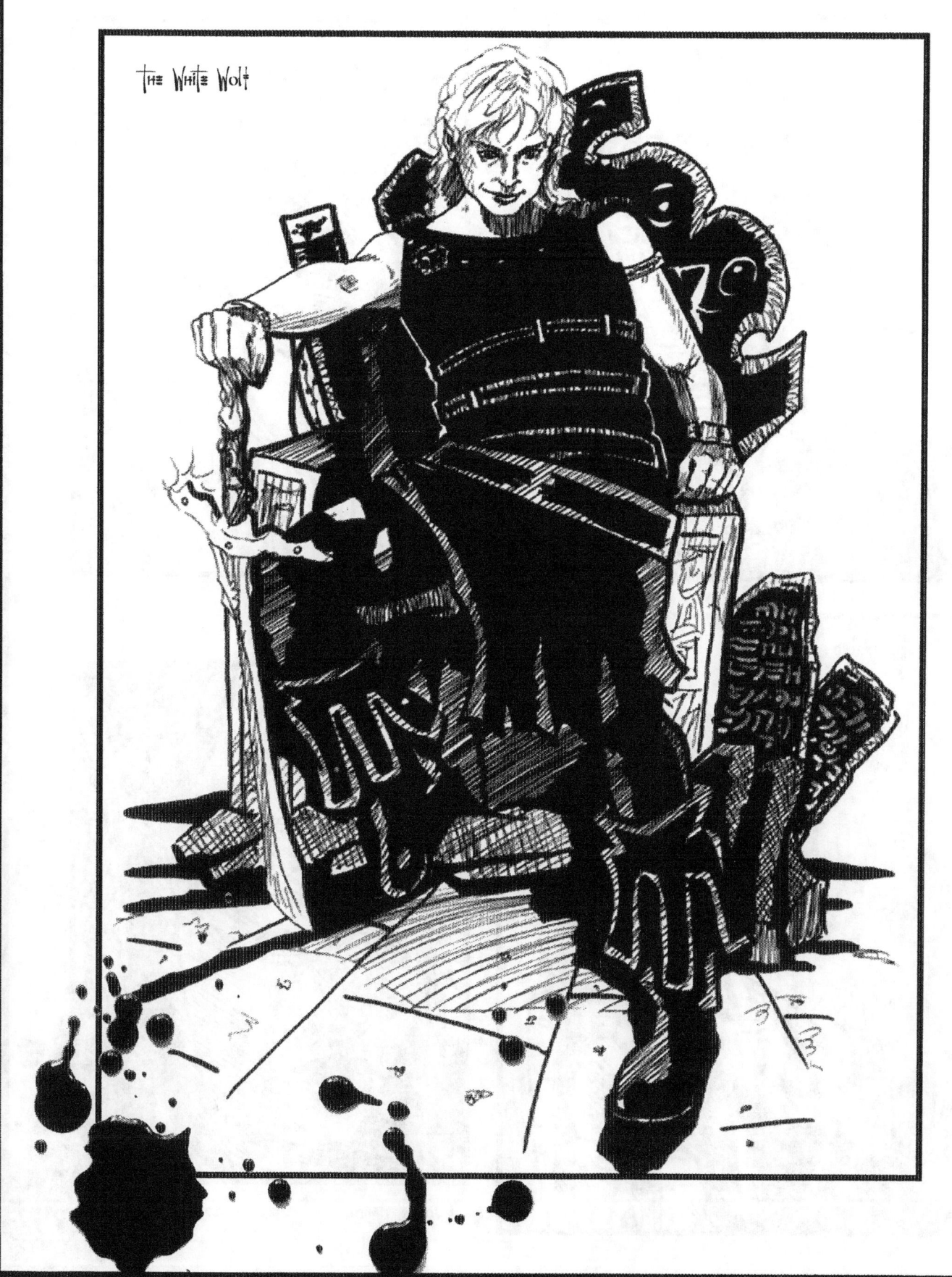

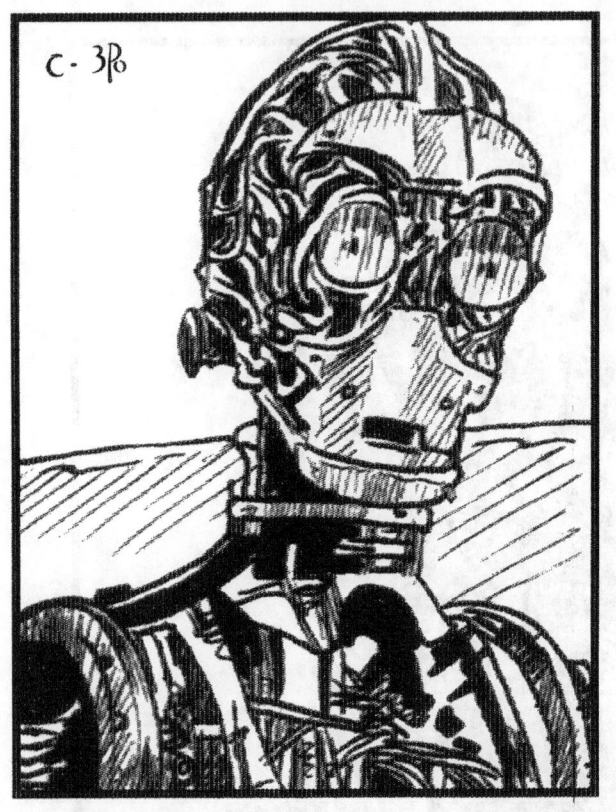

C-3PO

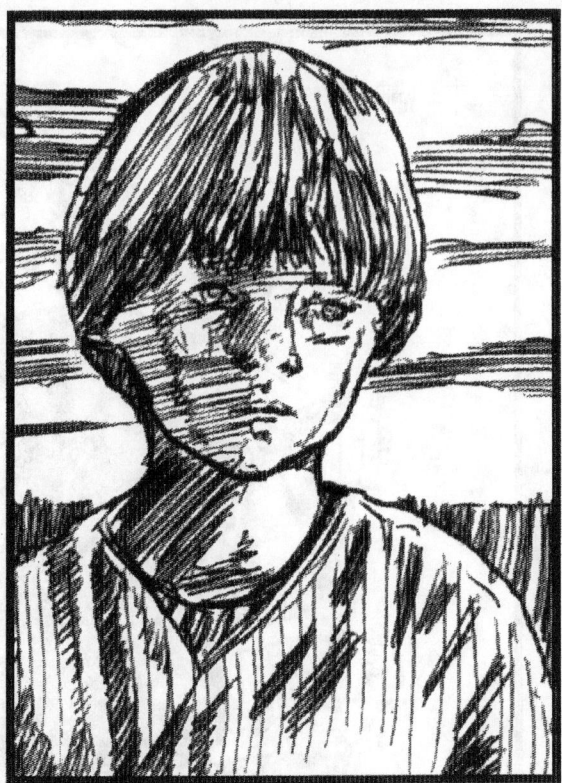

Anni

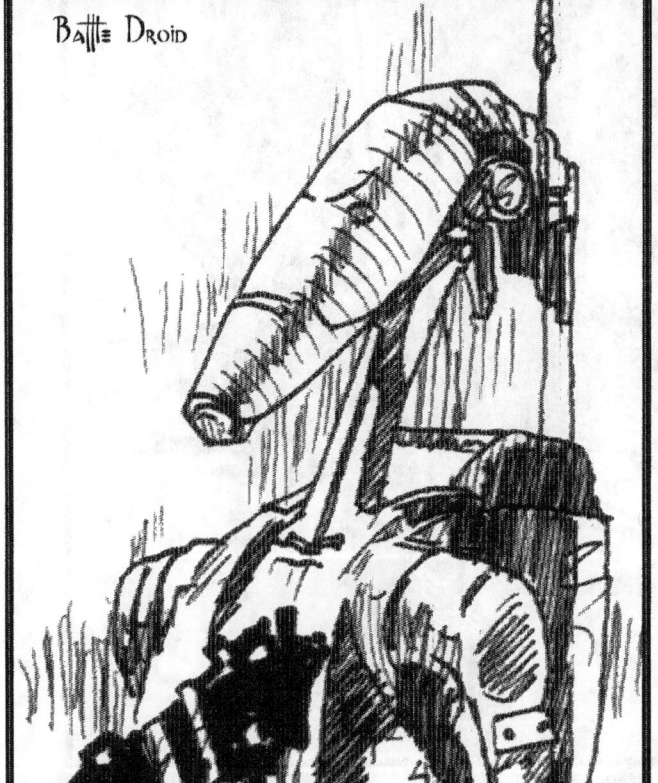

Battle Droid

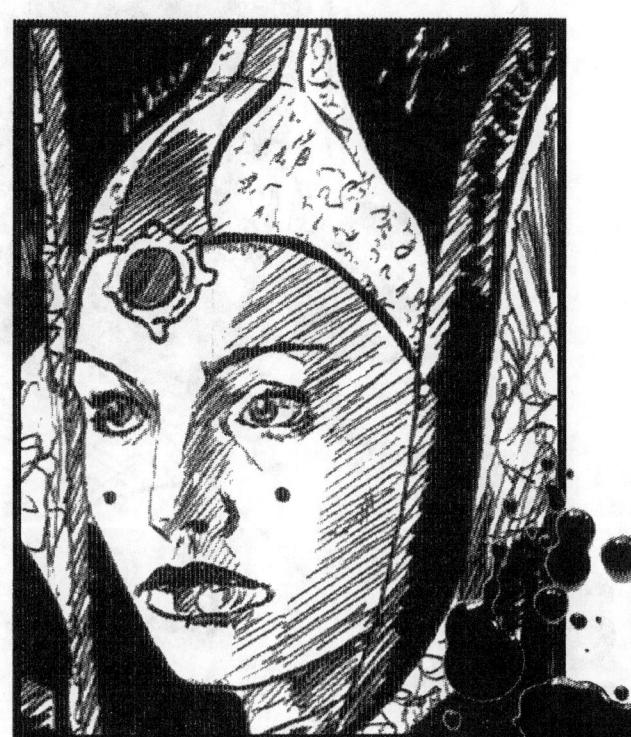

Queen Amidala

Obi-Wan Kenobi

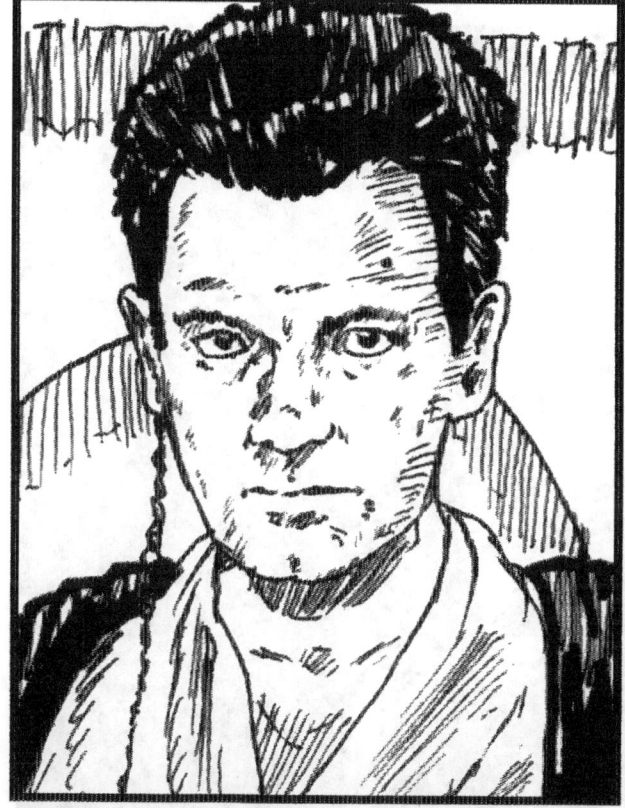

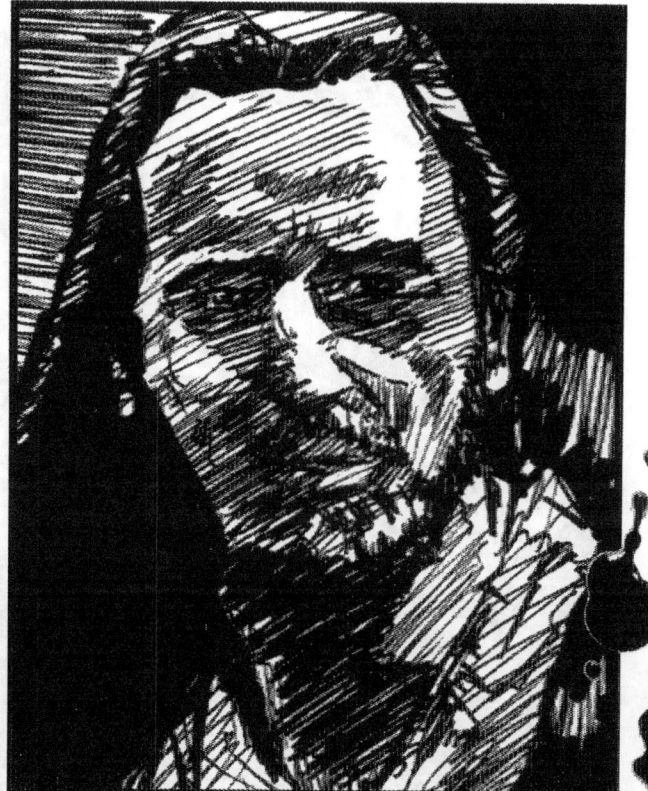

Qui-Gonn Jinn

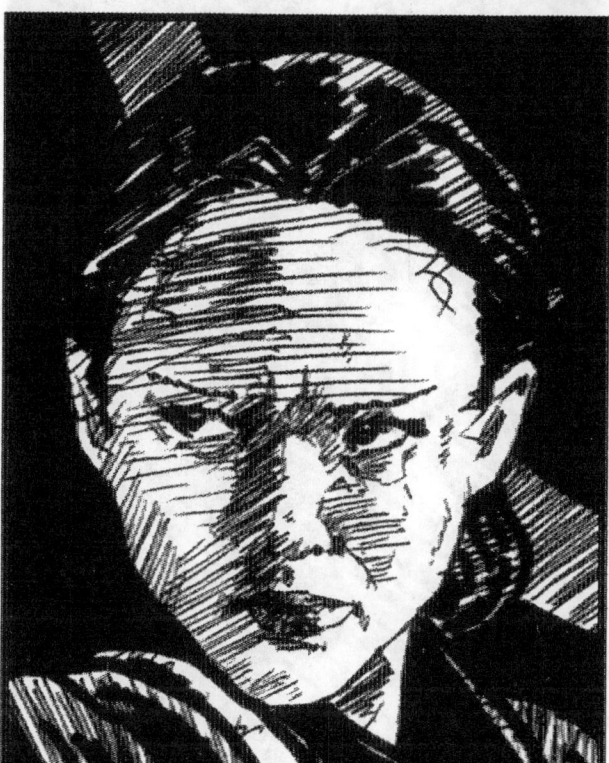

Padme Amidala

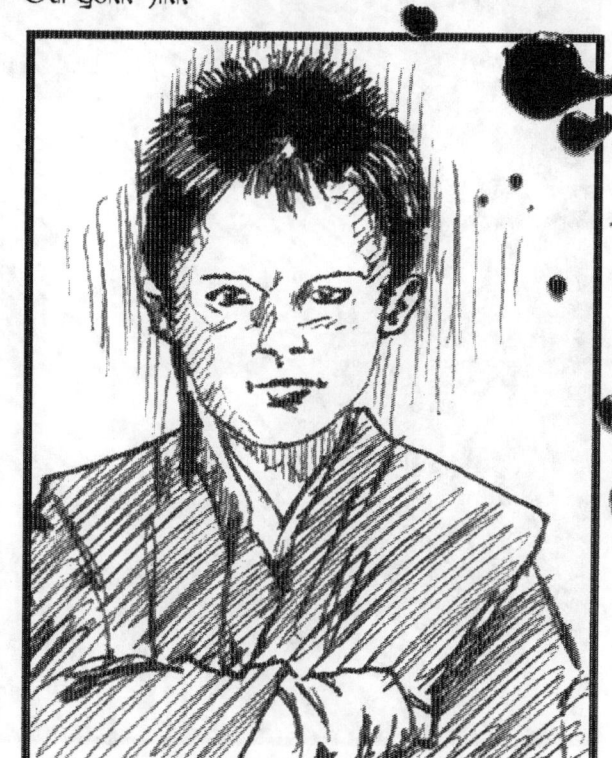

Anakin Skwalker

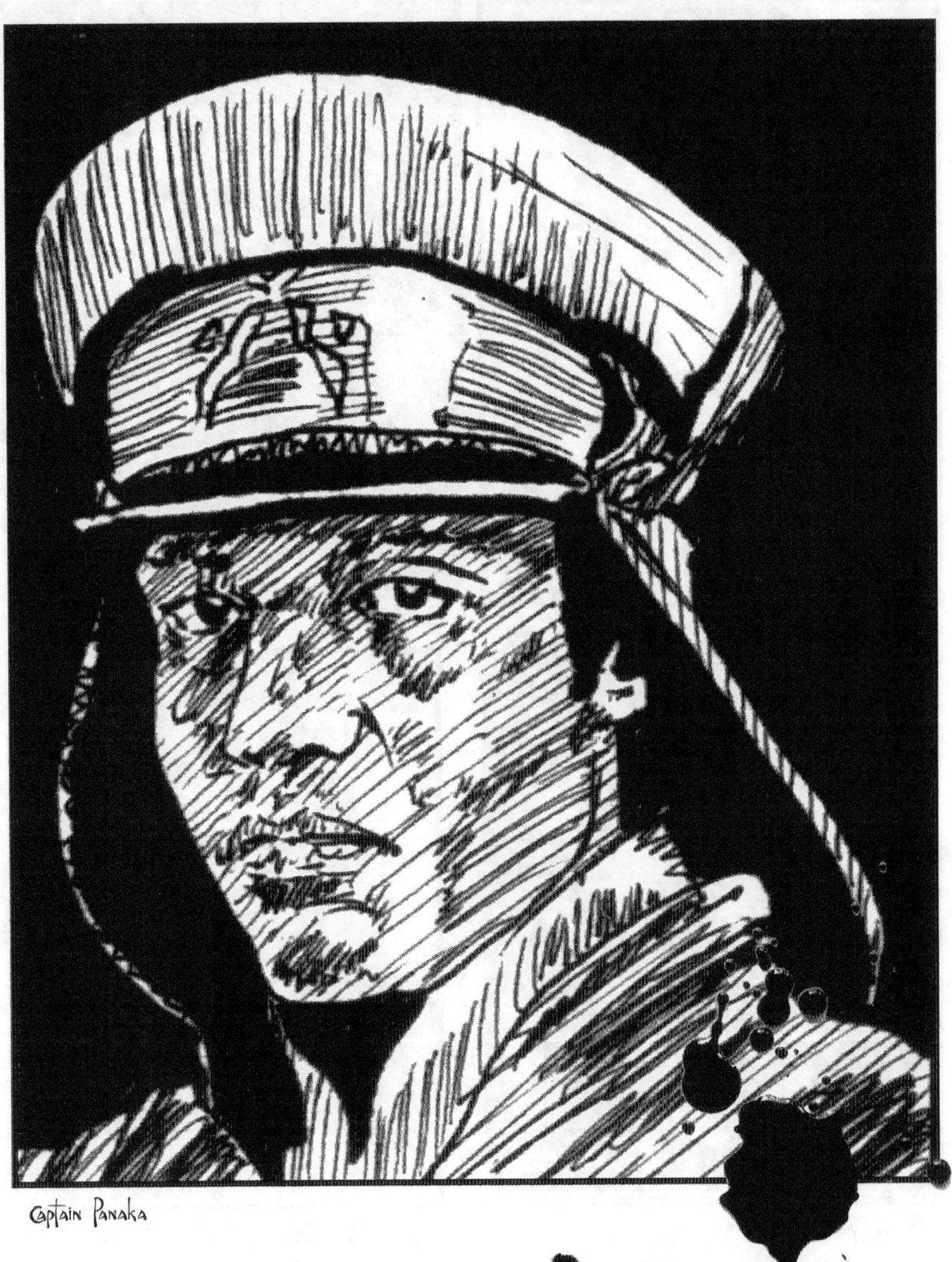

Captain Panaka

Cindel Towani

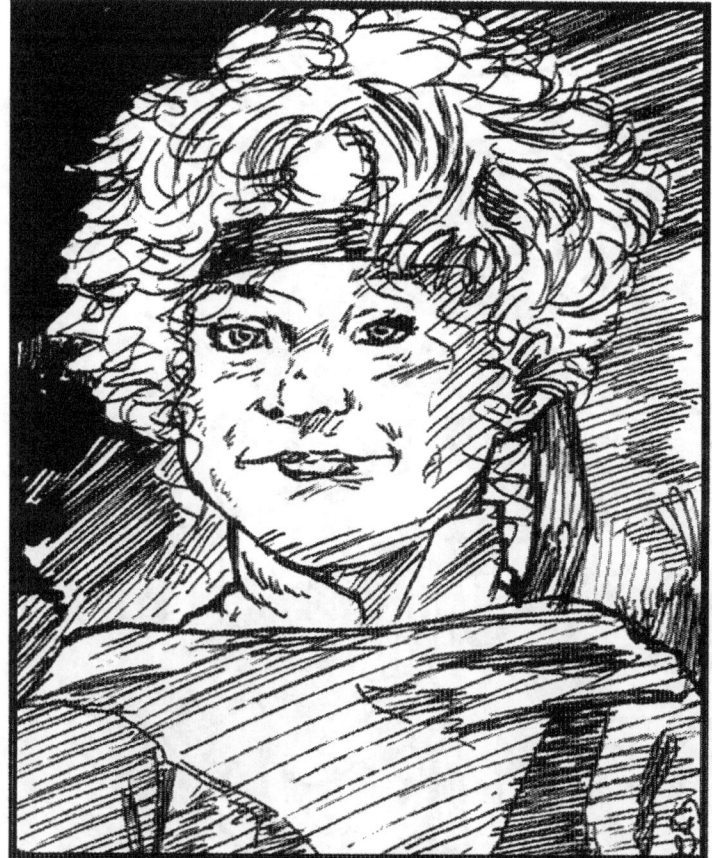

Cindel Towani

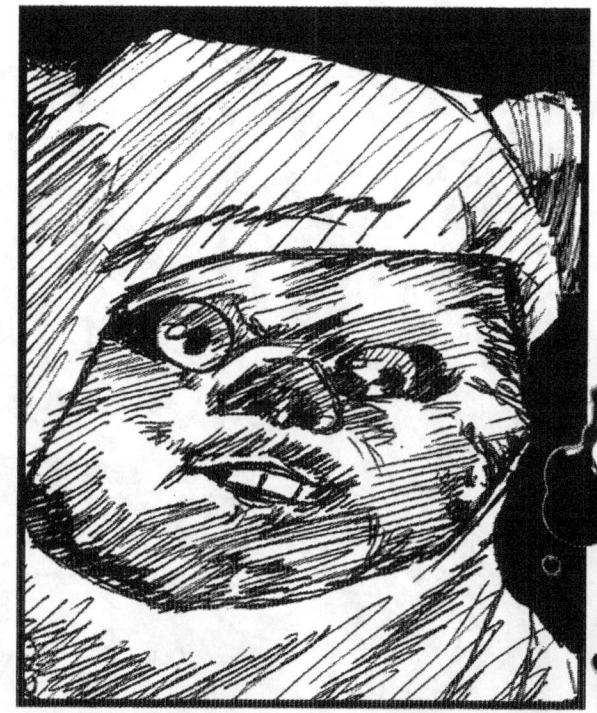

Wicket Warrick

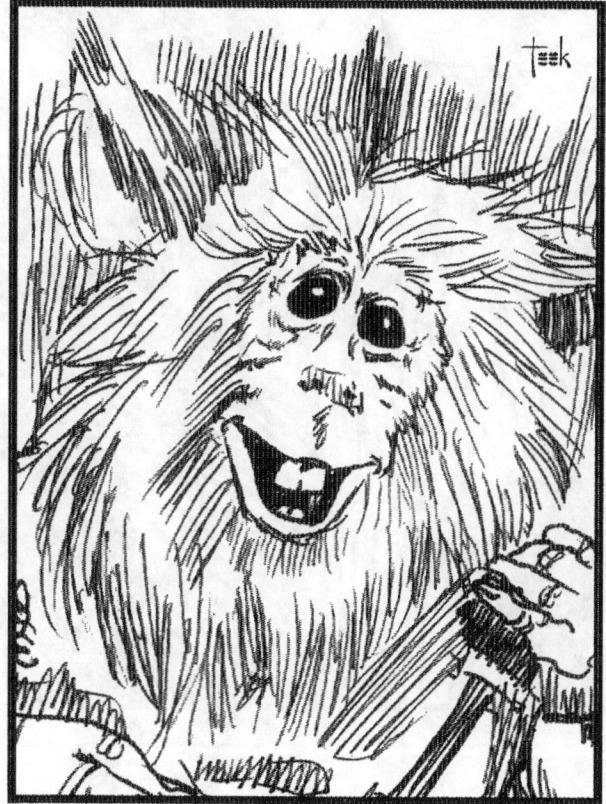

Teek

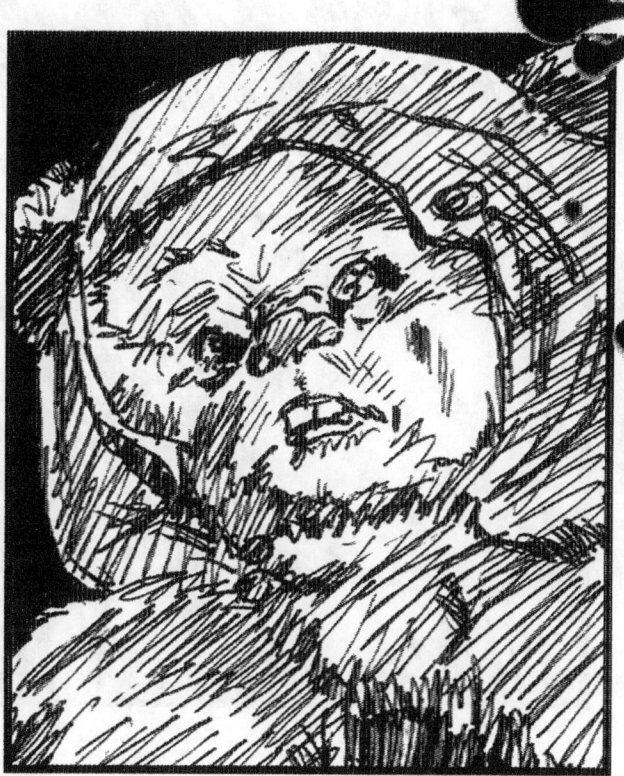

Deej Warrick

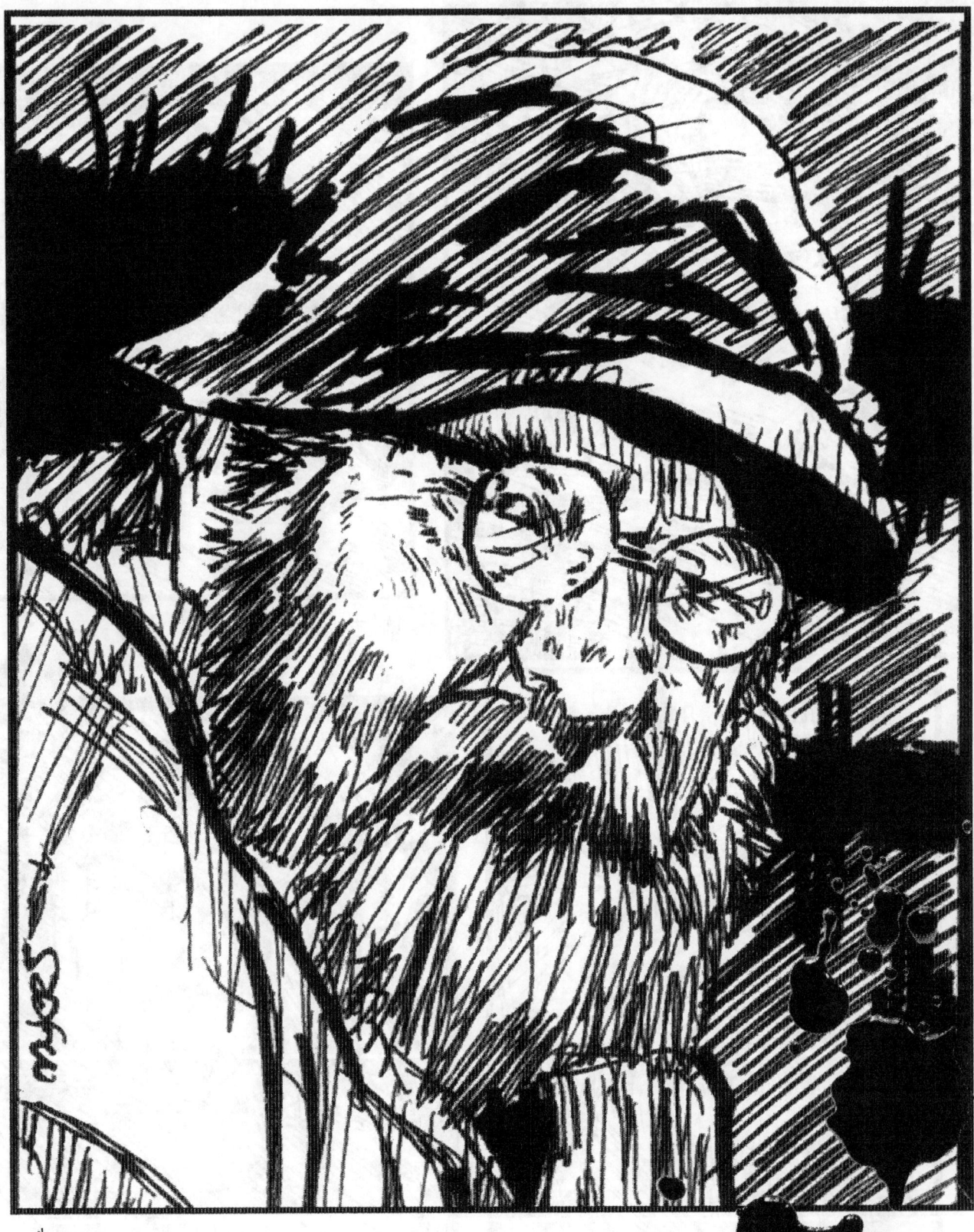

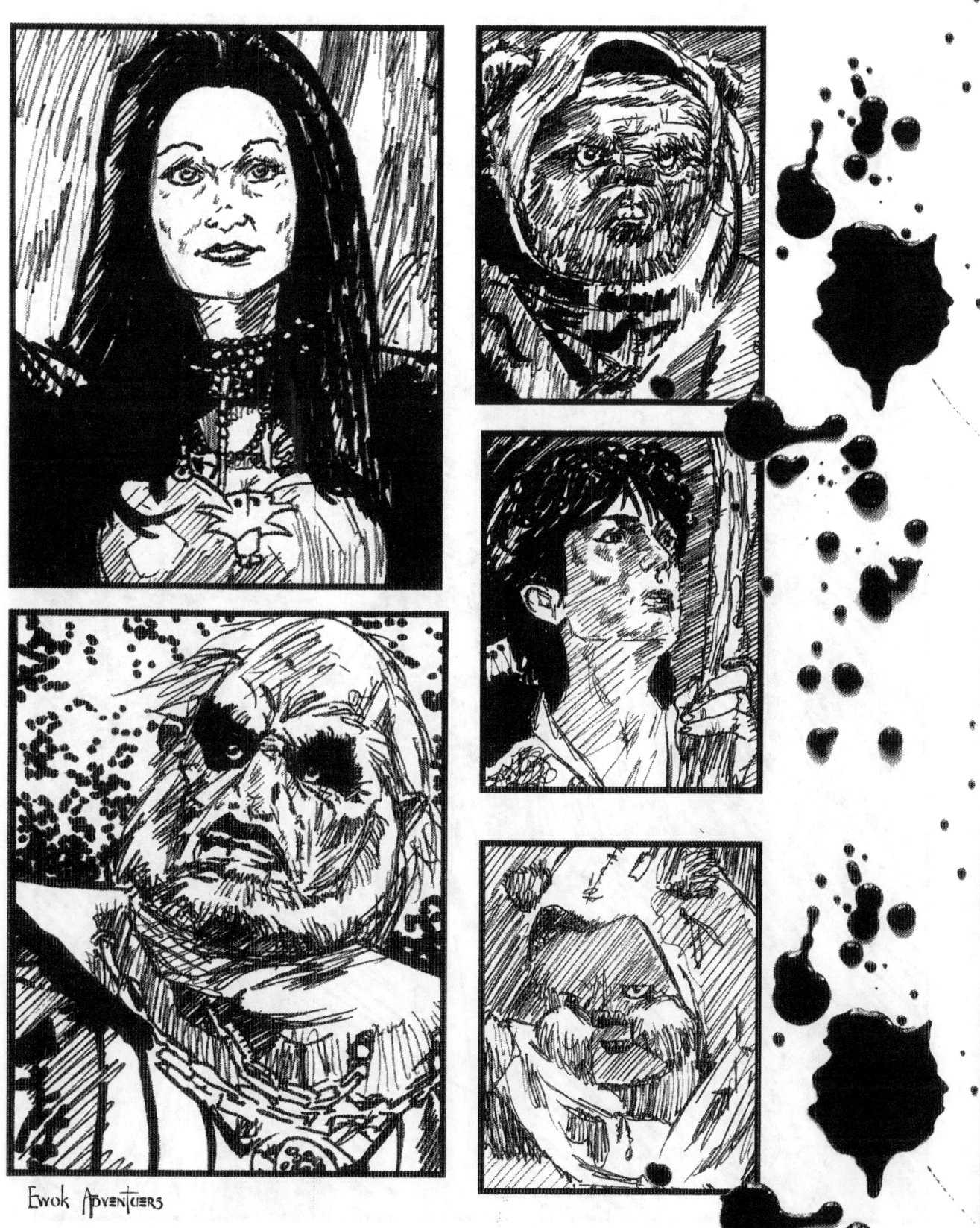

Ewok Adventuers

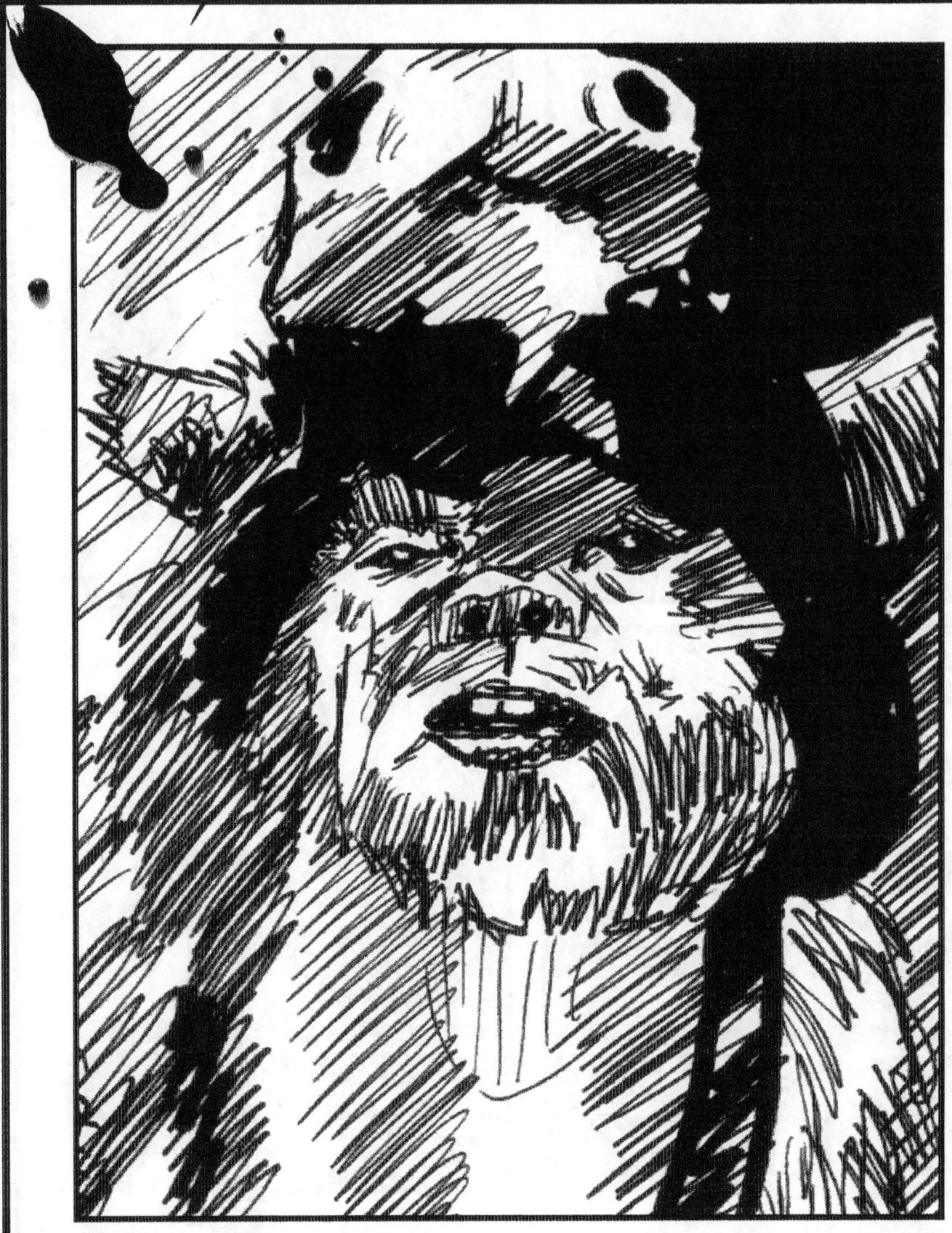

LOGRAY

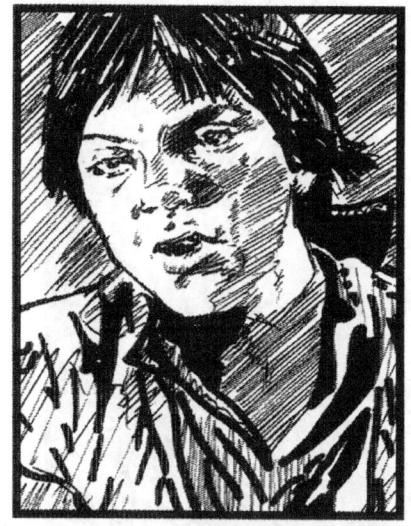
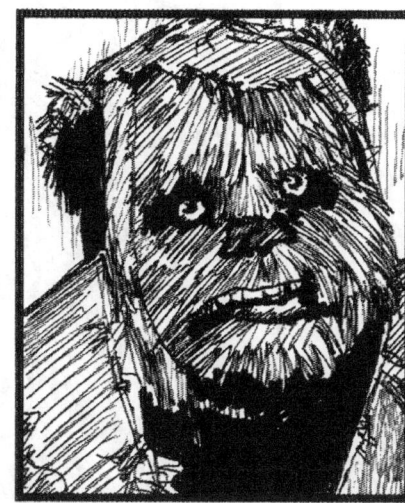
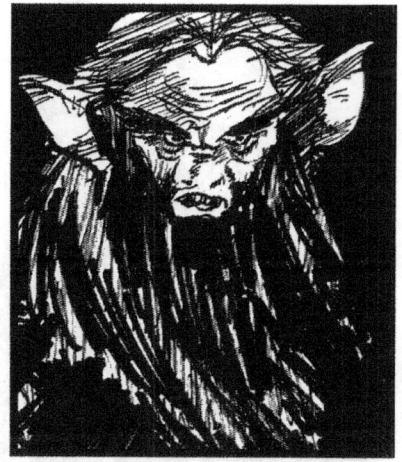

EWOK ADVENTURES II

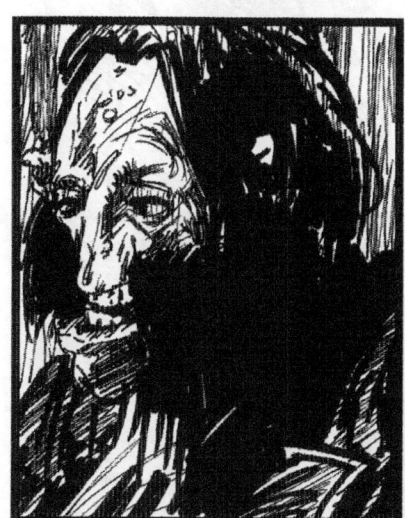
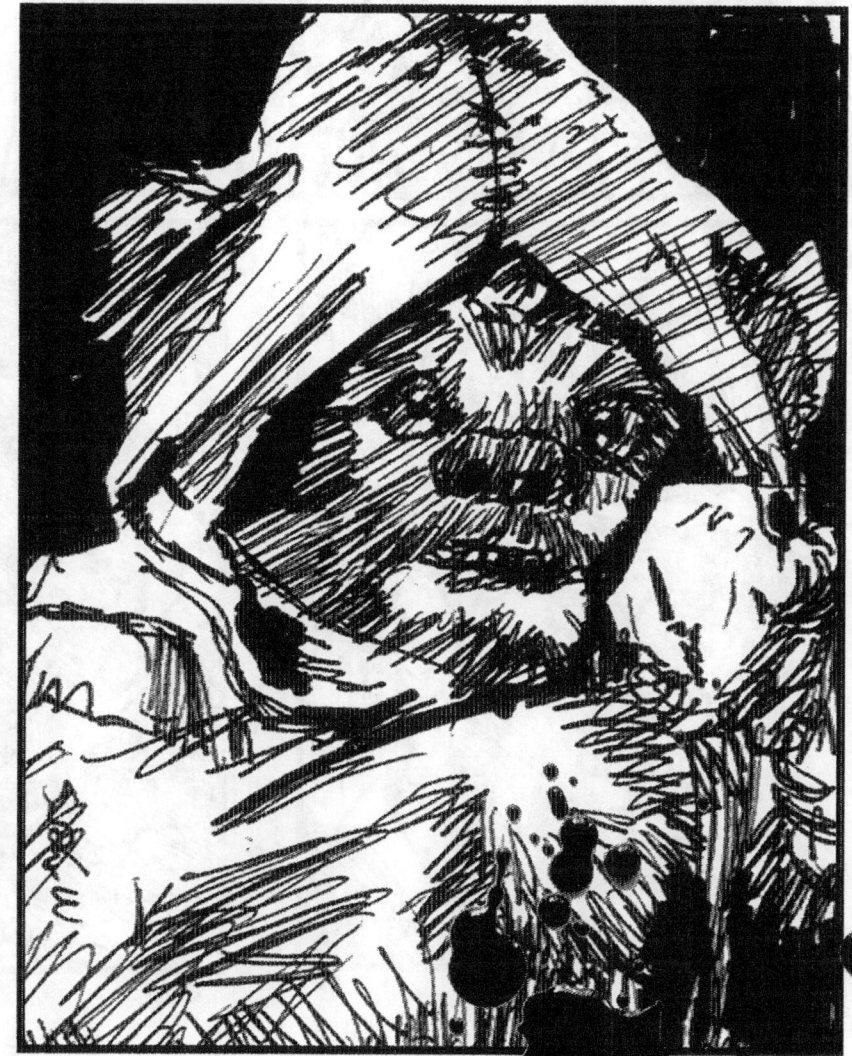
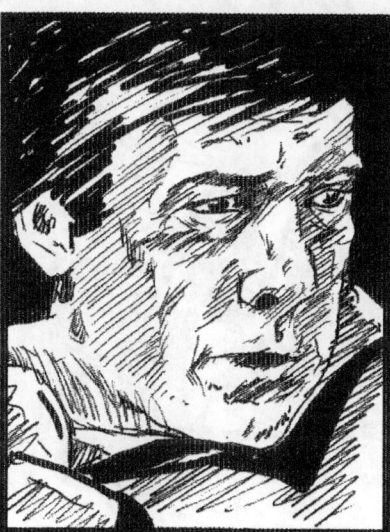

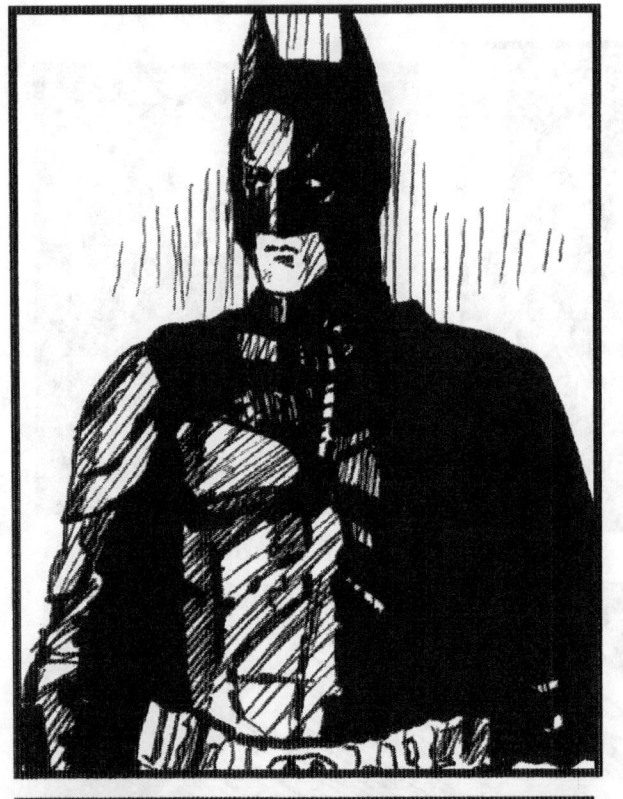
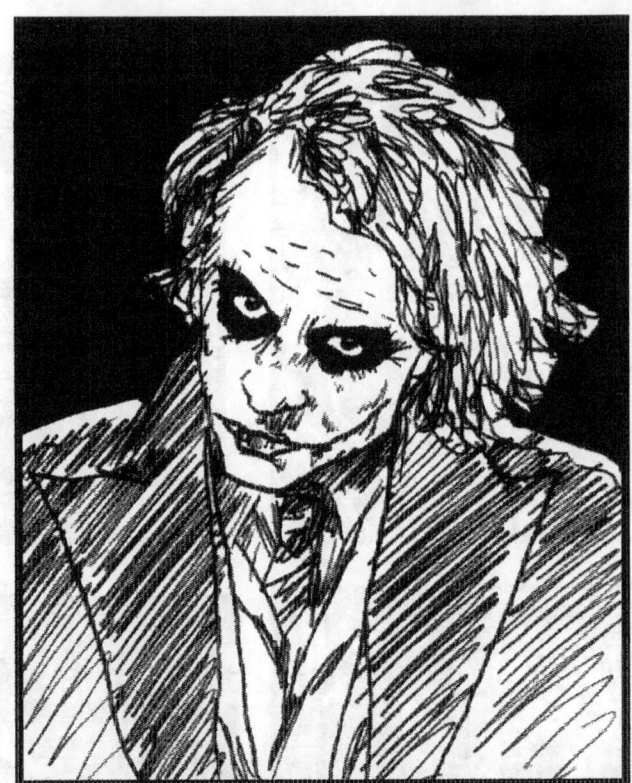
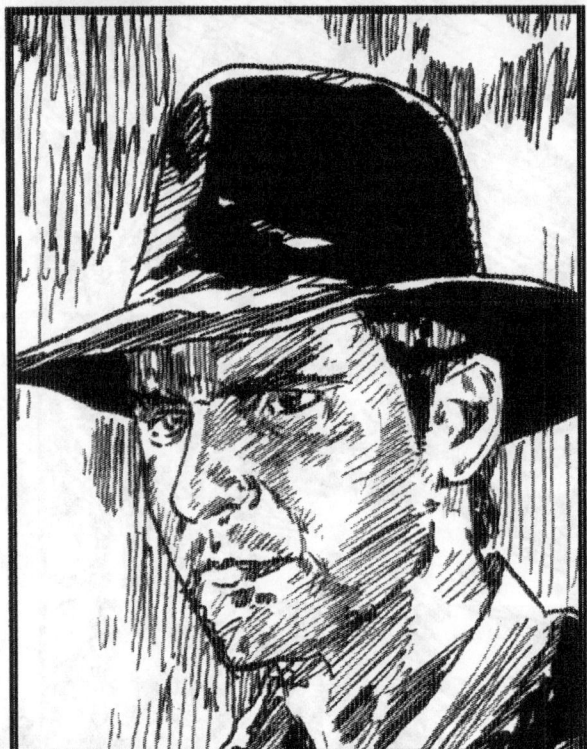
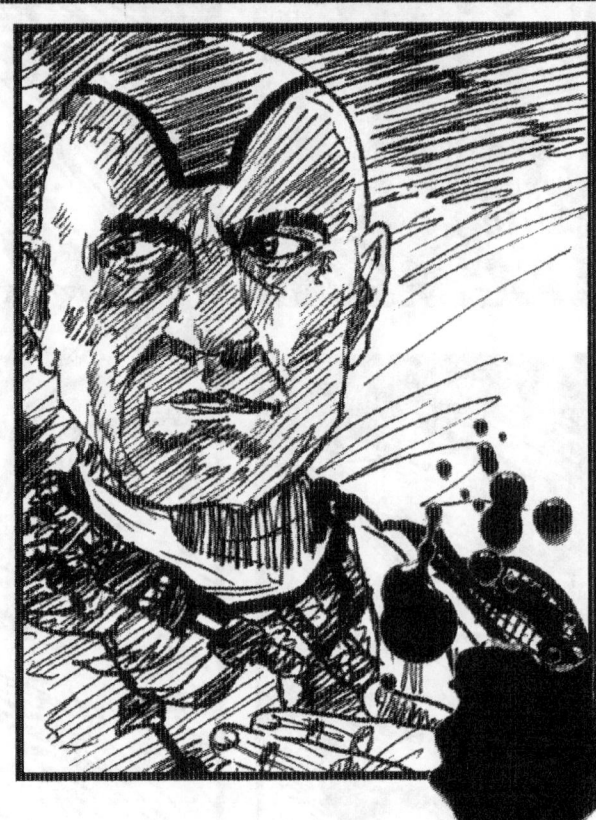

film Icons I

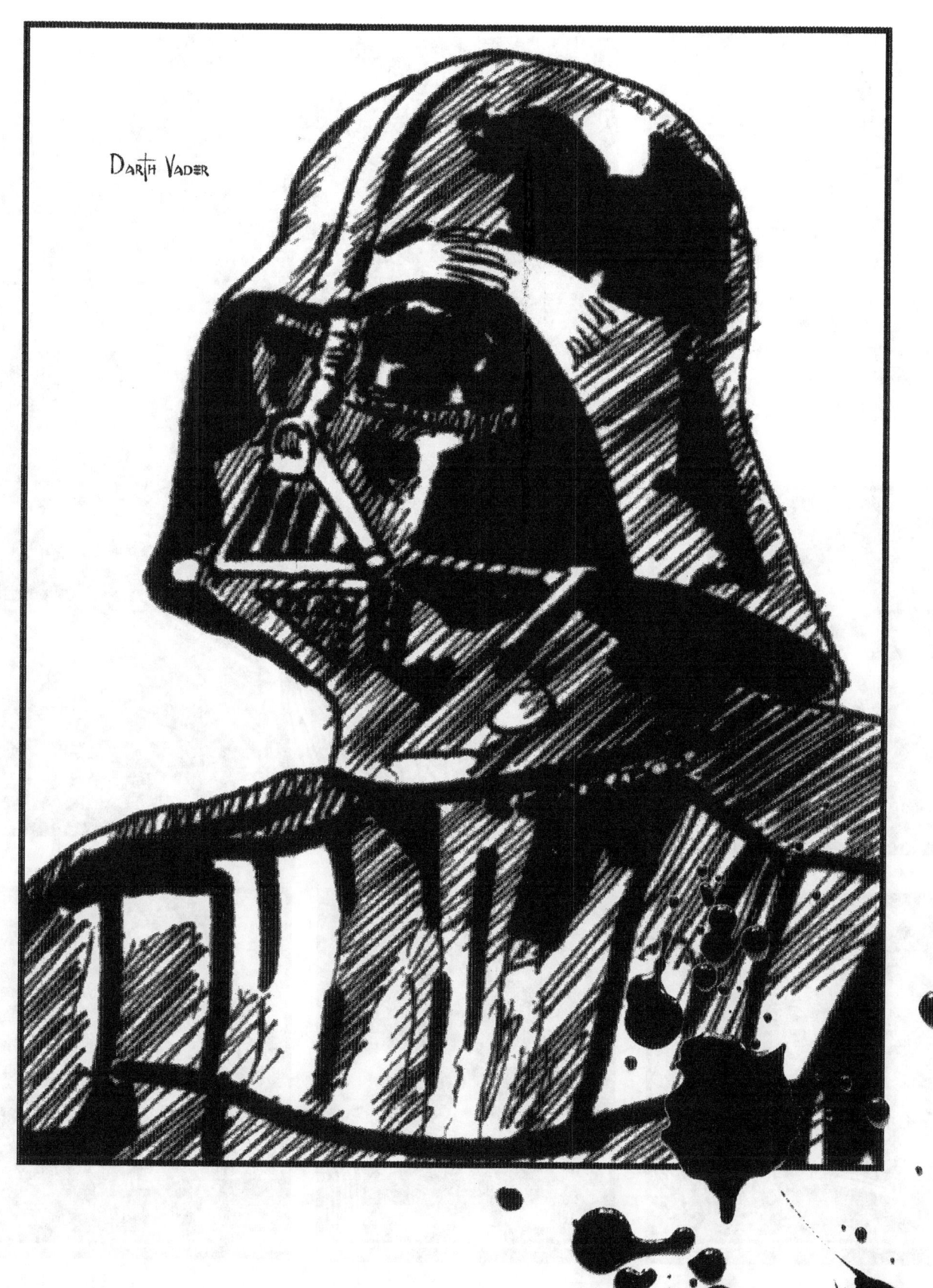

DARTH VADER

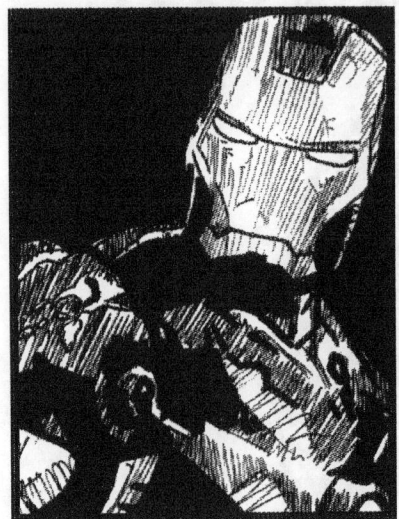

film Icons II

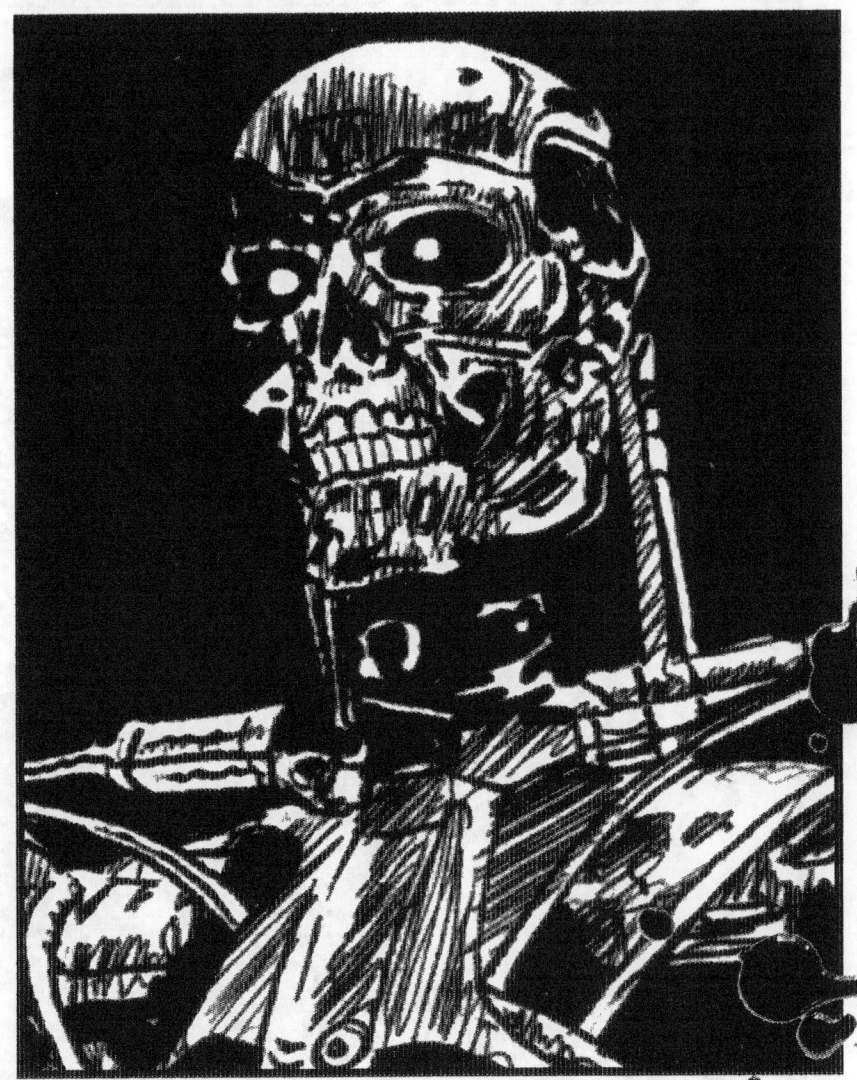

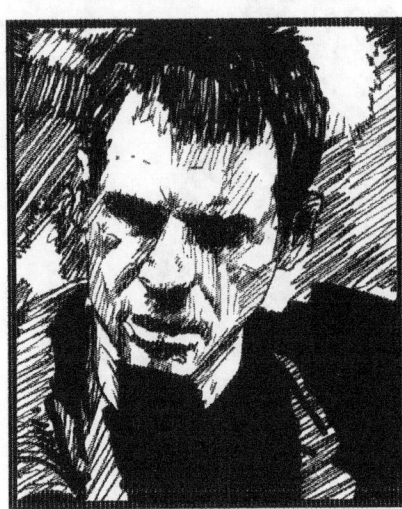

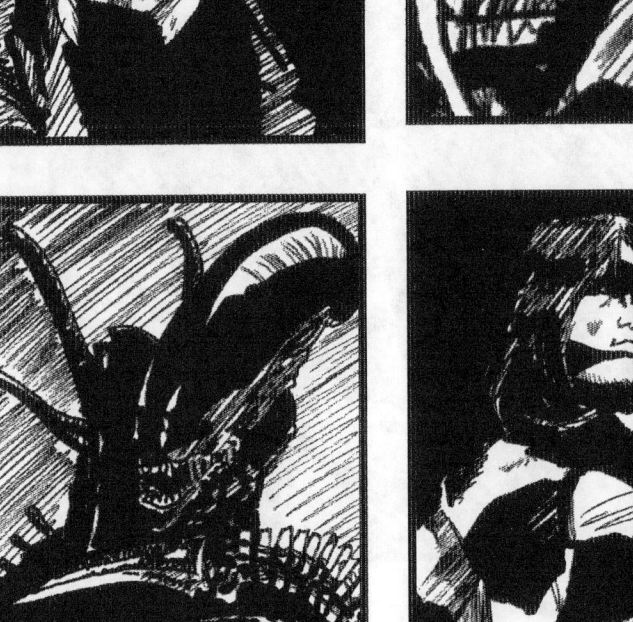

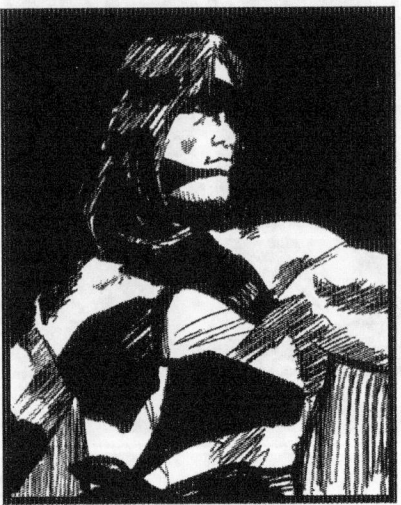

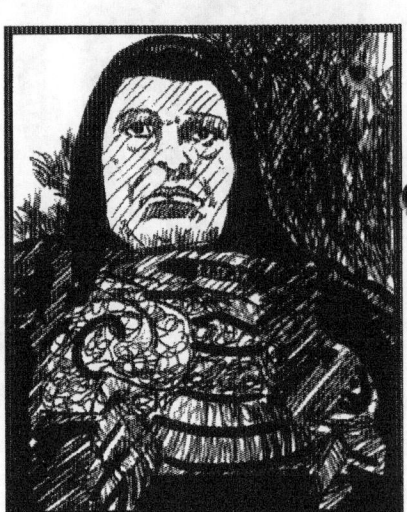

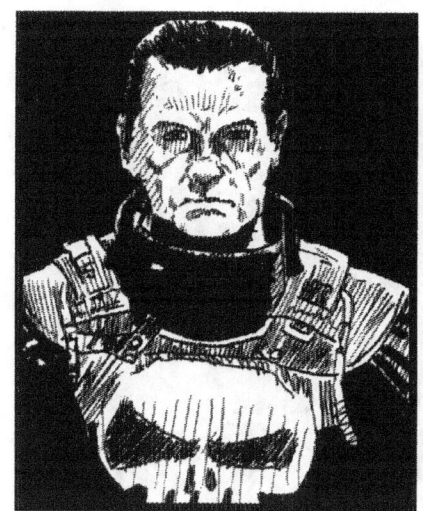

film Icons III

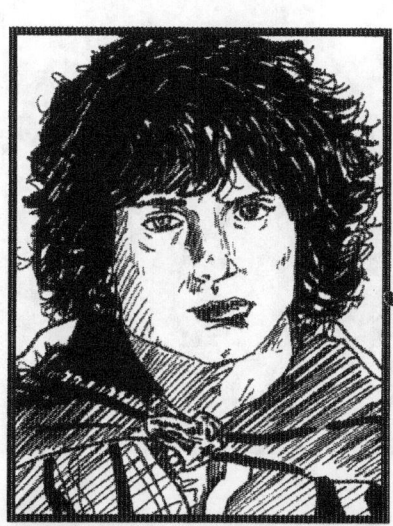

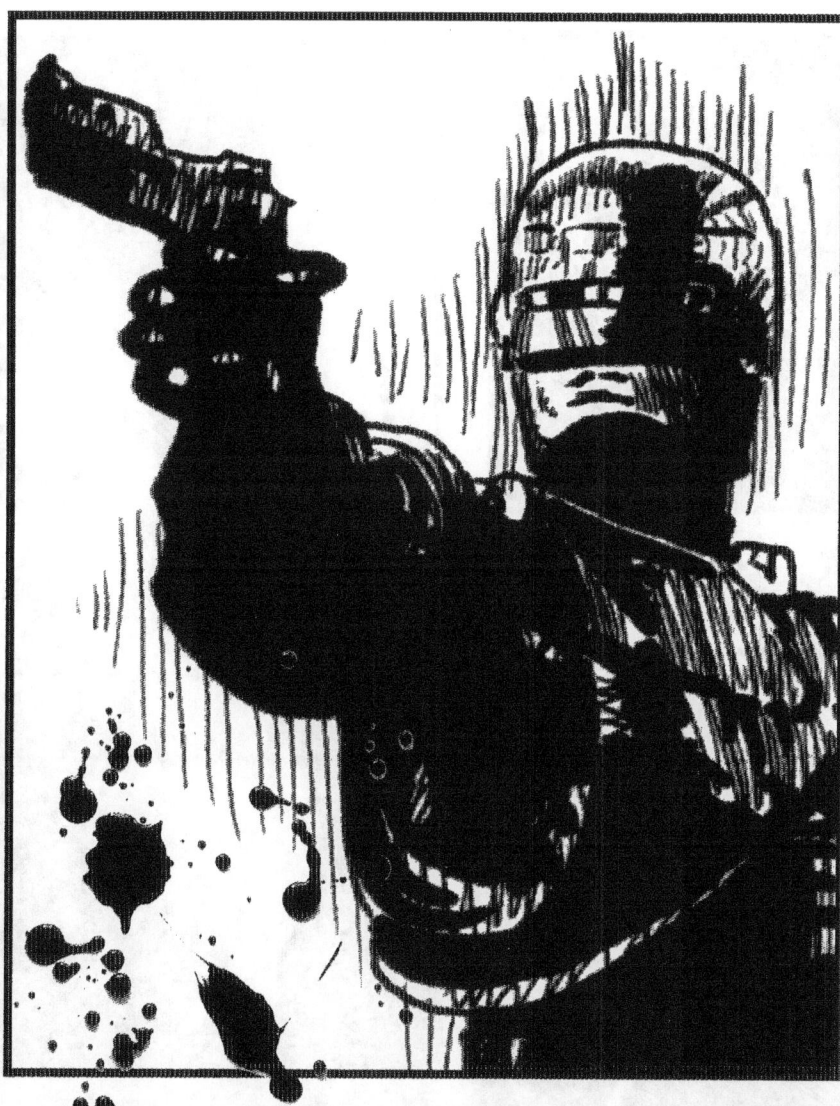

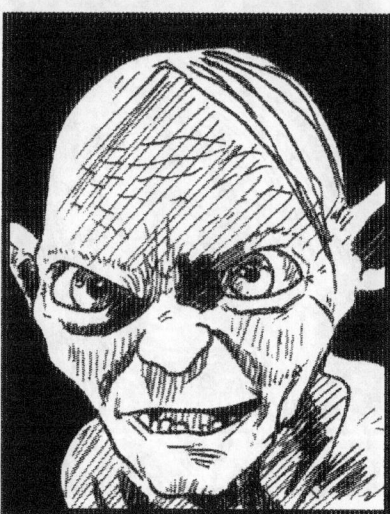

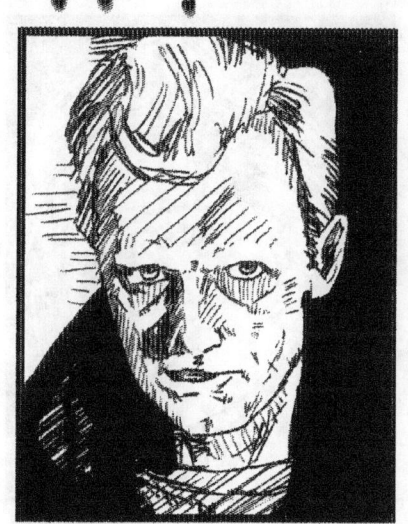

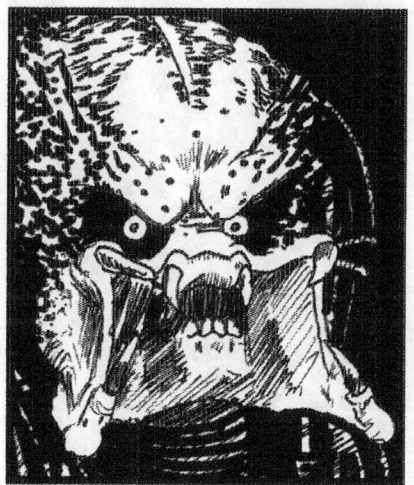

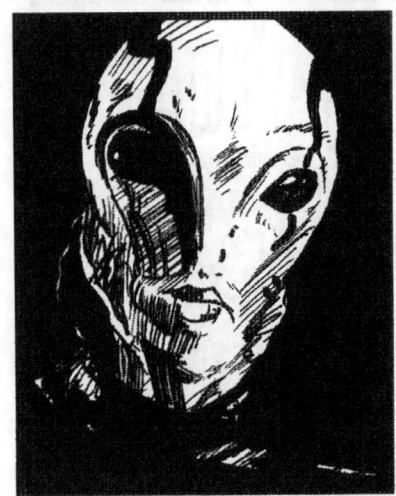

film Icons IV

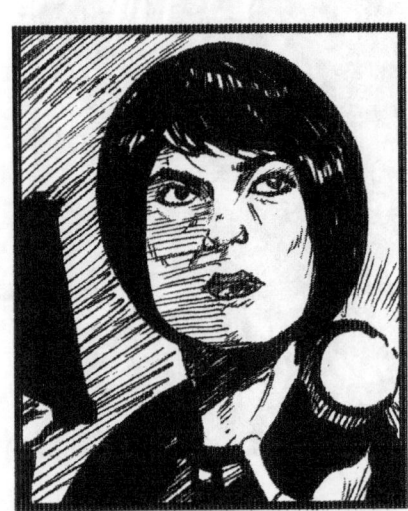

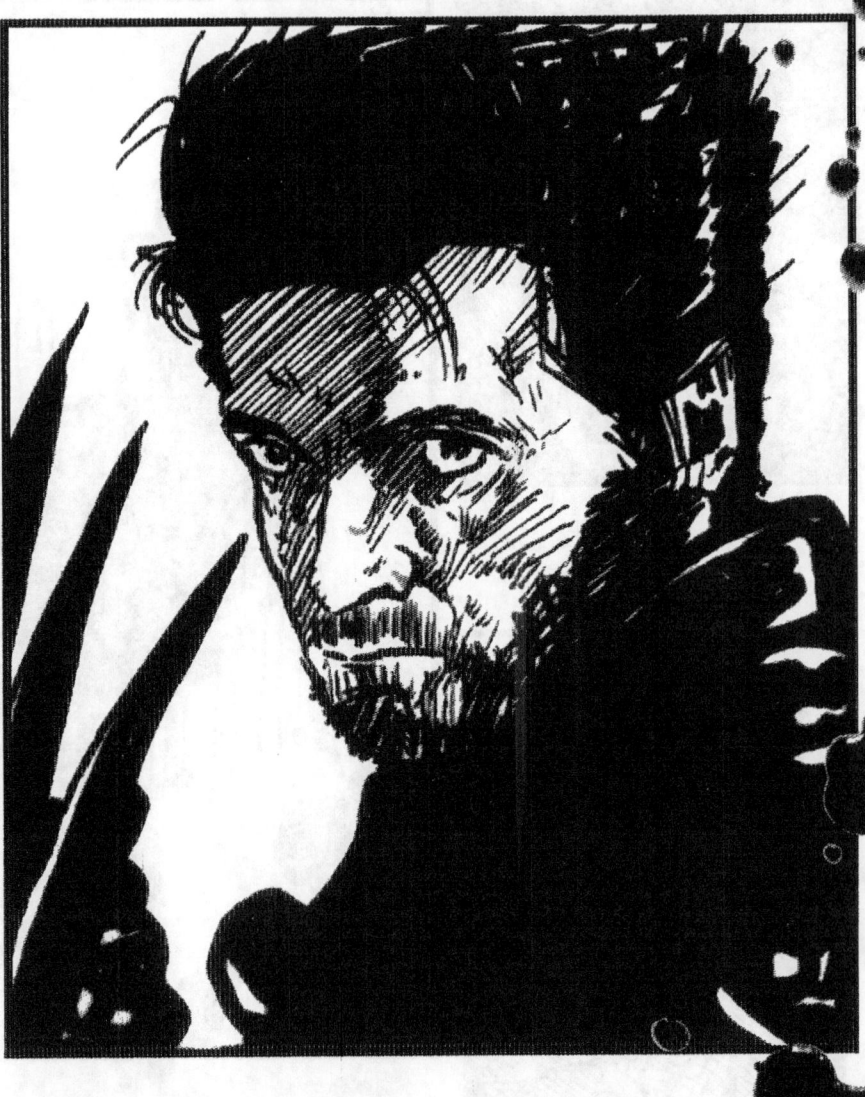

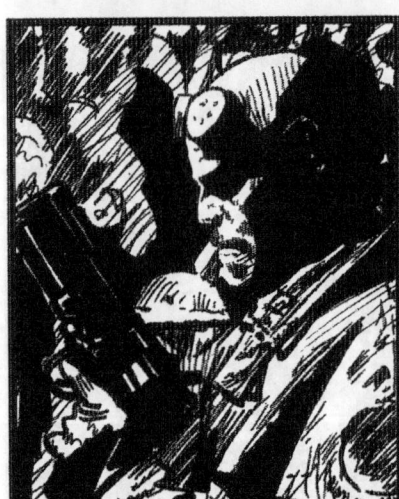

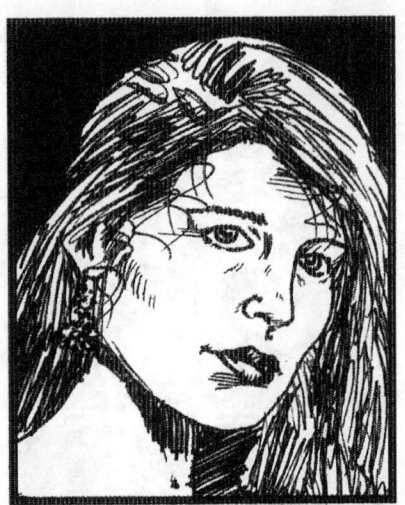

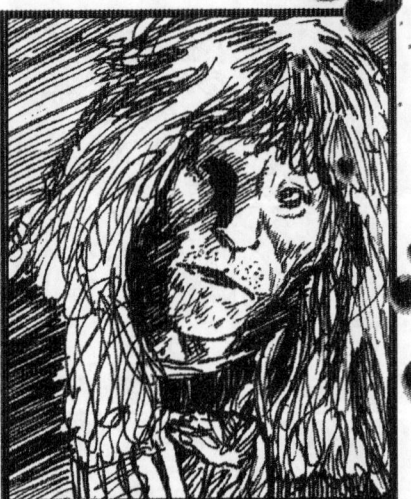

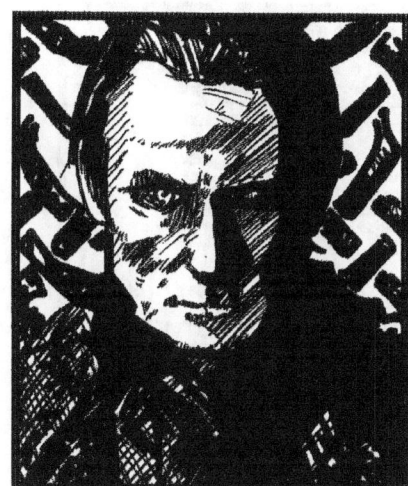

film Icons V

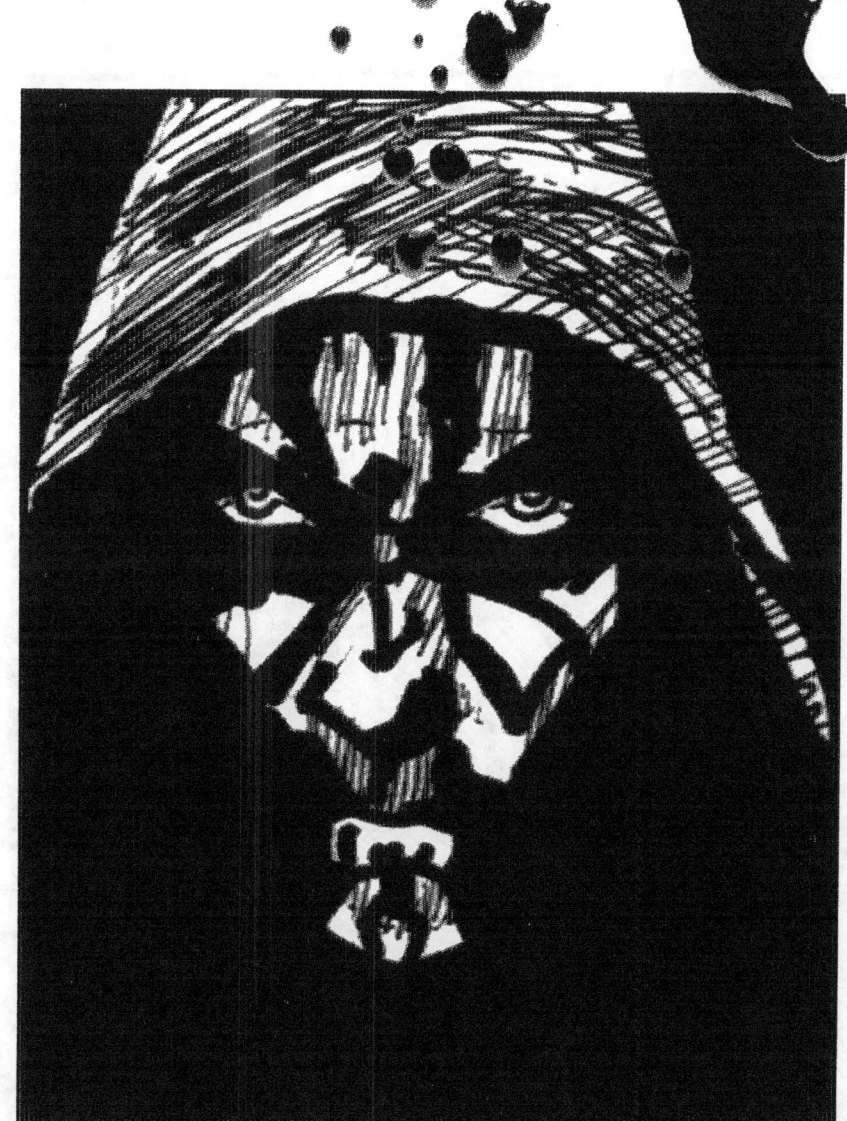

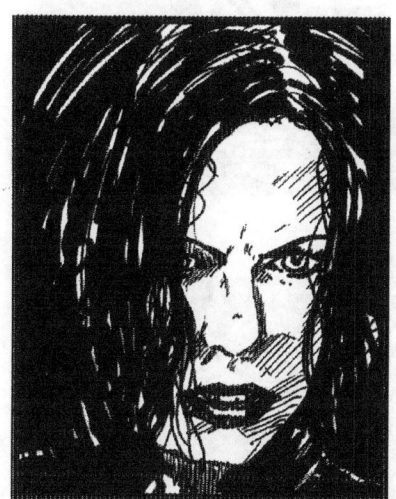

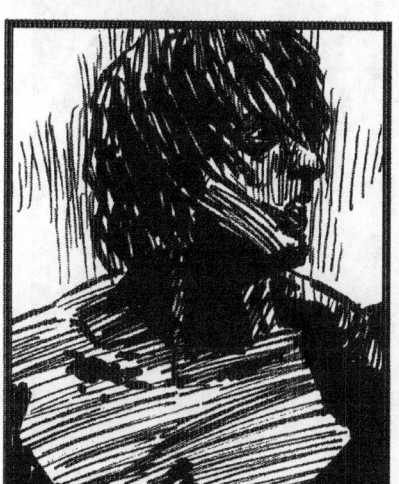

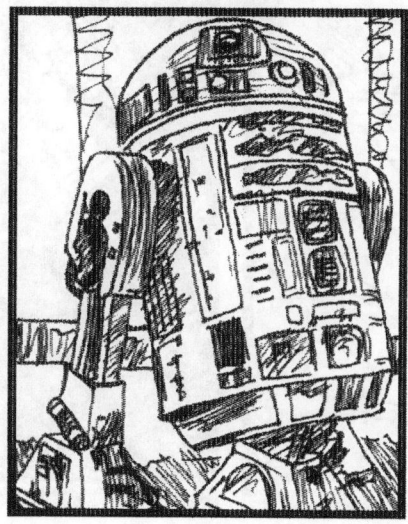

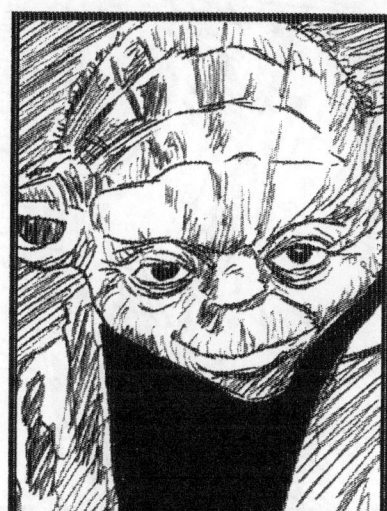

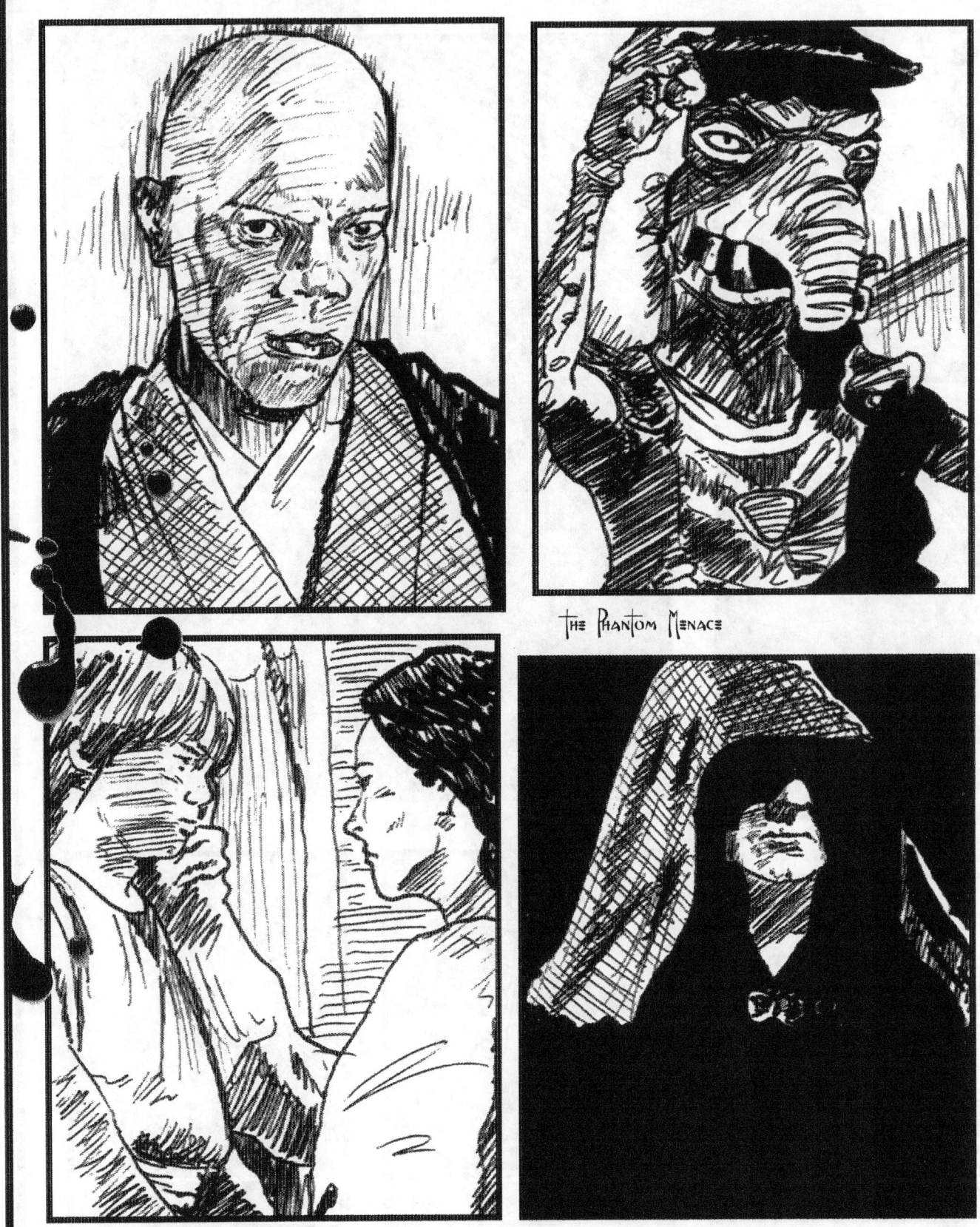

THE PHANTOM MENACE

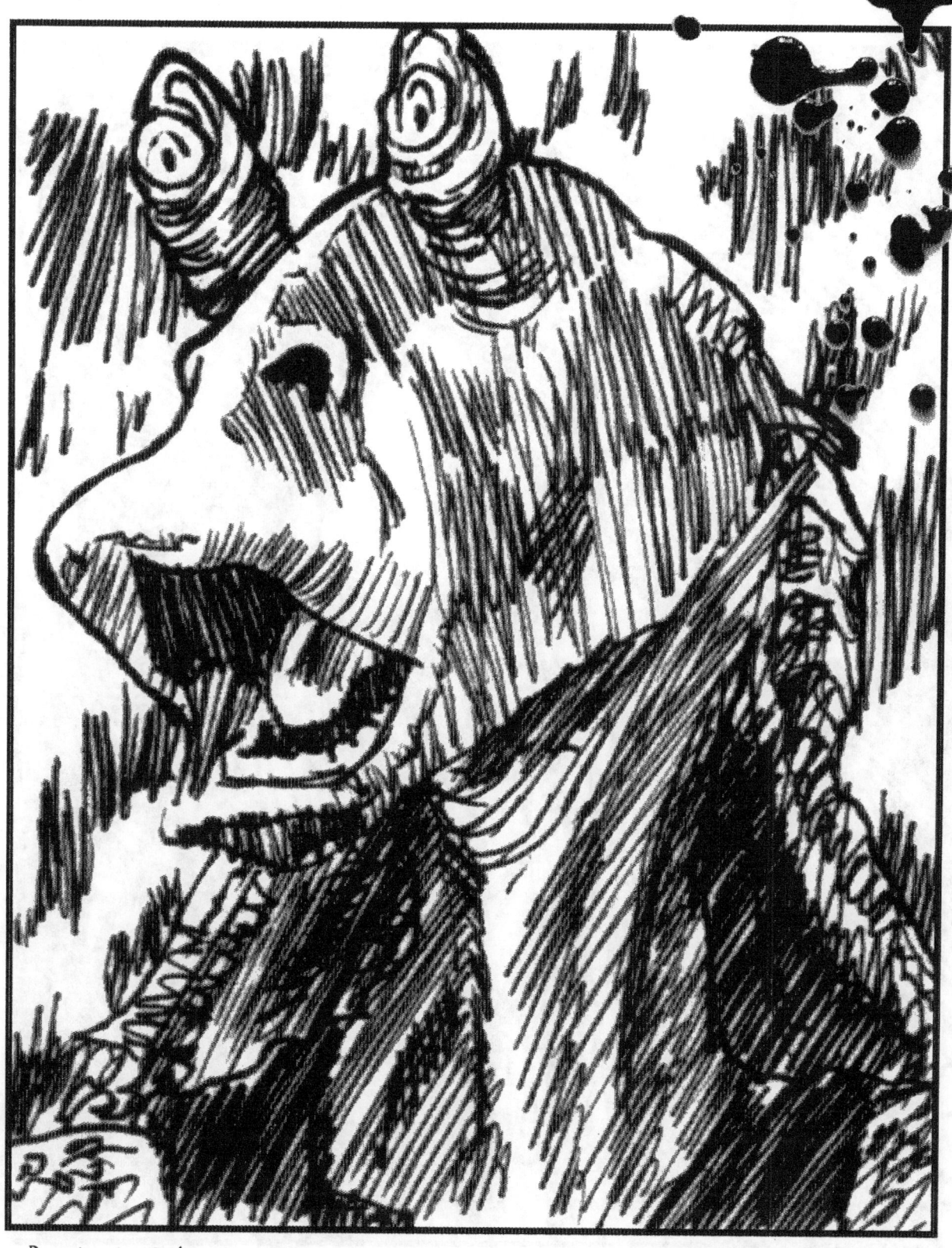

Poor Jar Jar Binks

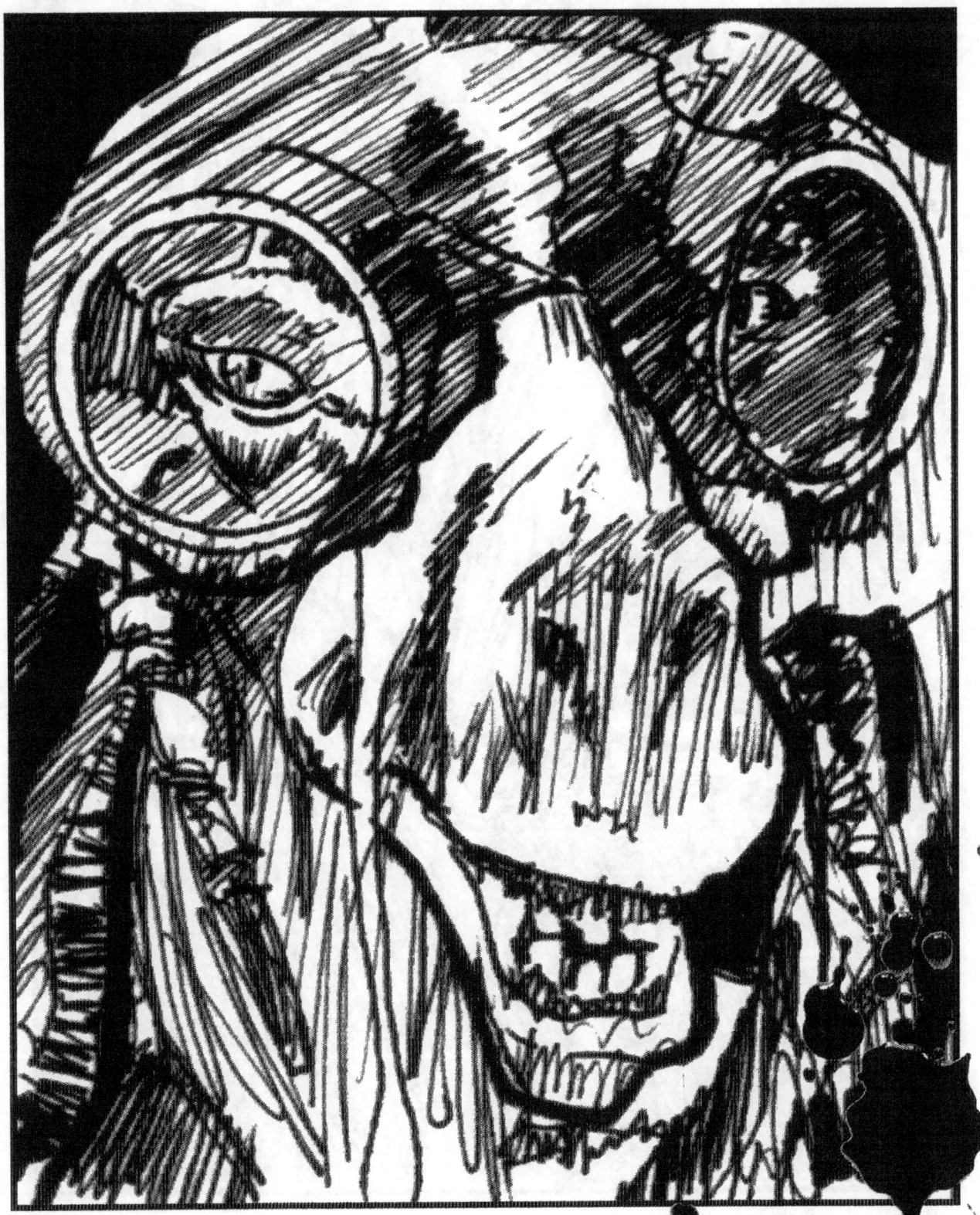

SEBULBA

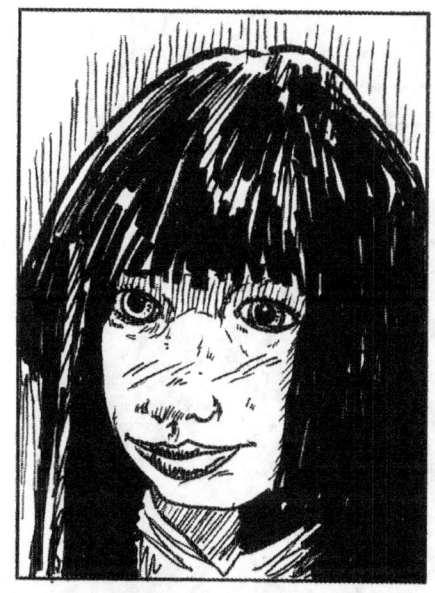
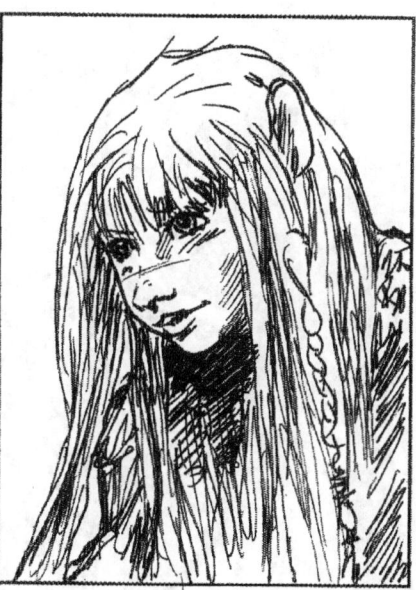
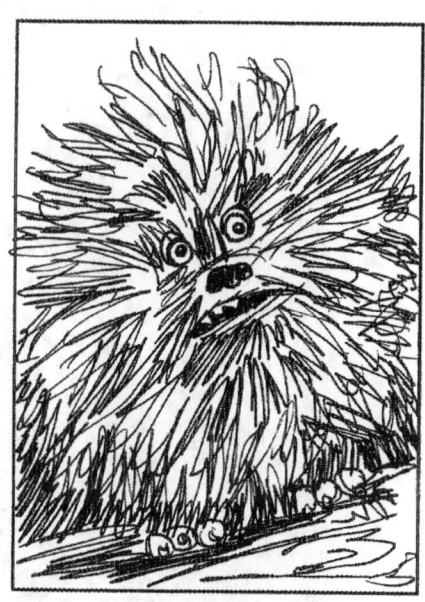

THE DARK CRYSTAL I

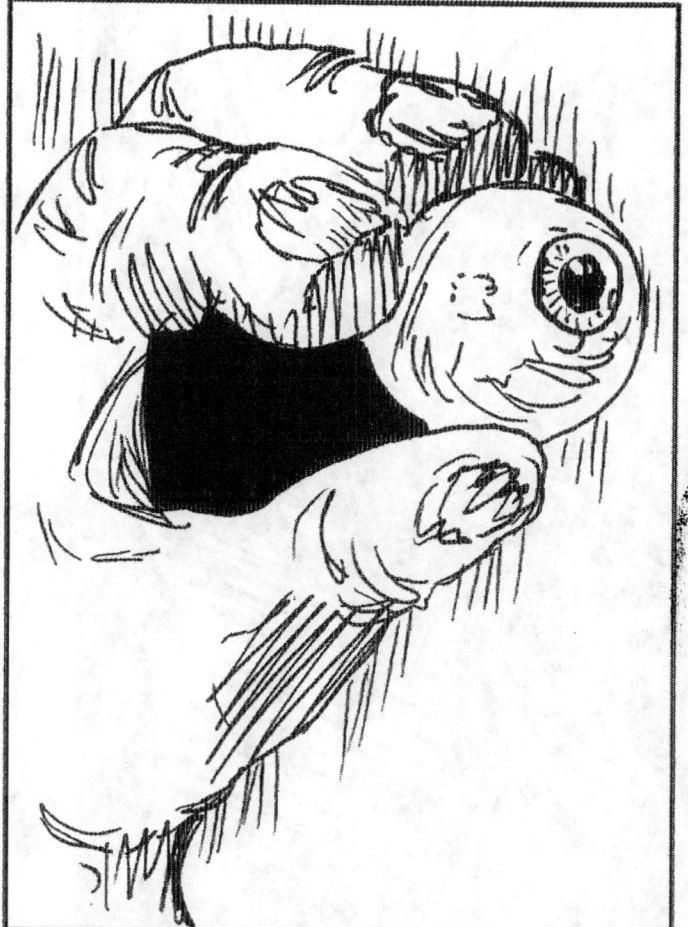

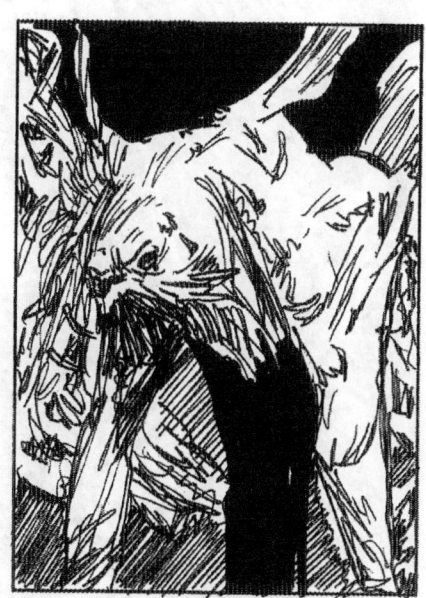

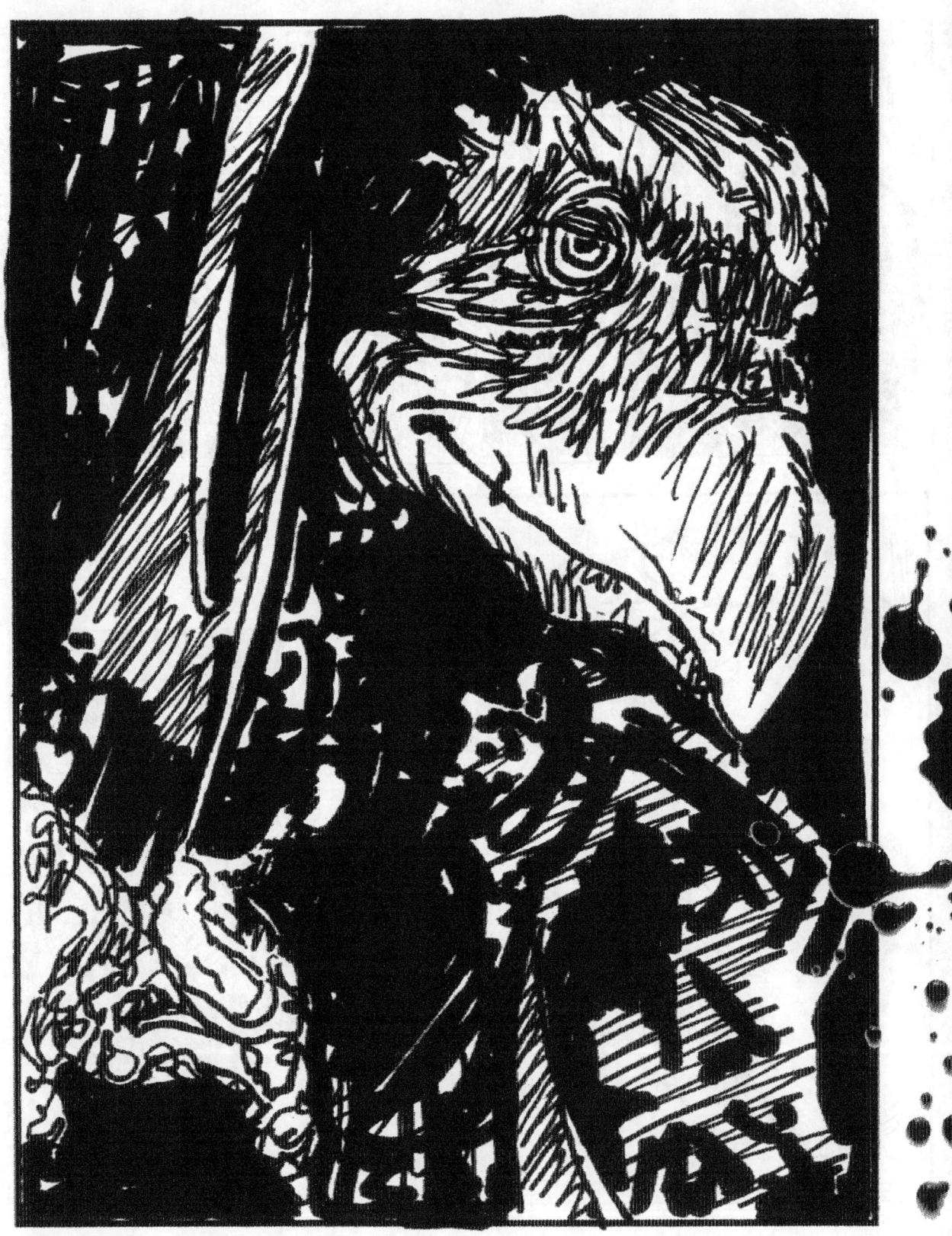

CHAMBERLAIN

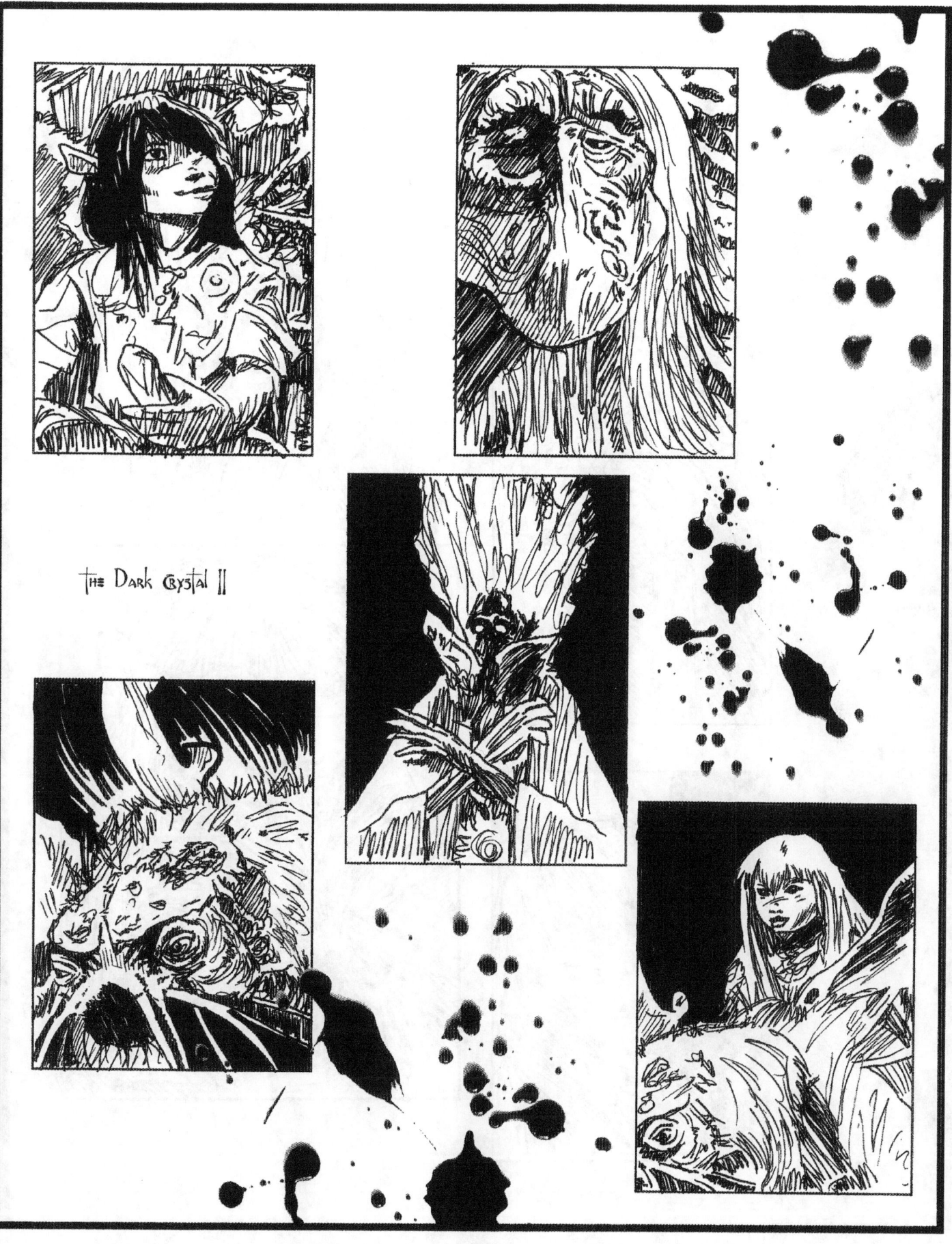

THE DARK CRYSTAL II

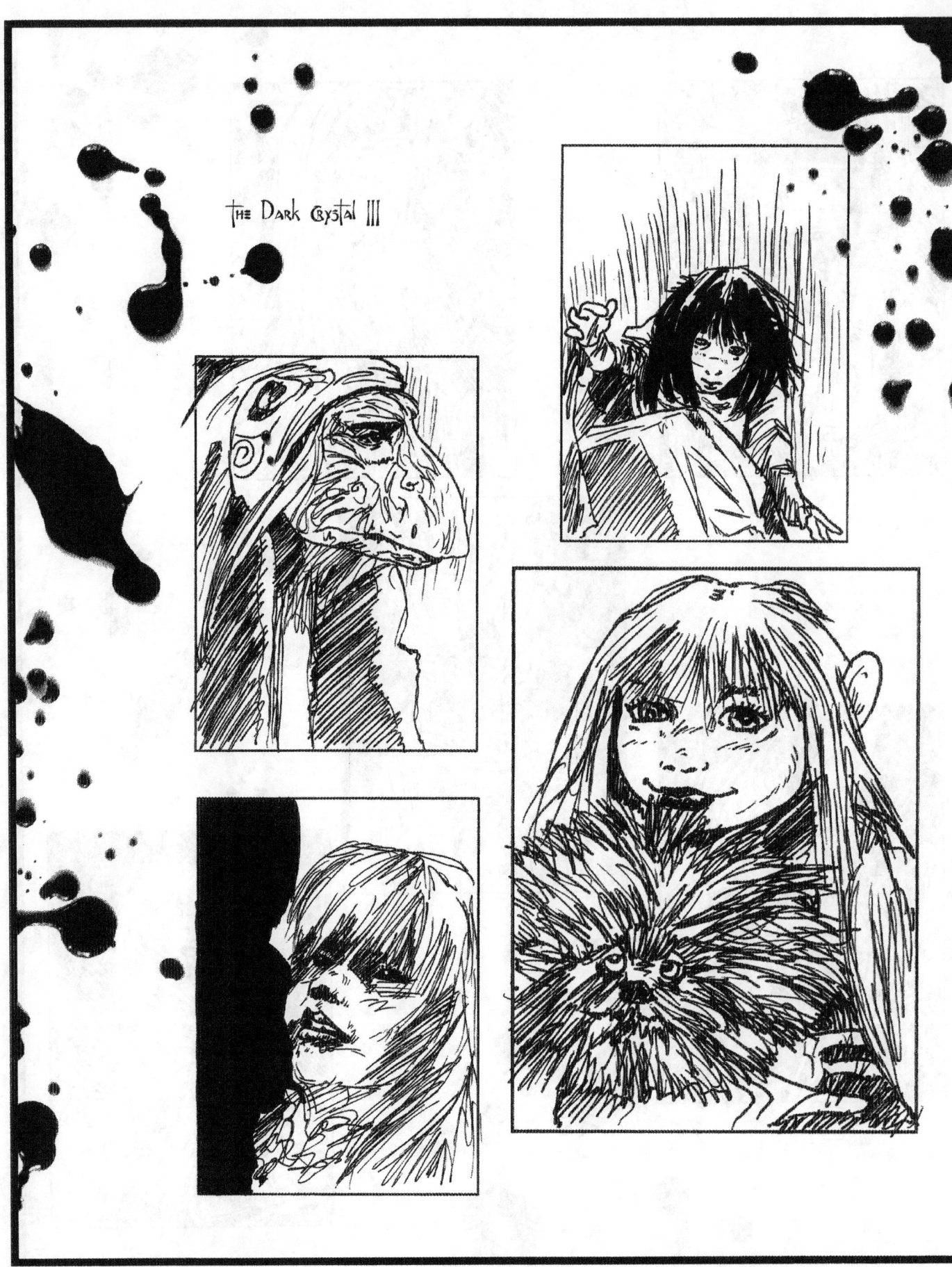

THE DARK CRYSTAL III

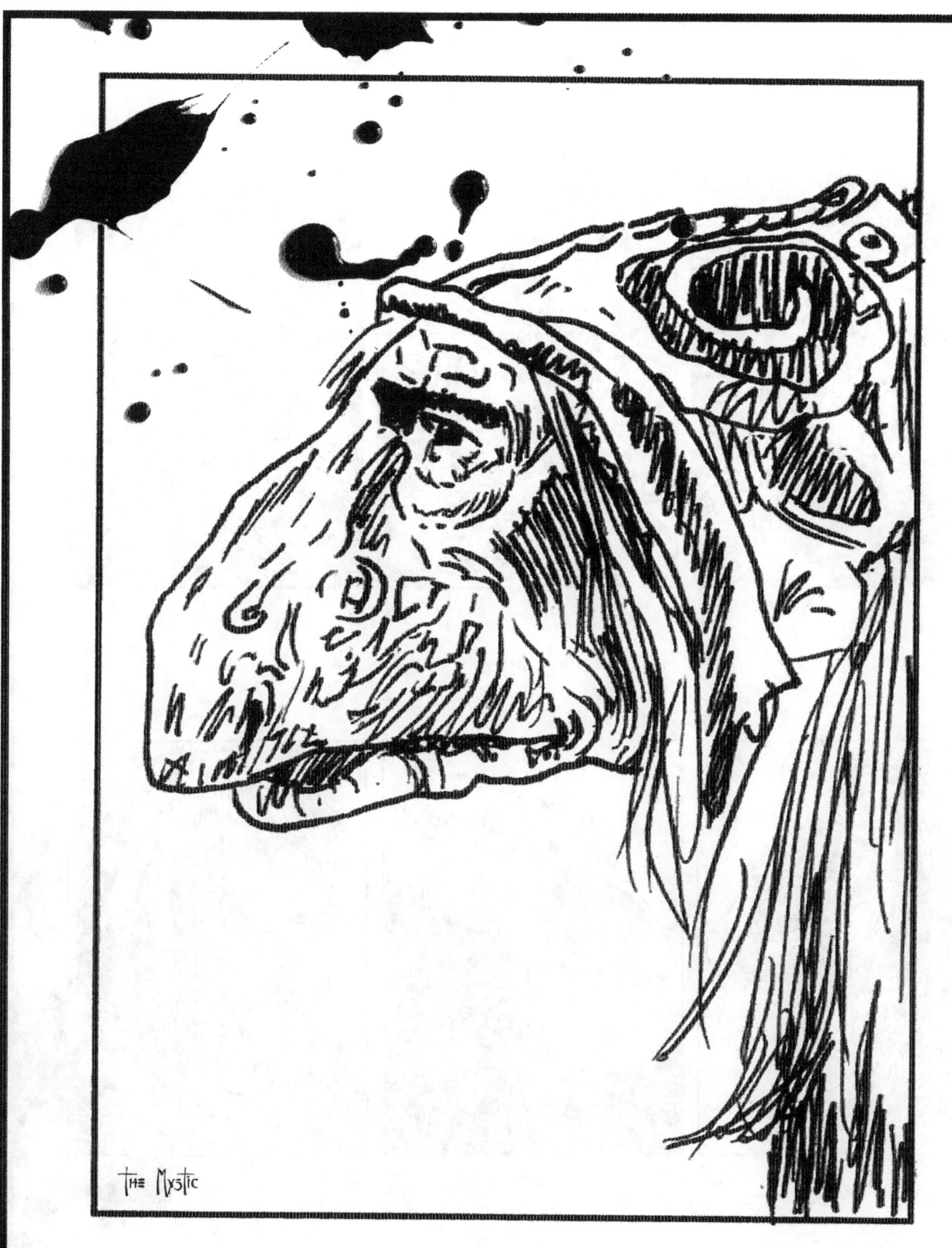

THE MYSTIC

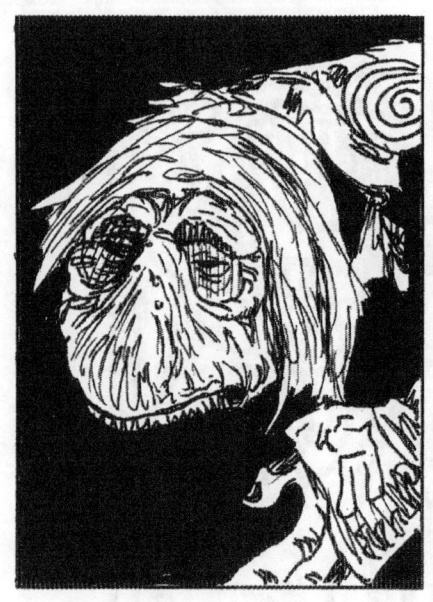 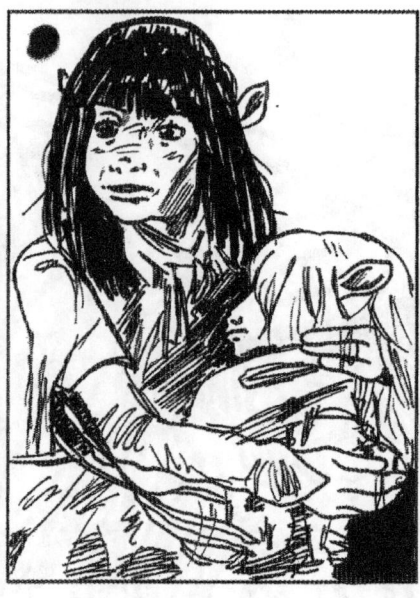 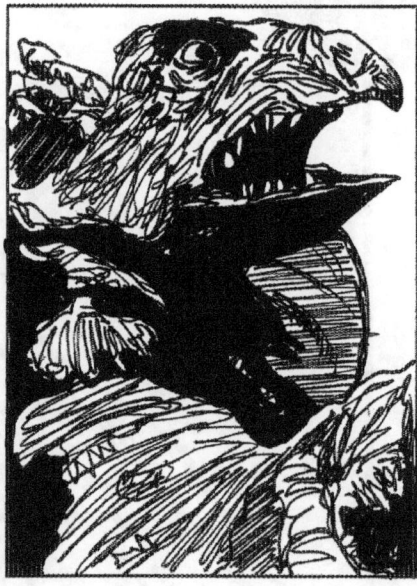

the Dark Crystal IV

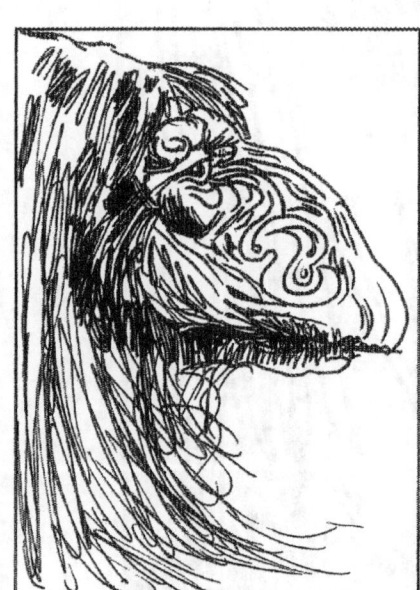 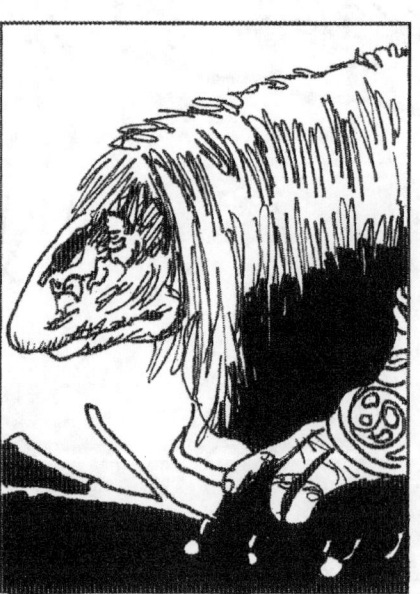 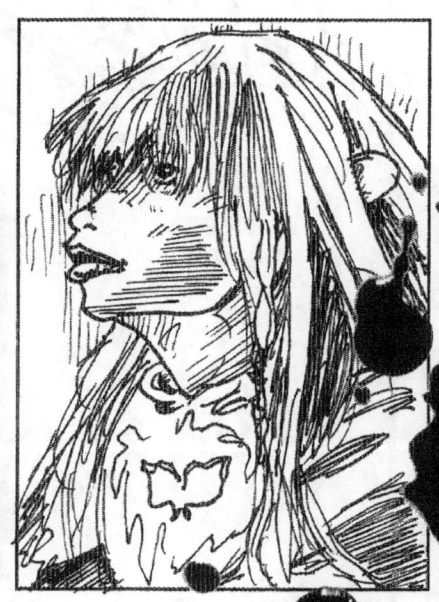

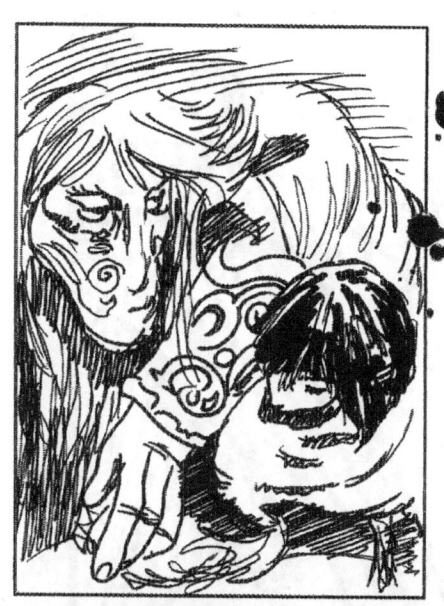

THE DARK CRYSTAL V

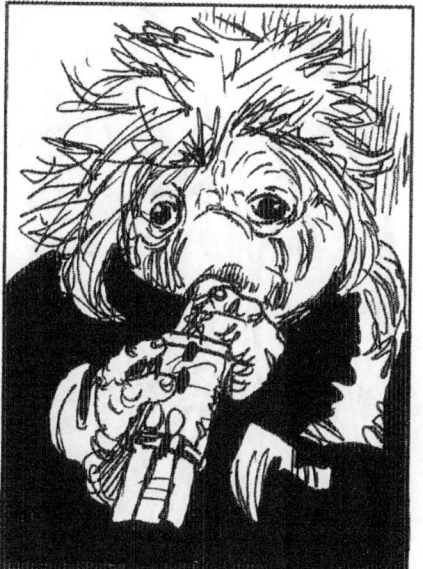
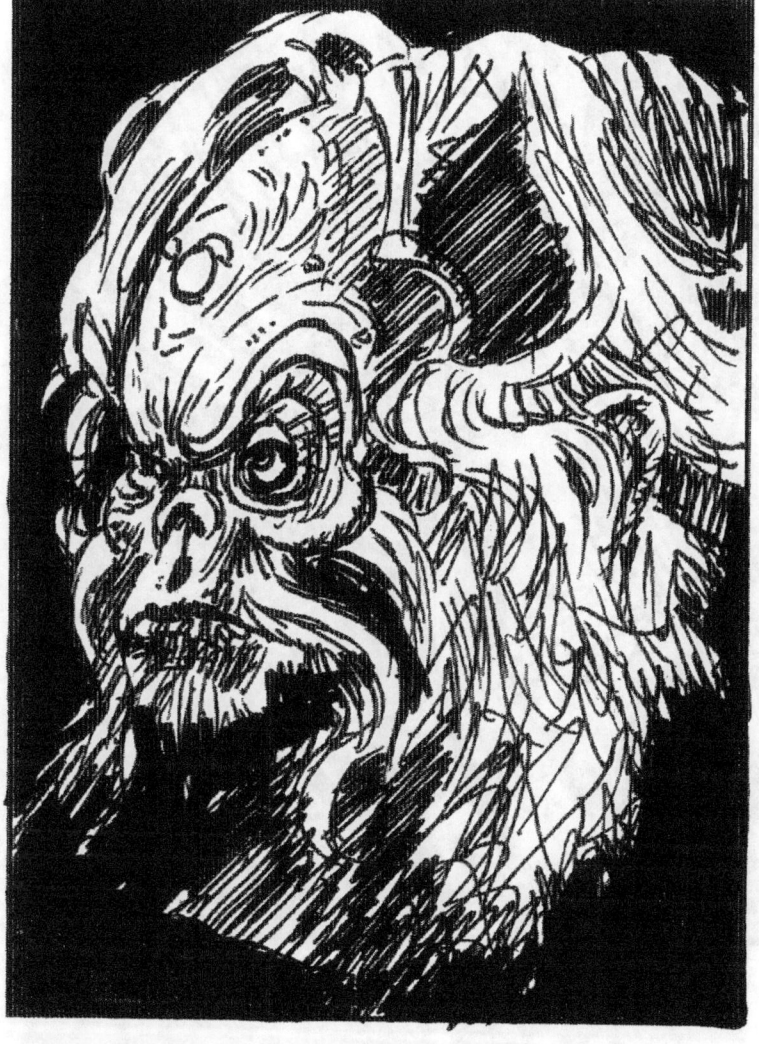
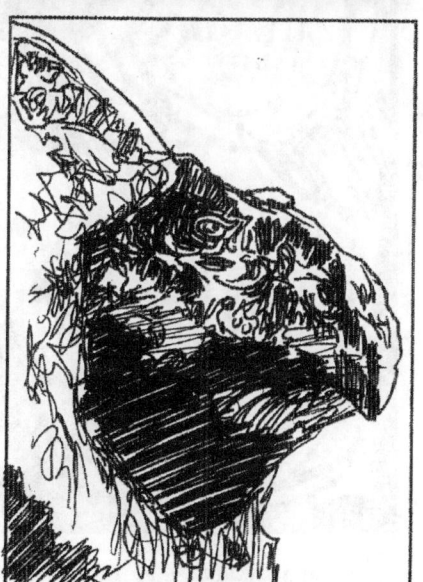

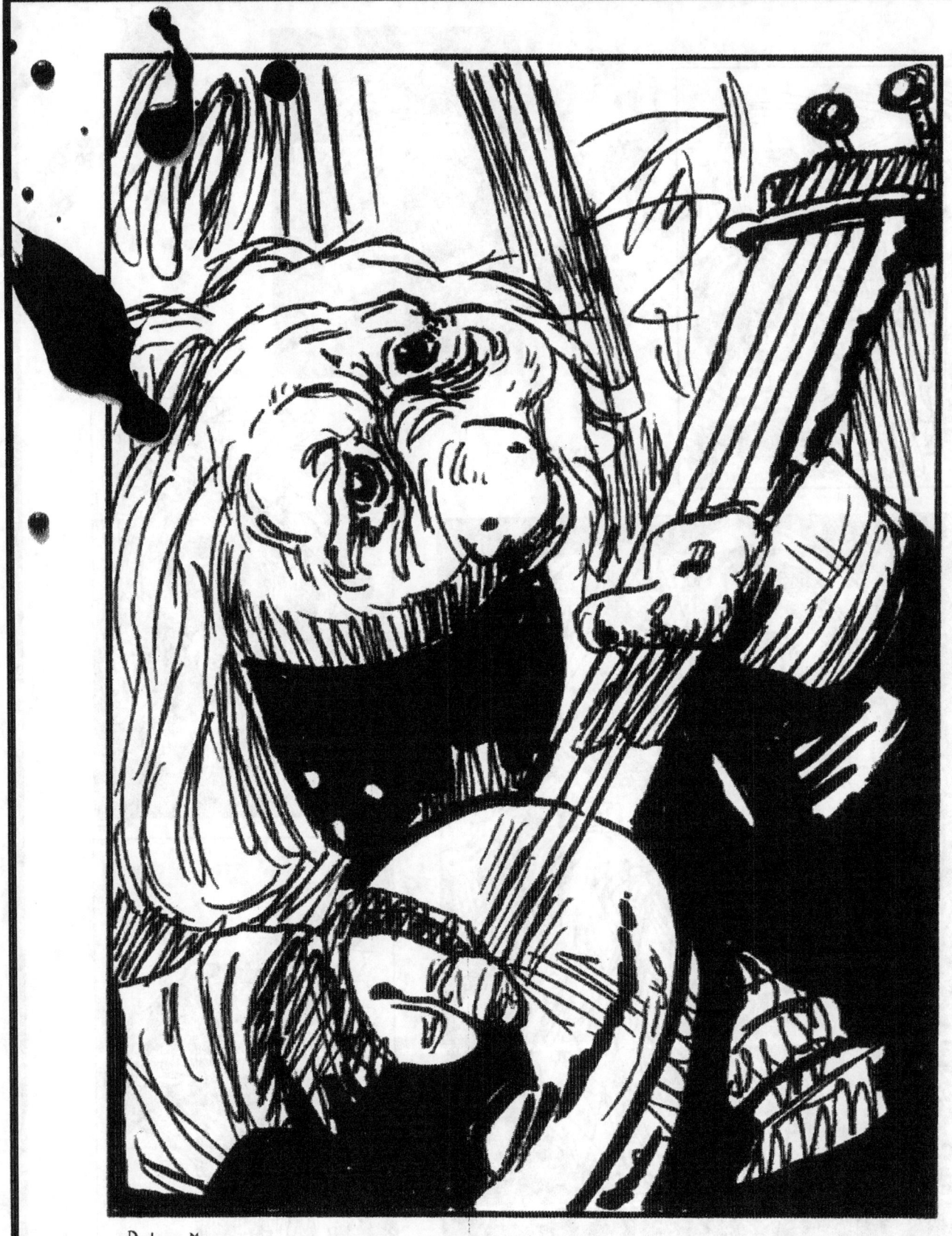

Podling Musician

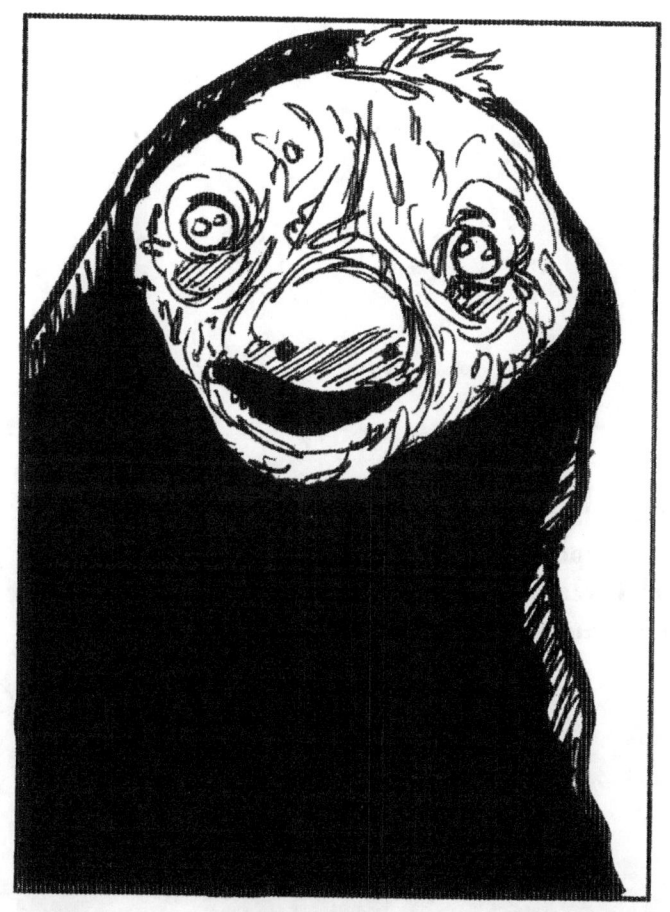

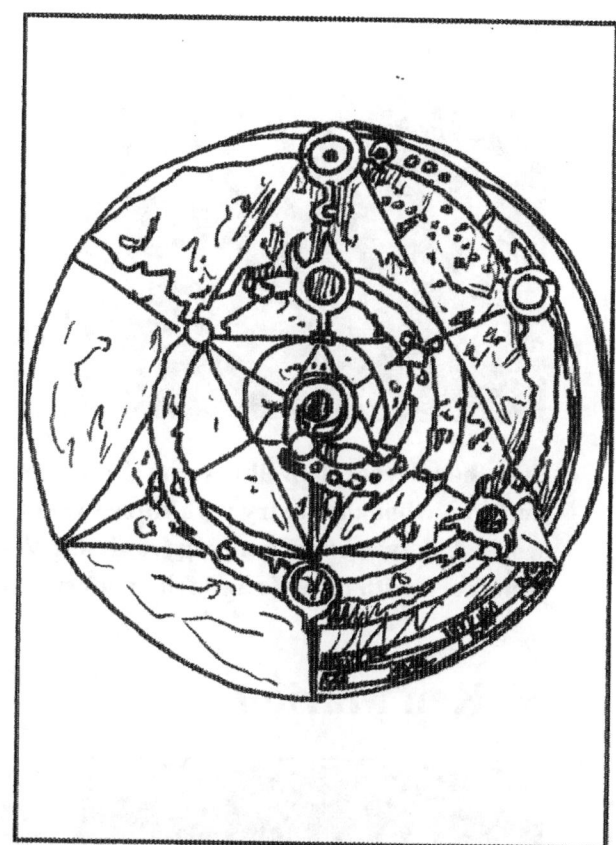

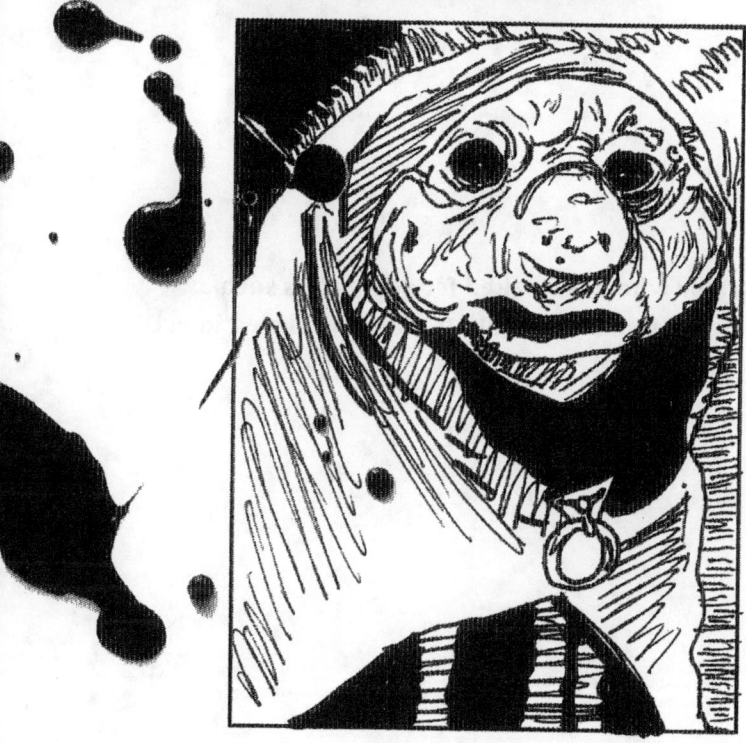

THE DARK CRYSTAL VI

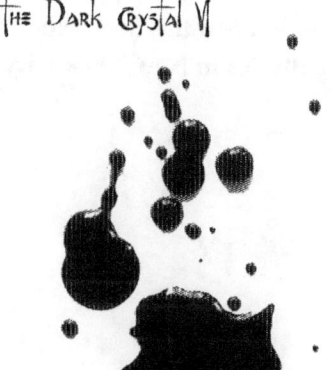

Jonathan Myers

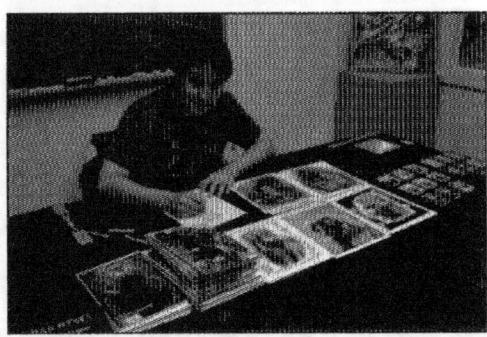

Jonathan Myers is an illustrator and cartoonist who has worked in the gaming, publishing and comic book industry with fifteen years of experience. He is a prolific artist who has worked on properties ranging from Star Wars to Tarzan. He currently resides in Upstate New York with his wife and fellow illustrator, Lola, and their daughter, Sara.

V. Ken Marion

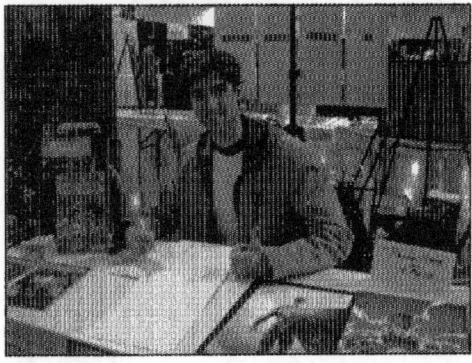

Ken Marion is a popular comic book illustrator who has worked for companies such as Boom! Studios and Aspen Comics. His work is regularly sought after and displayed in art galleries in New York City, where he currently resides.

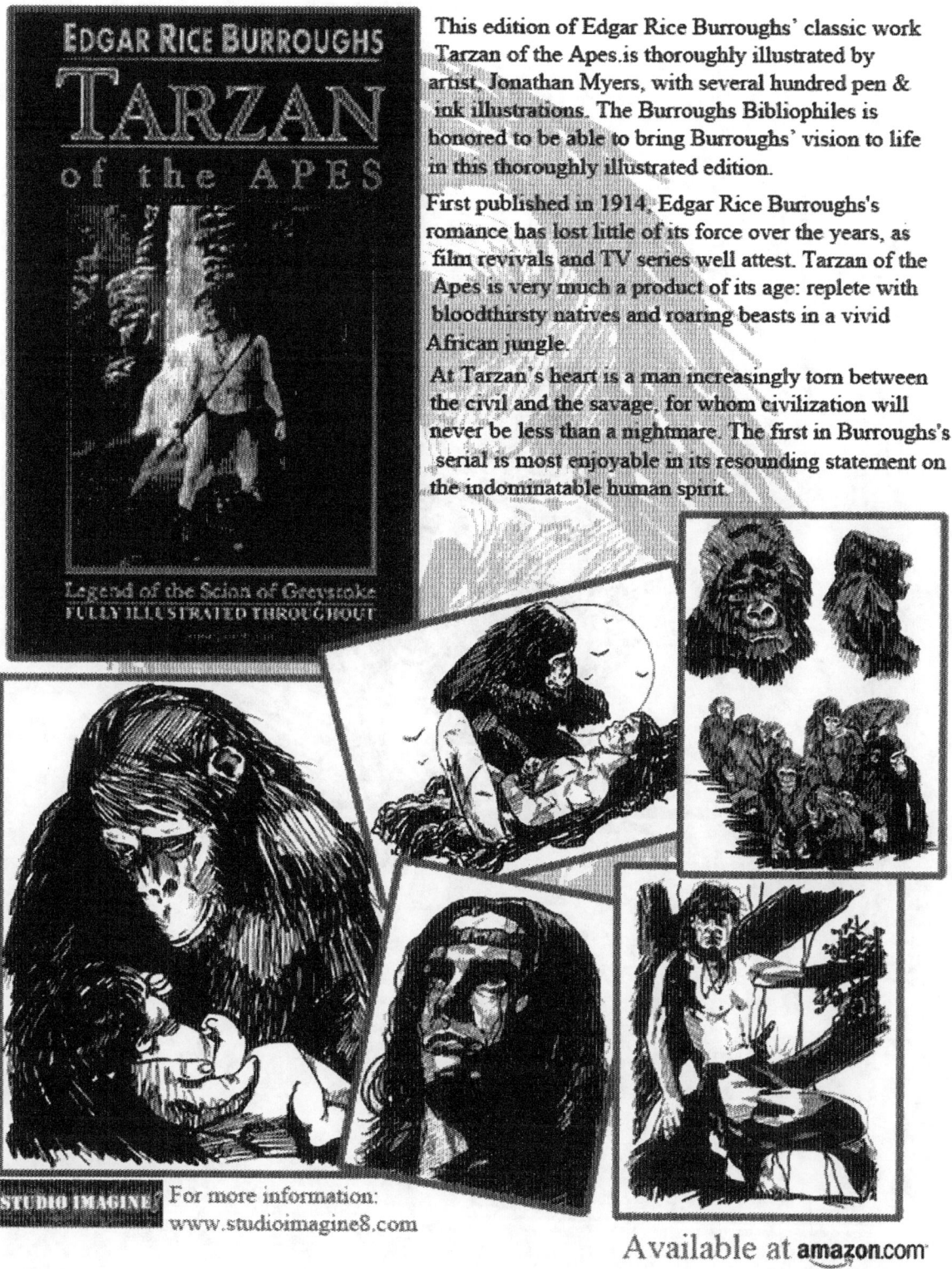

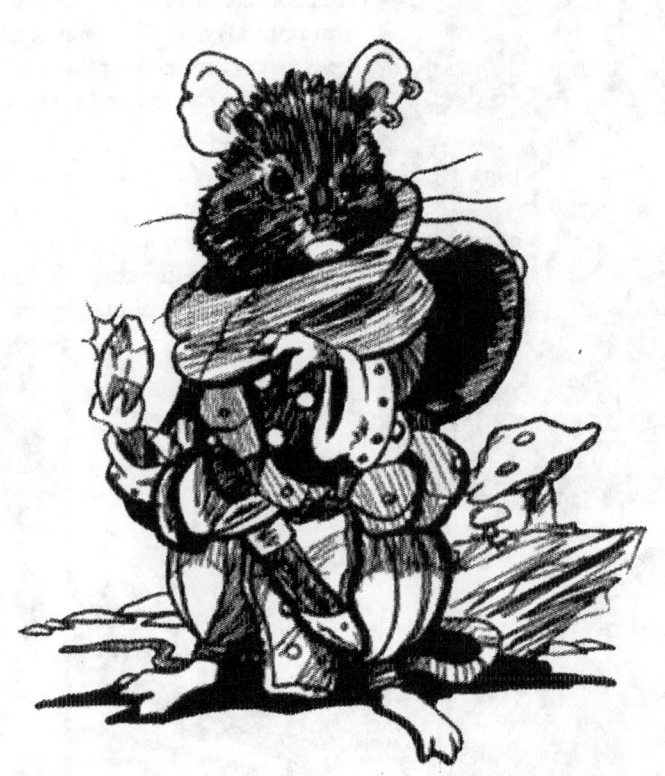

www.ingramcontent.com/pod-product-compliance
Lightning Source LLC
Chambersburg PA
CBHW080308180526
45167CB00006B/2726